T0275060

The
GREAT
AMERICAN
SONGBOOK

201 Favorites You Ought to Know (& Love)

ALSO BY STEVEN SUSKIN

Show Tunes: The Songs, Shows, and Careers of Broadway's Major Composers

Berlin, Kern, Rodgers, Hart, and Hammerstein: A Complete Song Catalog

Opening Night on Broadway: A Critical Quotebook of the Golden Era of the Musical Theatre, Oklahoma! *(1943) to* Fiddler on the Roof *(1964)*

More Opening Nights on Broadway: A Critical Quotebook of the Musical Theatre, 1965–1981

Broadway Yearbook 1999–2000

Broadway Yearbook 2000–2001

Broadway Yearbook 2001–2002

A Must See! Brilliant Broadway Artwork

Second Act Trouble: Behind the Scenes at Broadway's Big Musical Bombs

The Sound of Broadway Music: A Book of Orchestrators and Orchestrations

The Book of Mormon: The Testament of a Broadway Musical (with Trey Parker, Robert Lopez, and Matt Stone)

Natasha, Pierre & The Great Comet of 1812: The Journey of a New Musical to Broadway (with Dave Malloy)

Offstage Observations: Inside Tales of the Not-So-Legitimate Theatre (foreword by John Pizzarelli)

The GREAT AMERICAN SONGBOOK

201 Favorites *You Ought to Know* (& Love)

STEVEN SUSKIN

Backbeat
Books

Lanham • Boulder • New York • London

An imprint of Globe Pequot, the trade division of
The Rowman & Littlefield Publishing Group, Inc.
4501 Forbes Blvd., Ste. 200
Lanham, MD 20706
www.rowman.com

Distributed by NATIONAL BOOK NETWORK

Copyright © 2023 by Steven Suskin

All rights reserved. No part of this book may be reproduced in any form or by any electronic or mechanical means, including information storage and retrieval systems, without written permission from the publisher, except by a reviewer who may quote passages in a review.

British Library Cataloguing in Publication Information Available

Library of Congress Cataloging-in-Publication Data

Names: Suskin, Steven, author. | Pizzarelli, John, writer of foreword.
Title: The Great American songbook : 201 favorites you ought to know (&
  love) / Steven Suskin ; foreword by John Pizzarelli.
Description: Essex, Connecticut : Backbeat, 2023. | Includes
  bibliographical references. | Summary: "A carefully curated, cheerfully opinionated
  guidebook surveying 201 of the most significant selections from the Great American
  Songbook, ranging from celebrated masterpieces to forgotten gems" —Provided by
  publisher.
Identifiers: LCCN 2022041790 (print) | LCCN 2022041791 (ebook) | ISBN
  9781493070947 (paperback) | ISBN 9781493070954 (epub)
Subjects: LCSH: Popular music--United States—History and criticism. | Musicals—
  United States—History and criticism.
Classification: LCC ML3477 .S87 2023 (print) | LCC ML3477 (ebook) | DDC
  782.42164/0973—dc23/eng/20220902
LC record available at https://lccn.loc.gov/2022041790
LC ebook record available at https://lccn.loc.gov/2022041791

∞™ The paper used in this publication meets the minimum requirements of
American National Standard for Information Sciences—Permanence of Paper
for Printed Library Materials, ANSI/NISO Z39.48-1992.

to the songwriters

without whom
we'd all be just
whistlin' in the dark

CONTENTS

FOREWORD BY JOHN PIZZARELLI   xv

INTRODUCTION   xvii

SONGS!   1

SONGWRITERS!   205

ACKNOWLEDGMENTS   233

BIBLIOGRAPHY   237

INDEX   241

**A COMPLETE LIST OF SONGS WITH PAGE NUMBERS
APPEARS ON THE FOLLOWING PAGES.**

THE SONGS

Ac-cent-tchu-ate the Positive ("Mister In-be-tween")	1
After You've Gone	2
Ain't Misbehavin'	3
All of Me	4
All the Things You Are	5
Alone Together	7
Another Autumn	8
April in Paris	9
As Long as I Live	10
Autumn in New York	11
The Ballad of the Sad Young Men	12
The Best Is Yet to Come	13
The Birth of the Blues	14
Blue Day	15
Blues in the Night (My Mama Done Tol' Me)	16
Body and Soul	17
Born Too Late	18
The Boy Next Door	19
Brother, Can You Spare a Dime?	20
Can This Be Love?	21
Can't Help Lovin' Dat Man	22
Can't We Be Friends?	23
Carolina in the Morning	24
Charleston	25

Cheek to Cheek	26
Chicago (That Toddling Town)	27
Come Rain or Come Shine	28
The Continental	29
Crazy Rhythm	30
Dancing in the Dark	31
Darn That Dream	32
Day In—Day Out	34
Don't Get Around Much Anymore	35
Early Autumn	36
East of the Sun (and West of the Moon)	37
Everything I Have Is Yours	38
Ev'ry Time	39
Fascinating Rhythm	40
Fly Me to the Moon (In Other Words)	41
The Folks Who Live on the Hill	42
Georgia on My Mind	43
Get Happy	44
Good-bye to All That	45
Guess Who I Saw Today	46
Hand in Hand	47
Happy Days Are Here Again	48
Have You Met Miss Jones?	49
Have Yourself a Merry Little Christmas	50
The Heather on the Hill	51
Here I'll Stay	52
Here's That Rainy Day	53
Honeysuckle Rose	54
How About You?	55
How Are Things in Glocca Morra?	56
How High the Moon	57
How Long Has This Been Going On?	58
I Can't Get Started	59
I Can't Give You Anything but Love	60
I Cover the Waterfront	61
I Don't Want to Walk Without You	62
I Found a Million Dollar Baby (in a Five and Ten Cent Store)	63
I Get a Kick out of You	64
I Get Along Without You Very Well (Except Sometimes)	65

I Got Rhythm   66
I Gotta Right to Sing the Blues   67
I Guess I'll Have to Change My Plan (The Blue Pajama Song)   68
I Had a Love Once   69
I Left My Heart at the Stage Door Canteen   70
I Love a Piano   71
I May Be Wrong But I Think You're Wonderful!   72
I Only Have Eyes for You   73
I Remember You   74
I See Your Face Before Me   75
I Thought About You   76
I Want to Be with You   77
I Wish I Didn't Love You So   78
I Wonder What Became of Me   79
If I Love Again   80
Ill Wind (You're Blowin' Me No Good)   81
I'm All Smiles   82
I'm an Old Cowhand (From the Rio Grande)   83
I'm Beginning to See the Light   84
I'm in the Mood for Love   85
I'm Old Fashioned   86
Isn't It a Pity?   87
Isn't It Romantic?   88
It Had to Be You   89
It Never Entered My Mind   90
It's a Most Unusual Day   91
It's Only a Paper Moon   92
It's the Going Home Together   93
I've Always Loved You   94
I've Got the World on a String   95
Jeepers Creepers   96
Just in Time   97
Keepin' Myself for You   98
Laura   99
Lazy Afternoon   100
Lazy River   100
Let Yourself Go   101
Let's Call It a Day   102
Let's Do It (Let's Fall in Love)   103

Let's Face the Music and Dance 104
Let's Go 105
Little Girl Blue 106
Lorna's Here 107
Love Me or Leave Me 107
Love Turned the Light Out 108
Lover 109
Lover, Come Back to Me! 110
Lullaby of Broadway 111
Mack the Knife 112
Magic Moment 114
Make Someone Happy 115
Makin' Whoopee! 116
The Man I Love 117
The Man That Got Away 118
Maybe It's Time for Me 119
Memphis in June 120
Misty 121
Moonglow 122
More Than You Know 123
My Blue Heaven 124
My Funny Valentine 125
The Nearness of You 126
Never Never Land 126
Night and Day 127
Not Mine 128
Ol' Man River 129
Old Devil Moon 131
One for My Baby (and One More for the Road) 132
Over the Rainbow 133
Overnight 134
The Party's Over 135
Past the Age of Innocence 136
Pennies from Heaven 137
Personality 138
Pick Yourself Up 139
Put on a Happy Face 140
Puttin' on the Ritz 141
Satin Doll 142

Sentimental Journey — 143
Sentimental Rhapsody — 143
September Song — 144
A Ship Without a Sail — 145
Skylark — 146
A Sleepin' Bee — 147
Smoke Gets in Your Eyes (When Your Heart's on Fire) — 148
So in Love — 149
Some Girl Is on His Mind — 150
Some Other Time — 151
Someone to Watch over Me — 152
Something to Remember You By — 153
Something's Gotta Give — 154
The Song Is You — 155
Soon It's Gonna Rain — 156
Sophisticated Lady — 157
Speak Low — 158
Spring Can Really Hang You Up the Most — 159
Spring Is Here — 160
St. Louis Blues — 161
Star Dust — 162
Stormy Weather (Keeps Rainin' All the Time) — 163
Summertime — 164
Swanee — 165
Sweet Georgia Brown — 166
Swinging on a Star — 168
'S Wonderful — 169
Taking a Chance on Love — 170
Tea for Two — 171
Thanks for the Memory — 172
That Old Black Magic — 173
There But for You Go I — 174
There's No Holding Me — 175
They Can't Take That Away from Me — 176
They Didn't Believe Me — 177
This Is My Beloved — 178
This Time the Dream's on Me — 179
Thou Swell — 180
Time on My Hands (You in My Arms) — 182

Too Late Now   183
Too Marvelous for Words   184
Try to Remember   185
The Varsity Drag   186
The Way You Look Tonight   187
What Is There to Say?   188
When Did I Fall in Love?   189
When the Sun Comes Out   190
When You Wish Upon a Star   190
Where or When   191
Why Did I Choose You?   192
Why Was I Born?   193
Willow Weep for Me   194
Witchcraft   195
With a Song in My Heart   196
Without a Song   197
You Are for Loving   198
You Better Go Now   199
You Have Cast Your Shadow on the Sea   200
You Took Advantage of Me   201
You're All the World to Me   202
Zing! Went the Strings of My Heart   203

Note: The symbol ℅ within a song's entry indicates that the sheet music's cover image is reproduced in full color in the insert sections.

FOREWORD

John Pizzarelli

Everybody has a favorite song.

They carry them around like small photographs in their wallet and keep them near their heart.

When one of those songs is heard, it can trigger so many memories: sadness or joy, a place in time that no one else knows about, a wedding or a first date.

The Great American Songbook has provided these feelings for generations now.

When I flip through a Harry Warren or Cole Porter songbook, I have so many reactions from, "did he write that?" to "that is such an amazing song."

It is staggering to me how this Songbook has stood the test of time, but then again it isn't because the craftsmanship is central to it. The way Jerome Kern shaped the melody of "All the Things You Are" and the lyric Oscar Hammerstein put to it are sheer genius.

Hoagy Carmichael's "Star Dust" is still as popular today as it was when it was written . . . in 1927!

These songs recorded year after year have never ceased to be popular with the masses. No lyric or melody was left to chance. There were no rhymes like "rain and game" or "home and alone."

The care put into these works is why we remain singing these songs today.

I love thinking about Richard Rodgers and Larry Hart or Harold Arlen and Johnny Mercer sitting in a room contemplating a song that would become "My Funny Valentine" or "Come Rain or Come Shine," songs that generations after their writing are still sung today.

I am forever thrilled at the way some of these lyrics have become part of our everyday speech:

"Pick yourself up, dust yourself off"
"Who could ask for anything more?"
"Nice work if you can get it"
"Life is just a bowl of cherries"
"We're in the money!"

Nothing is better than being on a bandstand and getting a request for a song, and to watch the reaction of a person or couple when they hear it played for them.

I do not know if Johnny Mercer or Jimmy McHugh thought "I Thought About You" or "I'm in the Mood for Love" would be around and admired well after their days on this planet, but I think they would be pleasantly surprised to hear what this world has done with those songs.

Reading through this terrific guide that Steven Suskin has curated, you will find insightful essays on 201 songs. Let us hope they will bring to life memories tucked away near your heart and take you back again and again to another place in time.

INTRODUCTION

"If music be the food of love, read on."

So, purportedly, said a long-ago wise man. If it wasn't some Renaissance bard or other, it was likely a hackneyed Tin Pan Alley scribe. Man does not live on bread alone, or cake; or on wine, women, and song. (It's past time, methinks, that these archaic maxims be retooled, or even better cashiered.) But the sentiment is clear, especially in tunesmith terms: the moon belongs to everyone so long as you have a song in your heart and whistle a happy tune while you speak low of love.

Is there anything more perfect in this world than a perfect song?

Perhaps, in the larger scale of things: The sound of rain upon a window-pane? The breathless hush of evening? That magical moment a baby first sees a bubble burst before its eyes? All of these sentiments were formulated, it is only fair to admit, by one or another of those aforementioned scribes.

For our purposes, or the purposes of this book at least, nothing is more perfect than a song.

Stroll along, in village or town, and sooner or later music is likely in your inner ear (if not your inner earbud). Times of happiness bring melody sweeping into your soul; times of despair are so much more bearable with that aforesaid song in your heart.

Our memories, loaded with limitless information important and un-, are positively stocked with songs remembered and half-remembered—some justly loved, others so annoying that once we get them in mind, they lurk unwelcome for hours.

So many songs.

Hundreds of songs.

Thousands of songs.

Speaking of pop hits, a blacksmith's apprentice—walking the pike on the first sunny morn since March roared in like a lion in the blustery spring of 1581—passed a tarrier loafing beside the inn, awhistling.

"Whot's thot?" he exclaimed.

"'Tis called 'Greensleeves.' Number one on the Nottingham Hit Parade."

"Yoicks, I must download it," he retorted, trundling by.

As with many of the well-worn anecdotes on record about melodies and melodiemasters, I can't necessarily verify the accuracy of this exchange. But I can't say, either, that it *didn't* happen. And it does lead to the point of our discourse. Songs—at least good songs, whatever "good" may signify—are meant to be sung, played, whistled, and hummed. And *shared*.

Over the course of numerous books and columns, I have taken the opportunity to spotlight numerous songs, usually favorably so. But random citations within mountains of words tend to be hazily remembered or forgotten altogether. What did he say? What did *I* say? Where? And to what effect?

That is, conveniently, the precise purpose of this volume. *Here's* a song, I think, that you'll like. If you find "Greensleeves" or "White Christmas" or "Blues in the Night"—or even "Over the Rainbow"—catchy, have I got a song for you.

But just which song for you? Which songs? With a surfeit of worthy titles on the piano rack and the online playlist, how are we to settle on two hundred or so? (Aside to readers: my publishers suggested that *201* songs made a stronger subtitle, and there you have it.) What makes this song worthier, or more suited, than that one? More specifically, how does one determine which hundreds to include and which thousands, through omission, to leave for later?

One could select the all-time "best" songs, if there *were* a method to determine the all-time best songs. (Given the artificial taste and intelligence of today, there soon might be.) "Best" is indefinable; that implies that you or I have combed through all the songs that ever existed, across the scope of the genres and the centuries and the world. Wonderful songs, favorite songs, notable songs, vibrant songs; all such lists are only as good as the staff paper they're scrawled on.

Or I could compile my personal list of what I choose to be the all-time tops, with additions and deletions to taste. I have opted, however, for something so unjustifiably personal as to be practically reckless. "Best songs" implies, in absolutist terms, those that are indisputably better than all others. "Favorite songs" can be defined, more democratically, to include just about anything you or I choose.

At root, these are songs that I find arresting, impossible to bypass, and impelled to share with you. So *honi soit qui mal y pense*, as Larry Hart once found a niftily erudite rhyme for, within a comedy duet, and nobody blinked twice. Those were the days.

Are your personal favorite bests among those included herein? Quite a few, surely, assuming you are the sort of person who would pick up this book in the first place. *All* of them? Assuredly not; it's implausible that your list and my list precisely overlap. Are songs included that you never especially cared for? Perhaps. Songs you've never heard, nor even heard of? Definitely.

But that's the point.

If you agree with my assessment of songs that you already know and love, it follows that you might do well to track down those I similarly assess. If you perchance read discussion of songs such as "Blues in the Night," "All the Things You Are," or "A Ship Without a Sail" and think *he's all wet* (or whatever the internet-age equivalent might be), then it follows that this is the right book for the wrong reader. I will suggest, though, that if—for example—you love the chromatically bluesy titles on my list with which you are already familiar, you'll find the unknown-to-you chromatically bluesy suggestions worth ferreting out.

How, anyway, do you describe a song?

Although I wholeheartedly agree that there's a place for discourse on arpeggiated dominant tetrachords and descending Schenkerian dyads, that place is not here. Serious musicians looking for hard-core theory are advised to turn to some musicological academician or other who will be more than eager to comply to the extent that your eyes, and ears, might well cross.

This volume is geared not toward music theory but music *appreciation*. Far be it from me to explain why you should like this song or that. My aim is simply to direct you toward songs I find irrepressible, explain my reasoning, and suggest that you might find them equally rewarding.

The songs included—the earliest date from the years just before the twenties (the *last* twenties) started to roar—are, by any definition, old. The newest are from the sixties: songs I find exceptional that didn't stand a chance in the not-so-brave new musical world. Let it be added, though, that everything is relative. Speaking of relatives, I suppose it relevant to this particular point to note that my jazz guitar–strumming son, Charlie, loves the songs of the Beatles, who disbanded thirty years before he was born in 1999. He reveres their catalog, which I am nonplussed to relate that he labels within the realm of *classical music*. And I guess he has a point. Kind of. I have always considered Gershwin and Kern to be from way before our time; but Gershwin wrote his final song only fifteen years before I was born, and Kern, seven.

Although some of our 201 favorites have passed the century mark, today's song seekers will find most of them to be not nearly so obscure as formerly. There was a time when all but the most popular sheet music was hard to find, and "out of print" meant—literally—out of print. Thanks to our friends on the internet and the print-on-demand culture, many can be located and viewed (or purchased) at the flick of a mouse or a whisper to Siri.

And as each New Year's Eve rings in, another annum's worth of songs enters the public domain. As we go to press in 2023, any published song registered for copyright in 1927 or earlier is in the public domain in the United States (but not necessarily outside the United States). That includes Gershwin's *Rhapsody in Blue*, all the published songs from the original production of the Kern-Hammerstein *Show Boat*, and various songs discussed in this book. Copyright protection for published material expires ninety-five years after the year of the original copyright. If you are reading these pages in 2025, say, the entirety of the Roaring Twenties is freely accessible—with more joining the list each year.

Recordings of many of these songs—having been restored, remastered, and recirculated—can be handily located on various corners of the internet. We consider recorded versions secondary to actual printed music: arrangers were likely to—well, *arrange* the songs, omitting verses or refrains while altering harmonies or rhythms. Some vocalists (Frank? Ella?) seemed to pride themselves on haphazard attention to the words, to the extent that incorrect lyrics sometimes overtake public familiarity with what the writers in fact wrote. Even so, recordings are generally far more quickly accessible than printed sheet music.

That being the case, we have seen fit to assemble an extracurricular playlist for those readers who have access to the Spotify site. Recordings have been selected which most closely represent, in our estimation, the songs as written. At the time of publication of this book, this can be found by searching Spotify for "Suskin's Great American Songbook." This will enable readers to almost instantly hear many of the songs herein, in a manner that the songwriters could not have anticipated. Their initial response would likely by astonishment, followed by the almost-as-instant question: How do we get paid?

In whittling down to 201 favorites, we need to set at least some parameters, beginning with the qualification that we stay within the canon of what someone once decided to name the "great American songbook." That is a misnomer unless you want to start said songbook in 1775 with "Yankee Doodle" and his homegrown macaroni.

Now, we could easily pull far more than 201 incontrovertibly excellent songs from the catalogs of a handful of composers or four. This would result in a list upon which everyone (within limits) can agree and no one (within limits) can be surprised at. But what fun would that be?—especially given that I first embarked on this journey in a quest for forgotten and all-but-disappeared songs and was veritably smote by the numerous unknown-to-me treasures lurking on the top perimeter of my overburdened bookshelves.

Thus, I have determined that my offerings be divided among three inter-mingled categories:

1. songs that readers surely already have on their personal list;
2. songs that are vaguely remembered or pretty much forgotten, to which readers will react by thinking, "Oh, yes, I *like* that song"; and
3. a small but vibrant clutch of songs that I'd wager are unknown to most— and in at least some cases, all—who read these pages, but *demand* notice.

The latter group, the forgotten songs, decidedly have never been on anyone's best song list, except perhaps the songwriters in question and their mothers. That's all the more reason to give them a surprise spotlight on these pages. At least some present readers likely will search them out and—yes!—add them to their stack of favorites.

You undoubtedly will miss some iconic songs from legendary songwriters. Mi casa es su casa, as they say, but my favorite songwriters are not necessarily su composers favoriti. Ultimately, I decided to simply stock the list with the songs that fill my inner song stack and let the cadences fall where they may.

Let us interrupt ourselves mid-stanza to say a word for the people who wrote the words. Many lyricists make multiple appearances on these pages: Larry, Ira, Oscar, and Johnny among them. I bow low in admiration to all, without whom these songs would not be the treasures they are. Due to the nature of this par-ticular discussion, though, I have seen fit to concentrate somewhat more on the music and the music makers. That is not intended to slight the word slingers, who share credit, praise, and gratitude (and royalties).

You might well ask how and why I plowed through thousands of songs prior to determining my selections. Basically, I played through every song I could find; made a pile of a thousand or so; and kept playing them until I'd whittled down the stacks to about three hundred; and then, laboriously, further nar-rowed the field. The final 201 include many old favorites, along with others I'd never heard. Hence, we have at least some *new* old songs that I don't reckon anyone has tried at their piano in years. I find, though, that readers don't much care to get buried in explanations before they—in the parlance—get to the good stuff. My goal is precisely that. So, let's, forthwith, get to the good stuff.

But before we do . . .

Readers who choose not to read through these prefatory pages might wonder at what seems to be a black hole of songs from Broadway musicals. High among the elite I personally place the likes of *Carousel, South Pacific, The Most Happy Fella, Gypsy, She Loves Me,* and *Sweeney Todd.* I could, and have elsewhere, gone on at length about the scores contained therein.

In this volume, though, you'll find nary a song from any of them. The creators of those scores I see not as songwriters, but as *musical dramatists.* They weren't mere itinerant tunesmiths, scattered round the scarred upright with burnt-ash cigars and stubby pencils intent on turning out the next in their string of hopeful song hits. They were fully rounded dramatists intently concentrating on expressing character; providing plot, backstory, and subtext; thrusting the action on toward Act 2; and, as old habits die hard, turning out the next in their string of hopeful song hits.

That being the case, I can't justify pulling songs from the above-cited scores and adding them to our list. It would seem to trivialize the accomplishments, on the one hand; and, inevitably, monopolize our discussion by filling half the spots. So, songs from these musicals—along with other well-wrought scores (*Guys and Dolls, My Fair Lady, West Side Story,* and on)—are outside our scope. There is plenty of Rodgers and almost as much Hammerstein herein; but no selections from the later mating of Rodgers and Hammerstein. No Sondheim for that matter, as most (but certainly not all) of his career came outside the range of the *Great American Songbook*—not only by chronology, but by intent.

Given his exclusion-by-design from these pages, I asked our modern-day bard—at an early stage of this project—for insight on the use of standard song forms; specifically, the *A-A-B-A* pattern, which appears frequently within these pages. Where did it come from, did he think, and where did it go? Like Tevye in *Fiddler on the Roof,* Sondheim's answer was: I don't know. He suggested that it likely originated in the age-old sonata form of exposition, development, and recapitulation, although when I suggested that "everybody did it," he objected that this was *patently untrue!* Not Arlen, who was something of a hero to him and me, or Gershwin or Kern.

That, as we'll see in our pages, is not precisely accurate. When I respectfully pointed out that "Stormy Weather," "Ol' Man River," and "The Man I Love" are all written in *A-A-B-A* form, Sondheim let that pass and moved on. Now that I consider it, so are "Tonight," "Everything's Coming Up Roses," and—for that matter—"Losing My Mind" and "A Weekend in the Country." But *I'll* move on.

He ended our series of exchanges on the matter by pointing out that when he was collaborating with "the conservative and hidebound" Richard Rodgers on *Do I Hear a Waltz!*, he would occasionally "sketch out the rhythm of a tune" and hand it to the composer. "The first thing he would do is count the bars—before he gave the actual rhythms a glance—to be sure they were a number divisible by four."

All Great American Songbook songs are not composed within those standard thirty-two bars, of course. But very many are; not because they have to be, or because rules or publishers demanded it. Rather, songwriters were simply writing what sounded instinctively right.

Sondheim's final words on the subject were, "I can't wait to see what you write. Well, I can wait, but I do look forward to it." Alas, he did not wait, and is not here to see—and no doubt intensively parse—these pages.

And so, as Ira (with George) or Yip (with Harold) or Johnny (with just about everybody) once would have said, and possibly did:

> *Please pardon my ramble*
> *I'll skip the preamble*
> *So here's the refrain*

Or as Cole or Frank might suggest:

> *Just curse the verse*
> *And play on*

SONGS!

AC-CENT-TCHU-ATE THE POSITIVE ("MISTER IN-BE-TWEEN")

music by Harold Arlen, lyric by Johnny Mercer
from the motion picture *Here Come the Waves* (1944)

In the dark days of World War II, Harold Arlen and Johnny Mercer—who had only recently begun their collaboration, in 1941, with "Blues in the Night" [page 16]—contrived the spiritualistic **Ac-cent-tchu-ate the Positive**※ with the intent, in Mercer's words, to "spread joy up to the maximum." Rhythmic numbers with a revivalist slant had been a staple of Broadway songwriters since 1927, due to the lucrative popularity of such songs as Vincent Youmans's "Hallelujah!," the Gershwins' "I Got Rhythm [page 66]," and Cole Porter's "Blow, Gabriel, Blow." This one is explicitly revivalist: "feel a sermon comin' on me," we are told in the verse, "the topic will be sin, and that's what I'm a'gin.'" In this case, Arlen came up with a preliminary snatch of melody, marked by mostly eighth notes punctuated by a couple of well-placed quarter notes and those quarter rests:

♪♫ | ♩ 𝄽 ♩ 𝄽 | 𝄾 ♫♫♫♫ | ♩ 𝄽 ♩ 𝄽 | 𝄾 ♫♫♫♩

※ following the song title, here and elsewhere, indicates that the sheet music cover image is reproduced in full color in the insert sections.

Mercer duly and quickly matched it with the perfect words ("you gotta ac-cent-tchu-ate the positive"), after which the song, as they say, wrote itself. Mercer outdid himself with a string of four-syllable words (ac-cent-tchu-ate, e-lim-my-nate, af-firm-a-tive) and a granddaddy of five syllables, pan-de-mo-ni-um. After these, he wisely switched to multi-word phrases ("spread joy," "bring gloom"); no sense in setting yourself an impossible task. Arlen and Mercer also seem to have paid direct homage to the gone-but-never-forgotten George and his brother, Ira, in their "bridge"—the *B* section (of *A-A-B-A¹*)— citing Jonah and his whale (of "It Ain't Necessarily So" fame), all to a catchy rhythm that in the sheet music is marked "with a steady rock." Little did Arlen, Mercer, and their peers know that steady rock eventually would push them into virtual retirement.

AFTER YOU'VE GONE

music by J. Turner Layton, lyric by Henry Creamer
non-production song (1918)

Henry Creamer was one of the few black songwriters to make frequent visits to Broadway in the era between World War I—when he and Layton interpolated two songs to *Ziegfeld Follies of 1917*—and his death in 1930. Creamer and Layton's most enduring hit was **After You've Gone**, something of an early torch song of love lost.

The main phrase is instantly memorable: an ascending eighth-note figure in bar 1 ("after you've gone," with the word "gone" held through the rest of the bar). This is then continued in bar 2 with a five-note figure ("and left me crying"):

The first two bars are then repeated, a fourth lower; and Layton makes recurrent use of that initial phrase with the extended note ("gone"), which is heard in eight of the song's twenty bars. (The form is *A-B-A-C/A*.) Also prominent is the two-bar chain of eighth notes that tie the bridge to *A* ("you'll miss the dearest pal you've / ever had"). The *C* disrupts the flow, starting with a pair of half notes and concluding with a second chain of eighth notes ("some—day— / you'll grow lonely"). Following a startlingly chromatic progression, we're back to the title phrase to close the song.

AIN'T MISBEHAVIN'

music by Thomas Waller and Harry Brooks, lyric by Andy Razaf
from the stage revue *Hot Chocolates* (1929)

Thomas Waller, who called himself "Fats," burst into prominence in 1929 with two popular hits featured in Harlem revues, both of which became perennials. Both were written for floor shows at Connie's Inn, the not-quite-as-renowned competitor to the Cotton Club. The spring edition, featuring **Ain't Misbehavin'**,※ moved to Broadway under the title *Connie's Hot Chocolates*. The fall show, *Load of Coal*, did not meet with similar success—perhaps in part because the stock market crashed in the interim—but contained the equally enchanting "Honeysuckle Rose" [page 54].

Waller and cocomposer Harry Brooks start us off with a lazily mellow rhythmic pattern ("no one to talk with, all by myself") with a slightly delayed entry, beginning with eighth-note rests:

This features a leap of a fifth, from *e♭* (in the key of E♭) to *b♭* in bar 1 and then *f* to *c* in bar 2. In the next bar, they jump a fourth, from *b♭* to *e♭*, and build to a high *f* before descending to the title phrase ("ain't misbehavin' / I'm savin' my love for you"). The bridge (in *A-A-B-A*) is even more intriguing, with the first four bars built on a simple figure:

This is set on alternating tones: *e♭* ("like") *c* ("Jack") *e♭* ("Hor-") *c* ("ner"). On the fourth hearing, the *e♭* is raised to *e♮*. The underlying chords to these bars are intriguingly altered, eventually working their way back to the final *A*. All of this comes within a simple thirty-two bars, but one never tires of this playful ballad of unrequited love. And do seek out the verse, which starts out sweet before almost instantly running into out-of-kilter harmonics.

ALL OF ME

music and lyric by Seymour Simons and Gerald Marks
non-production song (1931)

How, why, and where I ran into composer Gerald Marks (1900–1997) I can't recall, but he told me that he and collaborator Seymour Simons couldn't get anywhere with their torch song **All of Me**. They finally wangled their way into the dressing room of vaudeville headliner Belle Baker, who had memorably introduced—among other items—"Blue Skies." After waiting hours, he said, she finally consented to hear them audition their song. (If Irving Berlin sculpted "Blue Skies" for you—on demand, overnight—do you really want to hear from itinerant Tin Pan peddlers?) As they launched into the refrain—"can't you see, I'm no good without you"—she broke down, hysterically. It turns out that she had recently buried her beloved husband and remained distraught.

She quickly launched the song in her act and on radio; it has been recorded many hundreds of times since. (Baker's departed husband was a songwriter himself: Maurice Abrahams, composer of the 1912 hit "Ragtime Cowboy Joe," which is a pretty nifty song by the way. And speaking of relatives, Baker's niece was Tony Award–winner Marilyn Cooper.)

The first half of the *A* consists of three three-note phrases ("All of me / why not take / all of me"); the first and last with descending intervals, the second being a set of triplets. The bridge (of *A-B-A-C*) changes the melody but more or less retains the pattern with those second-bar triplets. The *C* alters the gentle syncopation by starting each bar head-on with either a half or dotted half note ("YOU took the / PART that / ONCE was my / HEART"); and Marks leads into the final cadence with his bluest note ("so why NOT take all of me") of the thirty-two bars.

ALL THE THINGS YOU ARE

music by Jerome Kern, lyric by Oscar Hammerstein 2nd
from the musical *Very Warm for May* (1939)

Jerome Kern reached his most rhapsodic heights, and then some, with **All the Things You Are,**❋ which was written for what turned out to be his final Broadway musical. The refrain starts simply, with a whole note ("you") in the first measure jumping a fourth to a dotted half ("are") in the second ("YOU—ARE—the promised kiss of springtime," in the glorious words of Oscar Hammerstein). This is followed by four repeated quarter notes in bar 3, another jump of a fourth in bar 4, and another four repeated quarters in bar 5. In bar 6, though, the expected interval is raised to a diminished fifth; and the cadence at the end of the first *A* is out of key, being an *e♮* in what had been the key of A♭. The *A¹* is similar to the first section, although it starts four steps lower, on *e♭* instead of *a♭*. The bridge is altogether remarkable, featuring a drop of a diminished seventh ("you are the angel GLOW—THAT lights a star") followed by a leap of a minor sixth ("that LIGHTS—A star"). In *A²* (of *A- A¹-B-A²*)—which extends twelve bars instead of the eight in the prior sections—Kern fools us again, with a grand leap of a minor seventh going from bar 5 to 6 ("and SOME—DAY").

But these leaps and eccentricities aren't contrived; they're inspired, always resolving in a felicitous manner that seems inevitable. This is in good part why Kern paved the way for the next generation (Gershwin, Youmans, Rodgers et al.)—although ol' man Kern demonstrated, time and again, that time and the times hadn't passed him by. Let it be added that the refrain was preceded by a unique thirty-eight-bar verse. (If you search out a copy of "All the Things You Are," be advised that later printings truncate or in some cases thoroughly omit the intrinsically connected verse.)

This glorious love song was written to be sung—as part of a musical within the musical—by tongue-tied teenagers. (The director within the musical explains: "In this scene, the two lovers are too shy to express their real feelings, so this duet is sung by their heart voices.") At the start, they confess what they would say if they weren't so inarticulate and bashful. The refrain—or "burthen," as Kern insisted on labeling it throughout his career—was what their "heart voices" sang.

Nobody quite understands why Kern insisted on labeling his refrain as *burthen* (an archaic form of *burden*); the composer seemed to pull it from Shakespeare's stage directions within Ariel's songs in *The Tempest*. Whatever.

A funny thing happened when Stephen Sondheim, long after Kern's death, formed his own personal publishing company for *A Funny Thing Happened on the Way to the Forum*: he honored Kern by naming it Burthen Music. And I suppose it's now permissible to add that he used "burthen music" as his e-mail address. Sondheim, not Kern.

For those interested in such matters, be advised that there are three "original" published versions of this song. The preferred one, referred to above, is the second: the catalog number, on the bottom left of the five pages, is C-981-5. The verse is in G, burthen in A♭. The six-page initial printing (C-975-6) is titled "All the Things You Are, Are Mine." This was likely on sale at the theatre for the initial October tryout date, along with five other songs from the show. It is marked "Duet," with a second vocal line in places, and is in A♭ (verse) and B♭ (burthen). C-981-5 appears to have been published within the month, in time for the November Broadway opening. A truncated version (C-1007-4)—"simplified edition by Albert Sirmay," it says on the initial printing—was published in 1940 following the quick failure of the musical. This four-page version retains the keys of the second version but has a reduced sixteen-bar verse with a generic lyric ("time and again I've longed for adventure").

Further complicating the issue is that Kern wrote the music as "Cantabile," subtitled "a song without words," for his failed 1938 musical *Gentlemen Unafraid*. The copyright registration reveals that the original verse was a standard sixteen bars, later extended to justify the use of those "heart voices" in "All the Things You Are." The burthen remains as we know it until the bridge; in the original, Kern repeated the first four bars, whereas in the final version he keeps the pattern but lowers the actual note and provides an uncanny modulation. The *A2* in "Cantabile" is not the twelve-bar section we know but goes on for sixteen bars. Kern was famous for not altering his melodies to accommodate his lyricists; in this case, though, he did so with altogether glorious results.

ALONE TOGETHER

music by Arthur Schwartz, lyric by Howard Dietz
from the stage revue *Flying Colors* (1932)

Arthur Schwartz and Howard Dietz followed their memorable 1931 revue *The Band Wagon* with the troubled and quickly forgotten *Flying Colors*. Even so, they managed to match the power of the earlier show's instant classic—"Dancing in the Dark" [page 31]—with an equally worthy stunner, **Alone Together**.§ The two ballads conjure the image of a composer brooding in a Manhattan penthouse at twilight. This verseless song is decidedly unusual in form: after the initial two-bar title phrase, Schwartz moves to an ascending figure (three times, over six bars) before descending over the next six bars. This fourteen-bar *A* section (of *A-A-B-A¹*) is then repeated, intact. The eight-bar bridge is even more highly dramatic, marked by two inner bars containing quarter-note triplets ("our love —IS AS DEEP AS THE sea") with a hold over the penultimate (and highest) note in each four-bar half.

Schwartz begins his final section with the first four bars of the *A* and then cuts to a four-bar ending. Outlining this form seems almost trivial, given the power of the work from Schwartz and lyricist Dietz, the latter of whom provides equally moving words. It does suggest that the pair were so very inspired while writing this song that they simply ignored what they knew about the standard thirty-two-bar refrain, winding up with an unusual forty-four. That is not to say that there is something pedestrian about a ballad of thirty-two bars, as demonstrated in "Dancing in the Dark" and "I See Your Face Before Me" [page 75].

ANOTHER AUTUMN

music by Frederick Loewe, lyric by Alan Jay Lerner
from the musical *Paint Your Wagon* (1951)

The use of consistent repeated notes is not uncommon within our songbook. In many cases this is incidental, or subliminal, on the part of the composer; this varies so greatly that it is senseless to make pronouncements. **Another Autumn**, an expressive song of unfulfilled yearning, seems consciously devised by skilled craftsman Frederick Loewe around the use of repetition. It is unknown how this song was written, but from the sound of it we'd have to guess that lyricist Alan Jay Lerner—or more likely, the pair in tandem—came up with the title; Loewe devised the figure—three quarter-note pickups followed by two half notes, all on a repeated *a* (in the key of F) which in bar 4 resolves to *g*:

That was not incidental, mind you; he goes on to use those three repeated pickups in fourteen of the thirty-two bars. The *A* sections are loaded with repeated notes: eight of those *a*s in the first phrase, followed by nine *g*s. He shifts the pattern in the *B* ("for you can / dream in spring"), giving us four repeated *c*s (including the pickups) rising to six *d*s. He then finishes the bridge (of *A-B-A¹-C/A*) with a staggered scale (*c–c–d / d–e–e–f / f–g–g–g# / g#–a–a*). Loewe alters the melody in *A¹*, building to a climactic high *d* ("but how it haunts you / when all is WRONG"). He then drops an octave for the pickup notes to the final section. If this sounds mechanical, the effect is anything but. All those repetitions serve to express the unfulfilled yearning and unexpressed undercurrent of sexual frustration within the song—the musical was set in a rough gold rush mining camp, with hardly a woman in sight—as Lerner concludes, "if you're alone when autumn comes, you'll be alone all winter long."

APRIL IN PARIS

music by Vernon Duke, lyric by E. Y. Harburg
from the stage revue *Walk a Little Faster* (1932)

Vernon Duke's friend and mentor G. Gershwin and Yip Harburg's college pal I. Gershwin teamed the two up-and-coming songwriters in a match not quite made in heaven, one that would soon culminate in notably public backstage strife—but not before this odd couple turned out **April in Paris**.§ It was a song, mind you, that had nothing whatsoever to do with the production: a brash contemporary revue starring comedians Beatrice Lillie and Bobby Clark. The story goes that when the designer—a young, expressionistic Russian émigré named Boris Aronson—came up with a striking Paris streetscape, the producer demanded a suitable song to match. "April in Paris" was an instant classic that pushed newcomers Duke and Harburg into the rarefied rank of pedigreed songwriters at Harms, publishers of Kern/Gershwin/Rodgers/Porter et al. Harburg, from the rough-and-tumble Lower East Side, didn't know from Paris; but the Kiev-trained Duke, who had written for Diaghilev and the Ballets Russes in the City of Light, was altogether steeped in authentic atmosphere.

The sixteen-bar verse is as bright and airy as a morning ramble in the Tuileries, at which point the tang of wine in the April air (as Harburg puts it) turns exalted. The refrain is anchored by the title phrase, built on triplets:

This makes the song instantly imperishable and altogether unforgettable. This figure is used thrice in the each of the *A* sections (of *A-A¹-B-A²*), starting on *f* (in the key of C) the first two times, then down a minor third to *d*. After that Duke drops to *b* and then steps up to high *d* over only six beats. The bridge lightens the tempo with the use of a pattern of eighth notes and repeated quarter notes, after which we return to those "April in Paris" triplets.

AS LONG AS I LIVE

music by Harold Arlen, lyric by Ted Koehler
from the stage revue *Cotton Club Parade*, 24th edition (1934)

Harold Arlen demonstrated that his musical paintbox encompassed far more than just varied shades of blue with **As Long as I Live**, written for his final edition of the *Cotton Club Parade* and the swan song of his collaboration with lyricist Ted Koehler (of "Get Happy" [page 44], "Stormy Weather" [page 163], and other golden classics).

The refrain leaps forth with a breathlessly syncopated rhythm, interrupted only occasionally for sustained half notes:

Arlen centers his *A* sections on *a*—the third note of the scale, in the key of F: all of those syncopated notes in the first two bars are *a* except for slight pivots, on the sixteenth notes, to *b♭*. The *A* wends its way down to end on *f*, as it should; but then it's back to those *a*s. The bridge halts the word explosion—at least temporarily—by cutting down to four notes or so a bar, in a descending pattern: *e♭* (with a leap to *c*, a major sixth, and back) in bar 1, *d* (up a minor sixth) in bar 2, then *d♭* (up a major sixth), and finally landing on c. The notes then break out into dotted eighths and sixteenths set to a colorful torrent of words from Koehler such as the pert "I'm gonna take good care of me because, a sneeze or two might mean the flu and that would never never do."

"As Long as I Live" was sung and danced to great acclaim by a sixteen-year-old chorine named Lena Horne. When she came to Broadway a quarter century later heading the Arlen-Harburg musical *Jamaica*, Horne saw to it that a featured spot—billed "in a box," as they say—went to Adelaide Hall, the star of the 24th *Cotton Club Parade* who had memorably introduced "Ill Wind" [page 81].

Despite five years of memorable song hits with Arlen, Koehler receded into virtual anonymity; this is what can happen when you're displaced by the likes of E. Y. Harburg, Ira Gershwin, and Johnny Mercer. Koehler's name may have faded, but his songs certainly haven't.

AUTUMN IN NEW YORK

music and lyric by Vernon Duke
from the stage revue *Thumbs Up!* (1934)

Vernon Duke—having been deserted by Yip Harburg, who turned combative on their final revue and moved over to a collaboration with Harold Arlen—seems to have set out to prove that he didn't need Harburg or anyone to write another song as exquisite as "April in Paris" [page 9]. Surprisingly—English was Duke's second language—the Russian immigrant was able to do precisely that. If **Autumn in New York** is not quite so imperishable as the earlier song, that's more a question of the nostalgia of the case. (Every time I ponder returning to France, I pine for those chestnuts in blossom; as a lifelong New Yorker, I am no longer quite so enthused by dark benches in Central Park.) What's more, Duke's lyric—referring to "the thrill of first nighting" as well as "jaded roués and gay divorcees who lunch at the Ritz"—is perhaps overly erudite for present-day use.

The title phrase, which sets off the *A* sections (of *A-B-A¹-C/A*), is set to a descending phrase skipping from *a* to *c* (in the key of F). This continues ("why does it seem so inviting?") by ascending an octave up to *d* before settling on an *a*:

Duke, as is his tendency, grows adventurous in *A¹* and strays into exotic harmonies culminating with an extreme *d♭* whole note, initially against a B♭-minor chord but moving to G♭-major. Not incidentally, the word Duke uses in his lyric there is "pain." The thirty-two-bar refrain is preceded by a verse worth noting, which starts out gently melancholic but cycles through extreme harmonics while the singer stands "on the twenty-seventh floor, looking down on the city I hate—and adore." Note the four chords that lead into the chorus; the last bar of the verse ("a-DORE") starts on F-major, moving to G-minor for the refrain.

THE BALLAD OF THE SAD YOUNG MEN

music by Tommy Wolf, lyric by Fran Landesman
from the musical *The Nervous Set* (1959)

"Sing a song of sad young men," starts the lyric, and that's precisely what we get: a keenly provocative, and wrenchingly beautiful, lament for lost souls "drinking up the night trying not to drown." Fran Landesman was a beat-era poet; Tommy Wolf was a jazz pianist, playing at the St. Louis nightclub owned by Landesman's husband. They wrote songs and fashioned a satiric musical that played well at the club but was a total bust upon a misguided transplantation to Broadway. But **The Ballad of the Sad Young Men**⸸ is a marvel; I'm a strong proponent of "One for My Baby" [page 132], but this song speaks just as pointedly for the displaced young men of the next generation.

The form is unusual, in that what seems to be the verse turns out to be inseparable from the rest. Thus: *A-B-C-B-C¹*. As printed, they then circle back for a full repeat (including the *A* section) and end with an eight-bar coda, and I wouldn't want to hear the song without the entire lyric. "Tired little girl does the best she can," Landesman writes, "trying to be gay for a sad young man." Was she broadly hinting, in 1959, at a double meaning? Perhaps, as that connotation appears to have started to surface. In any case, her ballad—and all those sad young men choking on their youth beneath that grimy moon—remains universal.

THE BEST IS YET TO COME

music by Cy Coleman, lyric by Carolyn Leigh
non-production song (1959)

The team of Coleman and Leigh peaked with this sinuous, finger-snappin' hit. The song starts with an intriguing vamp—as does their 1957 hit, "Witchcraft" [page 195]—and follows a path so unprecedented that one can't efficiently describe it.

The first section is twelve bars, which could be broken down as *a-a-b*. The key abruptly shifts—from A♭ to C, in the original sheet music—for two identical four-bar *a* sections followed by a variation of the original *b*, in the new key, which is instantly repeated. The initial refrain then switches back to A♭ with a restatement of the *A* followed by a four-bar ending. That's thirty-six bars thus far, with Coleman repeating—*seven* times—the rhythmic pattern of the first four-bar section:

But it turns out that he is only halfway through. Next comes what is labeled Interlude, built on a second distinct rhythm that had been introduced at the very end of the first section (to the words "come the day you're mine"). The interlude repeats it, on different tones, four times. We then return to the rhythmic pattern of the original section for sixteen bars, starting the theme on *f* (twice) and then on *e♭* (twice). After all of this, a driving three chords move us into the key of A for a restatement of what had been the final eight bars prior to the interlude, albeit in the new key and with an extra bar added to the final phrase. Who's counting, but I get sixty-nine bars—all of them pulsatingly alive, with numerous surprises along the way.

The success of **The Best Is Yet to Come** quickly propelled Coleman and Leigh into what would be two failed Broadway musicals—*Wildcat* (1960) and *Little Me* (1962)—with the latter causing an acrimonious breakup of the team. As with "Witchcraft," Leigh's colorful lyric is so instantly arresting—"out of the tree of life I just picked me a plum"—that song lovers bemoan the fact that her self-sabotaging career dead-ended following the parting with Coleman.

THE BIRTH OF THE BLUES

music by Ray Henderson, lyric by B. G. DeSylva and Lew Brown
from the stage revue *George White's Scandals*, 8th edition (1926)

I expect that if you were looking for an authentic and/ or accurate representation of the origins of that ever-so-American form of music called jazz, **The Birth of the Blues**※—from DeSylva, Brown, and Henderson, purveyors of "Button Up Your Overcoat," "The Best Things in Life Are Free," and "The Varsity Drag" [page 186]—isn't it. But it is sure dynamic.

Henderson, the composer of the team, starts with a slow and sinuous verse: six of the sixteen bars consist of whole notes—all on *c*, in the key of C—whereas the rest are crammed with dotted eighths and sixteenths. Three chromatic descending chords lead into that powerful refrain ("they heard the breeze in the trees singing weird melodies, and they called it the birth of the blues"). The lyric, by today's standards, is practically unusable; but that doesn't diminish the power of the music.

Speaking of high Broadway ticket prices, the going rate for top-price entertainments in 1926 was $5.50. For the gala opening night of this edition of *George White's Scandals*, producer White demonstrated his entrepreneurial flair by charging a walloping $55—and, apparently, getting it from sensation-seeking sophisticates.

BLUE DAY

music by Abraham Ellstein, lyric by Walter Bullock
from the musical *Great to Be Alive!* (1950)

Among our most obscure selections is this song from a pair of first-and-only-time-on-Broadway songwriters from a show that practically collapsed during its tryout and staggered through a short run at the Winter Garden. Composer Abe Ellstein was a prince of the Yiddish Theatre, making his one and only foray uptown from Second Avenue. (His wife, Sylvia Regan, who wrote the book for *Great to Be Alive!*, returned to Broadway in 1953 with the long-running garment-industry hit, *The Fifth Season*.) Lyricist Bullock was thoroughly unknown to me, although it turns out that his little-known catalog of songs includes Oscar nominees written with Richard A. Whiting ("When Did You Leave Heaven," 1936) and Jule Styne ("Who Am I," 1940). Vinton Freedley—producer of Gershwin (*Girl Crazy*), Porter (*Anything Goes*), and numerous major hits—unaccountably came up with, and ended his career with, this one. The show was called *What a Day!* during the tryout; they changed the title but kept the story—about a couple getting married in a mansion haunted by ghosts—and kept the exclamation mark as well.

All of that aside, **Blue Day** is striking. Ellstein starts the main phrase with a quarter rest, marked by a dynamic chord in the piano accompaniment, followed by two *c*s (in the key of C), immediately dropping a minor seventh to *d* and running up to *a* in bar 2. He then moves this pattern down a step, with the resulting drop becoming a major seventh, *b* to *c*. The rest of the *A* (of *A-A-B-A¹*) features scale-like figures. Two-thirds of a triplet serves as a striking pickup into the second *A*. The bridge is built on sustained notes, bluesy chromatics, and three sets of well-defined triplets as Ellstein works his way from C-7—through F to F-minor to B♭ to E♭ and G-7—back to C, with a set of five pickup notes leading into the final section. (Could this sort of thing be typical of his Yiddish Theatre songs?) As a final fillip, Ellstein throws in a highly unexpected *e♮* for the second-to-last note. Find "Blue Day" if you can.

BLUES IN THE NIGHT

music by Harold Arlen, lyric by Johnny Mercer
from the motion picture *Blues in the Night* (1941)

There is little purpose in labeling this song or that song, among the many herein represented, as best, most important, or whatever. So, let's just leave **Blues in the Night**※ to stand on its own. It is also inefficient, given the unprecedented intricacies of this song, to attempt to explain the what and the why. Let it be said, though, that one Hollywood morn Arlen and Mercer were thrown together to write the blues, and they did. (They were not altogether unknown to each other: Mercer had in 1932 collaborated with his pal Yip Harburg on the lyric for the otherwise unexceptional "Satan's Li'l Lamb," with music by Arlen; and Mercer, in his singing days, had briefly partnered with Harold's younger brother Jerry as two of the Rhythm Boys with Paul Whiteman's Band.)

The music is keenly matched by Mercer's lyric, with that opening phrase—"my mama done tol' me"—instantly entering the lexicon. This is, indeed, a blues; that is to say, in this world of *A-A-B-A* songs consisting of eight-bar (or sixteen-bar) sections, most of "Blues in the Night" is composed in the twelve-bar sections common with the blues, purposely so. Arlen later confessed that while trying to write what he intended to be an authentic blues, he studied W. C. Handy's 1926 book "Blues: An Anthology." Arlen starts with a four-bar phrase built around a two-bar figure that is repeated as an echo; this turns out to be not so much an instrumental introduction as an intrinsic part of the song. Then comes the main statement in the *A* section, built around the musical phrase accompanying Mercer's colloquial catchphrase. Next comes the twelve-bar bridge ("now the rain is falling"), ending with the two-bar title phrase first heard at the end of *A*. This smoothly moves into *C* ("the evenin' breeze"), which consists of two almost-identical eight-bar sections. Then, thirty bars in, comes a two-bar reinstatement of the aforementioned introductory figure, with the singer instructed—per the sheet music—to whistle. This leads to a musical repeat of the twelve-bar *A* ("from Natchez to Mobile"). Then, as if to find the perfect way to finish this instant classic, Arlen forms a four-bar coda consisting of the introductory phrase followed by a tag: "My mama was right, there's blues in the night."

By 1941, Arlen (of "Stormy Weather" [page 163]) was already established as one of the most distinctive composers in the Broadway/Hollywood world, and the up-and-coming Mercer (of "Jeepers Creepers" [page 96] and "Too Marvelous for Words" [page 184]) was recognized for his folksy wordplay. "Blues in the Night," though, was something else again, and it turned out to be only the first of quite a few astonishing songs from the pair. But this is a song to be heard or sung, not clinically deconstructed.

BODY AND SOUL

music by John W. (Johnny) Green, lyric by Edward Heyman,
Robert Sour, and Frank Eyton
from the stage revue *Three's a Crowd* (1930)

This searing torch song appeared early in 1930 and immediately burst into international prominence. The sixteen-bar verse starts with a four-bar phrase ("life's dreary for me") in D minor, which is then restated in D major. The verse ends with a modulation to C for the refrain, initially, anyway. The haunting *A* section ("my heart is sad and lonely") is relatively straightforward and repeated in the customary manner. Then comes an abrupt detour to D♭ for four bars ("I can't believe it")—which then moves into E major ("are you pretending"), culminating in a remarkable modulation back to C for a final restatement of the *A*. Thus, the form is—quite surprisingly—a standard thirty-two-bar *A-A-B-A*, with a sixteen-bar verse, but nothing is standard about this song. While admiring those unworldly modulations, note how Johnny Green—in the sixth bar of the *A* sections—uses instrumental eighth-note triplets (on a low *e*) to thrust forward into the phrase "I'm all for you, **Body and Soul**"※).

The tangled tale of the song's creation bears unraveling. It was written by Green—a twenty-one-year-old piano prodigy from Queens—on commission from transplanted musical comedy star Gertrude Lawrence. She took it back to England and sang it on the radio, which led to multiple UK recordings and international acclaim, as a result of which it was purchased for inclusion in the upcoming Broadway revue *Three's a Crowd*. Green wrote it with his New York collaborators Edward Heyman and Robert Sour; Frank Eyton, a little-known

British lyricist, presumably made revisions for the premiere recordings in February 1930, meriting (or just taking) coauthor credit. Back in America, Howard Dietz—who assembled *Three's a Crowd*, which opened in October—rewrote the lyric for inclusion in the show. This version was duly published and circulated but withdrawn during the tryout in favor of the earlier Heyman-Sour-Eyton text. For those interested in such things, the authorized version credits Heyman, Sour, and Eyton as lyricists; the Dietz version ("my days have grown so lonely, for I have lost my one and only"), if you can locate it, credits Heyman and Sour but neither Eyton nor Dietz.

BORN TOO LATE

music by Vernon Duke, lyric by Ogden Nash
from the stage revue *The Littlest Revue* (1956)

Duke—whose esoteric roots as a White Russian escapee from the Bolshevik Revolution left him somewhat outside the Kern-Gershwin-Rodgers Broadway tradition—grew thoroughly out of fashion following one successful book musical, *Cabin in the Sky* (1940). He kept plugging away through numerous quick failures, his musicality overwhelmed by the work of his collaborators and compounded by the composer's own hardheadedness. **Born Too Late** demonstrates both his musicality and his tendency to write on a higher musical plane.

The song can be described, I suppose, as "unearthly"—harmonically, chromatically, structurally, and in overall effect. The *A* section, following a tentative sixteen-bar verse, is positively unsettling from the first pickup notes and the accompanying chords. (The lyric tells of a singer who bemoans that slumbering princesses no longer await rescue—this from famed versifier Ogden Nash, whose one claim to musical comedy fame is his collaboration with Kurt Weill on *One Touch of Venus*, which brought forth "Speak Low" [page 158].) The form, in six eight-bar sections, is a highly unusual *A-B-C-D-A-B/A*. It's unearthly but arrestingly lovely. Duke himself noted his increasing tendency to write "out of this world" tunes: "not heavenly, just plain uncommercial."

THE BOY NEXT DOOR

music and lyric by Hugh Martin (credited to Hugh Martin and Ralph Blane)
from the motion picture *Meet Me in St. Louis* (1944)

Hugh Martin, at his best, was a master of the unexpected note set to unexpected harmony. The initial four bars of **The Boy Next Door** make it instantly imperishable. This tender waltz of unrequited love is built upon the yearning expressed in the augmented fifth heard in the first two bars of the *A* section ("how can I IG-nore") and then repeated, down a step, in the next ("the BOY NEXT door"). In both cases, Martin immediately resolves the notes a half step up. The bridge (of *A-B-A¹-C/A*) switches to simple ascending runs, starting on *c* (in the key of B♭) in bar 1, *d* in bar 3, and *e♮* in bar 5. In the *C* section, he gives us a major sixth—descending, instead of ascending ("I JUST A-dore him")—before wrapping up with the title phrase on chromatically ascending notes. The extended verse is marked by half-note pickups (in ¾) in bars 4 and 8 of the initial eight-bar section and its repeat. Another distinctive touch comes in the final section leading into the refrain, with no fewer than twenty-four repeated notes as the lyric spells out the abodes of the neighbors. To wit: "though / I live at / fifty-one thirty- / -five Kensington / Avenue and / he lives at / fifty-one thirty- / -three."

At his best, Martin's colors were on a level with the likes of Gershwin and Arlen, which explains his outsized fan base even after all these years. But as Martin himself admitted, he was infrequently motivated to be "at his best." Although the song is credited to Martin and Blane, it was written by Martin— almost entirely. When Blane heard the verse, he thought it needed something more and suggested that Martin add that final eight-bar section spelling out the street addresses. (See authorship note on page 39.)

BROTHER, CAN YOU SPARE A DIME?

music by Jay Gorney, lyric by E. Y. Harburg
from the stage revue *Americana* (1932)

Rarely has a song—a song from a lavishly designed and staged revue, no less—had such outsized and long-lasting impact. But Yip Harburg, who worked with a selection of handpicked composers on this Shubert revue (with a "Cast of 100 Persons"), was strong on social significance. **Brother, Can You Spare a Dime?**—presumably a not-uncommon street plaint, circa 1932—hit a nerve, poignantly and evocatively capturing the burst dreams of a couple of generations worth of Americans.

Composer Jay Gorney provides a suitably dramatic setting in this thirty-two-bar A-A-B-A^1 song, with the plaintive A leading into a martial-paced B as the lyric recounts what they used to call the Great War. There is a remarkable device through the A section. The melody, in bar 1, ends on high c (in the key of E♭). Bar 2 starts on $b♮$ and ends on $b♭$; bar 3, $a♮$ and $a♭$. Bar 4 is a whole note, g; and the descent continues until the middle c, which ends bar 7 and is held through the cadence. Wherever has there been a song like this? And how fitting for this imperishable theme of the forgotten man? Except Yip relates that Gorney's music was written earlier, with someone other than Harburg, for a forgotten and apparently never-used torch song ("I could go on crying / big blue tears"). Which is to say, the spark of creation—even in the case of a perfect song representing an imperishable marriage of music and words—doesn't necessarily strike at the same time, the same place, or even the same year. At any rate, the plaintive sixteen-bar verse ("why should I be standing in line, just waiting for bread?") surely was created specifically for the occasion.

Politics and the blacklist eventually caught up with both songwriters. Harburg did fine, thanks to his gilt-edged ASCAP residuals. Gorney, who despite an active career on Broadway and Hollywood doesn't have another song you're likely to be familiar with, pretty much lost it all. He also lost his first wife—to Harburg, who married her. Bruce Pomahac recalls meeting Edelaine Harburg and expressing surprise that she had been married to both. "Oh, my dear," she said with the manner of someone who had delivered this line hundreds of times, "I wouldn't marry anyone who *didn't* write "Brother,

Can You Spare a Dime!'" Still, Gorney retained the memory of his opening night review from Brooks Atkinson in the *New York Times*: "You are likely to feel that Mr. Gorney has expressed the spirit of these times with more heart-breaking anguish than any of the prose bards of the day." Talk about immediate impact.

CAN THIS BE LOVE?

music by Kay Swift, lyric by Paul James
from the musical *Fine and Dandy* (1930)

The success of "Can't We Be Friends" [page 23] led Kay Swift and her pseudonymous lyricist-husband to be commissioned to write the full score for *Fine and Dandy*. This vehicle for the rambunctious comedian Joe Cook included the familiar title song—which for reasons not quite understood is indelibly linked to magicians and magic acts—and the moodily romantic **Can This Be Love?**❦ As far as I can tell, Swift was only the second woman composer to write a full-scale Broadway musical; the first to write an entire score; and the first to write a hit show, at least by post-crash standards. (Preceding Swift was the altogether forgotten Alma Sanders, who served on a half dozen negligible musicals as cocomposer/lyricist with her husband—a Dane whose pseudonym was, get this, Monte Carlo.)

"Can This Be Love?" features a strong melody with a jump of a sixth in bar 1 ("I'm ALL AT sea"). Upon restatement, this becomes a full octave. The bridge (in *A-B-A-B¹* form) ends in a deft harmonic progression of remarkable colors. The verse, it should be noted, is so strong that it might well have served as a song of its own. As for the course of true love, Swift and James finally divorced in 1934 after eight years of her on-and-off affair with George Gershwin. The last time I saw Kay was in 1991 at William Finn's *Falsettoland*, a show I produced. (Burton Lane, who'd been there a week before, told her she must see it.) "Oh," Kay said to me, "do you know Frankie Godowsky?" It took a moment to realize that the octogenarian I was shaking hands with was George's adored kid sister, Frances Gershwin.

CAN'T HELP LOVIN' DAT MAN

music by Jerome Kern, lyric by Oscar Hammerstein 2nd
from the musical *Show Boat* (1927)

Kern and Hammerstein start the instantly memorable **Can't Help Lovin' Dat Man** in a bright and open manner—accentuated by friendly intervals of fourths and fifths—but with a sense of foreboding overshadowing the merriness. "Fish got to swim and birds got to fly" fills the first two bars with mostly eighth notes:

These jump from *b♭* to *e♭* (in the key of E♭) and back. The next bars repeat the rhythm, with the interval now a fifth (*G* to *C* to *G*). Then comes the title phrase, with Kern intruding a disharmonious *c♭* (and then *g♭*) for "LOV-in' dat MAN" before resolving the final cadence of the *A* (of *A-A-B-A*). He offers a different sort of surprise in the bridge: after his note-filled *A*, he moves to four quarter notes (*f*) followed by an *f#* whole note ("When he goes a-WAY"); moves it up a step for the next two bars, and then up a step further. This progression builds its way to a high *f* (the highest note of the song) on "fine," after which he takes us back down to the *b♭* that begins the final *A* section. The foreboding signaled by that errant *c♭* is not merely imagined; in dramatic context, it serves as one of the themes of the musical *Show Boat*, in that the two leading ladies endure dismal marriages because, indeed, they truly can't help lovin' dat man.

The authors devised the song so that it would work both slowly (in "Tempo di Blues") and in a quicker manner (when reprised in Act 2). It is effective either way and quite grand, and don't overlook the joyous verse. Hammerstein, as a lyricist, didn't have the same silvery tongue as many of his peers, who regularly matched unforgettable words to melodic snatches. "Fish got to swim and birds got to fly" makes a notable exception. Some of the dialect writing, here and elsewhere in *Show Boat*, is long outdated for our time and place. But in the context of when it was produced, and when Hammerstein revised it for subsequent stage and screen productions prior to his death in 1960, *Show Boat*—as typified by "Ol' Man River" [page 129]—was a powerful force for racial tolerance.

CAN'T WE BE FRIENDS?

music by Kay Swift, lyric by Paul James
from the stage revue *The Little Show* (1929)

Novice composer Kay Swift attracted immediate notice with **Can't We Be Friends?**, a smoky ballad of love lost interpolated into the 1929 Arthur Schwartz–Howard Dietz revue *The Little Show*. Providing the words was her husband, an amateur lyricist whose pseudonym masked the fact that he was James Paul Warburg, scion of the banking family and later a key financial adviser to Franklin D. Roosevelt. Their marriage was already on the rocks, alas, irremediably busted by Swift's relationship with another man: George Gershwin, who early on recognized and encouraged Swift's musical talent. (Wanting to expand the experience of his protégé, George arranged for Kay—who prior to her marriage had been a professional musician—to serve as rehearsal pianist for the 1927 Rodgers and Hart musical, *A Connecticut Yankee*.)

"Can't We Be Friends?" is stunning, thoroughly fulfilling Gershwin's confidence. The *A* section offers a long-lined melody (starting "I—thought I'd found the / man of my dreams") that ascends an octave and a third (*c* to high *f*, in the key of F); descends an octave, in bar 4; and then scales back up to high *d* before ending with the abrupt title phrase. The bridge (of *A-A-B-A*) is marvelously chromatic, building to a severe drop from *e♭* to *f♯* in the fifth bar. If the first two bars are colorful, bar 3 is uncanny, with an unexpected *d♭* that I suppose can be described as Gershwin-esque; but my guess is that it's purely, fully Swiftian. Based on numerous accounts, it appears that George valued Kay more for her musicianship—and freely involved her in his creative process—than for her charms. And, it also appears, vice versa.

CAROLINA IN THE MORNING

music by Walter Donaldson, lyric by Gus Kahn
from the stage revue *The Passing Show of 1922* (1922)

Tin Pan Alley, back in the 1920s, was awash with nostalgic "take me back home songs" that soon became a cliché of their own—these by tunesmiths who, for the most part, had never set foot south of Delancey Street. (The most successful specimen, perhaps, was the 1919 "Swanee," by George Gershwin from Brooklyn.) Falling within this sphere—but standing out because it really is quite effective—is **Carolina in the Morning**.* Walter Donaldson was already a song-selling force, with the wartime hit "How Ya Gonna Keep 'em Down on the Farm (After They've Seen Paree)?" and Al Jolson's mammy song to end all mammy songs, "My Mammy." Although Donaldson and his "Carolina" lyricist, Gus Kahn, lie outside the ranks of hallowed songwriters, both make multiple appearances on these pages.

Here, Donaldson (who was also born in Brooklyn) hit upon a musical phrase as simple as can be: start on *g* (in the key of C), go down a minor third to *e* and back eight times over two bars, and end the phrase on an *f* whole note: "Nothing could be finer than to / be in Carolina in the / mor-or-or- / ning." He then goes up a step to *a* and pivots down a major third to *f*. Thus, an A section (of *A-B-A-C/A*) that you can't help but find catchy. The bridge ("where the morning glories") is lighter of note and more varied of tone, moving down and up. The four-bar *C* brings the comfortable rhythm to something of a surprising martial rhythm, with a new melodic pattern of *c–g–a–g* ("if I had Aladdin's lamp"), after which he ends with a phrase derived from those initial minor thirds. Kahn, meanwhile, blithely indulges in triple rhymes ("butterflies all flutter up and kiss each little buttercup"). I'm not all that fond of the modern-day term earworm, which can be seen to belittle the accomplishments of accomplished tunesmiths. But those teeter-tottering thirds of "Carolina in the Morning" make something of a visualization of an earworm, and just try to forget this melody.

CHARLESTON

words and music by Cecil Mack and Jimmy (James P.) Johnson
music by Jimmy (James P.) Johnson, lyric by Cecil Mack
from the musical *Runnin' Wild* (1923)

Here's a song that launched a thousand imitations, few of them anywhere near so vibrant. "Jimmy Johnson" was James P. Johnson, a renowned black pianist considered to be the originator of the overactive, octave-leaping left hand playing that came to be called stride piano. In the wake of the success of the 1921 musical *Shuffle Along*, that groundbreaking musical's book writers (and stars) Flournoy Miller and Aubrey Lyles assembled a follow-up—conspicuously *without* the participation of songwriters Eubie Blake and Noble Sissle. Producer George White, an ex-*Follies* dancer who determined to out-Ziegfeld Ziegfeld, started his own annual series (*George White's Scandals*) in 1919, with an emphasis on roaring twenties dance crazes. These included songs such as "The Birth of the Blues" [page 14] and "Black Bottom." But first came **Charleston**,※ a song about a dance "made in Carolina":

It promises that "if you' ain't got religion in your feet, you can do this prance and do it neat." The world did. Despite the song's topicality a century back and its less than presentable lyric, it still packs quite the wallop.

CHEEK TO CHEEK

music and lyric by Irving Berlin
from the motion picture *Top Hat* (1935)

The studio heads at RKO, realizing that they had stumbled into a potential gold mine with Fred Astaire and Ginger Rogers, saw the wisdom of importing Broadway's top songwriters—at top dollar—to write original scores with new songs for the team. Thus, they invited Berlin to Hollywood for *Top Hat.* Astaire had achieved stage stardom singing Gershwin songs such as "Fascinating Rhythm" [page 40] and film stardom with Porter's "Night and Day" [page 127]. Astaire did seem to bring out the best in composers. Berlin certainly outdid himself on the occasion with several intriguing songs, including "Top Hat, White Tie and Tails," "Isn't This a Lovely Day to Be Caught in the Rain," and the even more remarkable **Cheek to Cheek.**

The first four bars of the sixteen-bar *A* section are simple enough ("heaven, I'm in heaven"). Berlin then builds a string of quarter notes, in stepwise fashion, up to a high *e* (in the key of C), after which he reverses the process down to a low *e* and ends the section with a couple of Astaire-syncopated bars to the main phrase ("when we're out together dancing cheek to cheek"):

The *A* then repeats, in typical fashion, after which Berlin eschews formula altogether. The eight-bar bridge is conversationally syncopated ("oh, I love to climb a mountain"), culminating again with the title phrase. After this section is repeated, we go not back to the *A* but to a distinctive and significantly more romantic *C* section ("dance with me, I want my arm about you"). This is the only minor-key section of the song—elsewhere he's describing what it's *like* to dance with her; here he's *asking* her to dance with him—and Berlin features somewhat severe interior melodic drops, from *e♭* to *g♭* and then *d* to *f*. All of this dovetails, smoothly, into the final restatement of the *A*. Thus: *A*(sixteen bars)-*A*(sixteen)-*B*(eight)-*B*(eight)-*C*(eight)-*A*(sixteen). That's seventy-two bars from Tin Pan Alley Irving, remarkable not so much for the form but the sterling result.

CHICAGO (THAT TODD'LING TOWN)

music and lyric by Fred Fisher
non-production song (1922)

Fred Fisher was a prolific Chicago songwriter/publisher with a large, and largely undistinguished, thousand-song catalog including the 1913 sentimental favorite "Peg o' My Heart"; the 1914 Jolson hit "Who Paid the Rent for Mrs. Rip Van Winkle (When Rip Van Winkle Went Away)?"; and the 1919 novelty smash "Dardanella." Fisher is best known, in Broadway circles at least, for his million-dollar suit against Jerome Kern for stealing the distinctive bass accompaniment of "Dardanella" (the initial recording of which is said to have been the first 3-million copy seller, ultimately hitting the 6.5 million copies), which Kern used as the basis for the more moderate hit "Ka-Lu-A" (from the 1921 musical comedy *Good Morning, Dearie*).

Fisher won a Pyrrhic victory, the judge determining that although the charge had merit, he found it unintentional and determined to give the distinguished Kern what he termed "the benefit of the doubt." Fisher was awarded the legal minimum for such cases of $250, but Judge Learned Hand pointed out that he was specifically declining to hold Kern responsible for Fisher's hefty legal fees.

With so many songs to his credit, I suppose it is not unlikely that at least one of Fisher's works retains its original appeal. That turns out to be **Chicago**, a blustering or—as self-described—todd'ling a big hit that is as emblematic of the Windy City between the wars as Rodgers and Hart's 1925 paean to "Manhattan." Fisher keenly stresses the pronunciation of his adopted city by using a pickup note ("Chi-") followed by an accented dotted-quarter ("-ca-") and then the final "-go" in a descending pattern:

This sets the tone, with this figure repeated ten times over thirty-two bars (*A-B-A¹-C/A*). Add in a colorfully site-specific lyric, which has been necessarily cleansed of objectionable matter over the years; a ragtime-like triplet-filled verse, with prodigious if indiscriminate rhyming; and a swift twelve-bar interlude simplistically built on descending chords to allow for joke after joke. "They've got the Stock Yards, so I heard the people say, I just got wind of it today."

COME RAIN OR COME SHINE

music by Harold Arlen, lyric by Johnny Mercer
from the musical *St. Louis Woman* (1946)

I promised myself on a stack of vocal scores that I wouldn't play favorites, so let's just say that Harold Arlen and Johnny Mercer's **Come Rain or Come Shine**⸎ is pretty good. This is, by definition, a romantic ballad. The music, though, expresses a deep melancholic strain, one that other writers might alleviate by moving from minor to major for the final *A*. Not here. The lyric suggests loving someone forever, come rain or come shine; but the musical atmosphere of this love story is less a shining sun than—if you'll pardon the expression—stormy weather.

The first half of the *A* (of *A-B-A¹-C/A*), spread over four bars (of the standard thirty-two), is straight and simple: "I'm gonna love you like / nobody's loved you, come / rain or come shine / —." That's six notes (a combination of quarters and eighths) in each of the first two bars, four in bar 3:

Remarkably, Arlen starts on an *a* (in the key of F) and repeats it thirteen times unrelieved, moving to *f* for the final three words. He does precisely the same over the next four bars with one exception, a remarkably bluesy *c* at the start of bar 5 ("high as a mountain and / DEEP as a river"). Mathematically minded readers might calculate an *A* section compiled of twenty-five repeated *a*s and little else, but who's counting? The four-bar *C* ("days may be cloudy or sunny") consists wholly of seventeen *d*s, which in two cases drop a full octave. Despite the deliberative tempo (marked "slowly and very tenderly"), the repetition is the opposite of monotonous. In terms of those repeated notes, it's interesting to look at the four-bar introduction in the original sheet music arrangement (with the tempo marking: Freely). Virtually all are repeated notes: *c* in bars 1, 2, and 4, against chords of A♭, G-7, and C-7, interrupted by an otherworldly *e♭* over an F♯ diminished-7 in bar 3. This leads to those twenty-five repeated *a*s of the *A*. And while you're at it, look at the four-bar chord progression Arlen provides under the final note ("shine").

The deep melancholy expressed might well be autobiographical on Arlen's part. (The composer didn't write the lyric, but he devised that initial fifteen-note strain; Mercer came up with words to suit; and they together rushed eagerly to the finish.) Arlen remained devoted to his wife, a former model who over the years demonstrated severe emotional problems requiring occasional institutionalization. When their Beverly Hills house burned down in 1943, rumor among the Arlen set was that the unstable Anya might have lit the match. Everything was destroyed, but Harold dashed back into the flaming house to rescue a picture from the living room wall: George Gershwin's final painting, a portrait of Jerome Kern. Days may be cloudy or sunny, indeed.

THE CONTINENTAL

music by Con Conrad, lyric by Herb Magidson
from the motion picture *Gay Divorcee* (1934)

The song hit of Cole Porter's 1932 Broadway musical *Gay Divorcee* was "Night and Day" [page 127]. The song hit of the 1934 film version, which catapulted the recently formed team of Astaire and Rogers to stardom, was not "Night and Day"—nor any other piece of Porter, as the rest of his stage score was scrapped—but an extended dance number called **The Continental**.§ The success of this song was so great that it took the first-ever Oscar for Best Song. (The composers of subsequent Astaire-Rogers classics—Kern, Berlin, Gershwin—carefully decreed: no interpolations!) Although composer Con Conrad was and remains little known—"Barney Google," anyone?—"The Continental" is quite a song. This is one of those dance songs *about* a dance, the lyric literally including step-by-step instructions. (André Sennwald, the *New York Times* film critic of the day, spent roughly 20 percent of his review of *Gay Divorcee* on this new song, noting that "it provides Mr. Astaire with a musical theme to match his nimble feet, although, when executed domestically, it probably will lack something of his polish.")

The song features four distinct themes, all quite winning. After a gently chromatic vamp that turns out to be an intrinsic part of the song, it begins with what we'll call *A* ("beautiful music"). The first main theme (we'll call it *B*) is introduced with "it's something daring, the Continental" and repeated with a different lyric. After thirty-two jaunty bars, we move to *C*, a swaying theme ("your lips whisper so tenderly") distinguished by notes held for more than six beats, contrasted with triplets. Then comes another restatement of the *B*, followed by a second vamp leading into *D*, perhaps the best theme of all ("you kiss while you're dancing"). After a second *D*, we go to the *E* ("you'll know before the dance is through"), which features interrupted triplets likely patterned to Astaire steps:

There then comes another *D*, another *E* (with a tag); and then—just to further astound us—Conrad returns to the *A* section and that initial vamp. Thus, it can be mapped—if it must be mapped—as something like *A-B-B-C-B-D-D-E-D-E-A*. The sheet music version runs some ninety-eight bars, and there is nothing you'd want to omit. It leads us to say that if you are unfamiliar with this first Oscar-winning Best Song, you might want to look it up—even if it left the great "Night and Day" somewhat in the twilight.

CRAZY RHYTHM

music by Joseph Meyer and Roger Wolfe Kahn, lyric by Irving Caesar
from the musical *Here's Howe!* (1928)

How does a nineteen-year-old bandleader get his photo on the cover of *Time* magazine? It helps, I suppose, if your father is not a bandleader but Otto Kahn, renowned banker, chairman of the Metropolitan Opera, and patron of the arts and artists (notably including George Gershwin). Roger Wolfe Kahn, though, was musically perceptive, with—at the time of the cover story, in what must have been a quiet news week in September 1927—ten orchestras operating under his name. This led to two 1928 Broadway musicals, the first of which included **Crazy Rhythm**—which has a rhythm as crazy, and fascinating, as that "Fascinating Rhythm" [page 40] of the Gershwins. (*Here's Howe!* was produced by Alex Aarons and Vinton Freedley, who in 1927 built their Alvin (Al-Vin) Theatre on profits from their Gershwin musicals.)

The rhythm here is highly syncopated, the main phrase ("[cra-zy rhythm / here's the door-way") consisting of a sequence of twice-repeated notes centering around the key note:

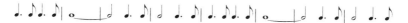

This two-bar figure is repeated verbatim seven times over thirty-two bars, with another three appearances starting on different tones. All of this is preceded by a humorous verse in which lyricist Irving Caesar—who had already peaked with "Swanee" [page 165] and "Tea for Two" [page 171]—compares fiddling in Nero's Rome with dance bands in Father Knickerbocker's Manhattan. Kahn and cocomposer Joseph Meyer introduce a strident discord on the third note of the first bar, which gets repeated twice more along the way, but it's that altogether crazy rhythm that controls the beat.

DANCING IN THE DARK

music by Arthur Schwartz, lyric by Howard Dietz
from the stage revue *The Band Wagon* (1931)

Schwartz and Dietz made a name for themselves with cleverly witty songs for two sophisticated intimate revues, *The Little Show* in 1929 (just before the stock market crash) and *Three's Company* in 1930 (just after). *The Band Wagon* was a sophisticated *lavish* revue; unlike the others, which were stocked with interpolations by other writers, Schwartz and Dietz wrote the full *Band Wagon* score themselves. Standing out—for its serious nature, and its haunting beauty— was **Dancing in the Dark**,* the first of a clutch of similarly exquisite ballads from the team.

The song starts simply, with repeated notes matching the title phrase over the first two bars:

This figure is repeated in bars 5–6 (of *A-B-A-B'/A*), in the first bars of the bridge, twice more in the second *A*, and again at the start of the final section. The suspense of the song—and it keeps you wholly engrossed—just might come from the way Schwartz shifts the tone of those repeated notes. The initial phrase is on *b* (in the key of C); the next on *f*, then *g*. The second *A* section and the partial bridge once again cycle from *b* to *f* to *g*. It's only at the restatement of the title phrase, in the final phrase of the refrain, that Schwartz finally hits the *c* that our ears have been listening for all along. As if in recognition of the power of the melody, Schwartz and Dietz omit a verse altogether. Instead, they opt to include a plaintive sixteen-bar interlude—marked "plaintively" on the sheet music—which, as with most of the refrain, refuses to find C major. Given the inclusion of the interlude, the song cannot realistically be performed without playing the refrain a second time—although I can't imagine any listener not wanting to hear the refrain again.

The singer Barbara Cook, who worked directly with Dietz and Schwartz later in their careers and championed "Dancing in the Dark" during her cabaret years, said that Dietz claimed this song was about death: "we're waltzing in the wonder of why we're here / time hurries by, we're here and gone." Perhaps so; but I'd say the meaning of the song, more pertinently, is what's in the mind and heart of the listener.

DARN THAT DREAM

music by Jimmy Van Heusen, lyric by Eddie De Lange
from the musical *Swingin' the Dream* (1939)

Jimmy Van Heusen—or sometimes James, as this was a spur-of-the-moment pseudonym inspired by an advertisement for a men's shirt manufacturer—came to Manhattan in 1933 or so and immediately started collaborating with Arlen at the Cotton Club. Well, exactly but not exactly; Harold, between the *Cotton Club Parade*s that brought forth "Stormy Weather" [page xxx] and "Ill Wind" [page 81], went off for a brief Hollywood sojourn. His replacement: little brother Jerry, who called on his Syracuse University roommate—the former Chester Babcock—to write lyrics. Thus, Van Heusen's initial published songs, "Harlem Hospitality" (1933) and "There's a House for Sale in Harlem" (1934), were as a lyricist. After several years toiling as a publishing house staff pianist, composer Van Heusen broke through in 1938 with a dozen "band songs" led by a couple of collaborations with Jimmy Dorsey. This led to two simultaneous assignments in the fall of 1939, writing three songs with Johnny Mercer (including "I Thought About You" [page 76]); and a full-scale Broadway extravaganza, *Swingin' the Dream*.

Said dream the tunesmiths were chromatically darning was Shakespeare's midsummer one, although the bard likely wouldn't have recognized it. The cast was led by Benny Goodman, Louis Armstrong, and Maxine Sullivan; the credits boasted "scenery after cartoons by Walt Disney." The musical was an instant failure, after which Van Heusen instantly departed for Hollywood and a highly successful collaboration writing Bing Crosby songs with Johnny Burke. But Van Heusen's five *Swingin'* songs, written with lyricist Eddie De Lange, included the imperishable **Darn That Dream**.⁂ And what a song!

Van Heusen contrives what otherwise might simply have been a nifty little rhythmic ditty: Except he gives us an astonishing harmonic roadblock. Our ear wants to hear (in the key of G) *d–g–e♭–e♭ / e♮–a–f#–f#*. In the second bar, though, Van Heusen makes that third note a jarring *f♮* (over a chord that can be described, if it must be described, as F7♭5), before immediately resolving to the expected *f#*. I call it a roadblock, because it more or less does block our way; the rhythm goes on, but our inner ear briefly pauses to absorb what the composer has just done. Being a wise melodist, he provides that detour thrice (*A–A¹-B-A¹*), jolting us every time with that errant *f♮*. "Darn That Dream" would be a swell song without it, yes; but that little surprise augurs the almost-immediate prominence of Van Heusen of Hollywood.

DAY IN—DAY OUT

music by Rube Bloom, lyric by Johnny Mercer
non-production song (1939)

This is one of numerous Mercer lyrics written to fit music by a working musician/colleague, in this case bandleader/pianist Rube Bloom. In such cases, the music does not necessarily fall into the usual patterns; this one is a verse-less song of fifty-six bars. The four-note title phrase is strung over four full bars: a quarter-note pickup (on the word "day") followed by a note (on the word "in") held for seven beats, with the same treatment of "day out":

Breaking the song down into seven eight-bar sections gives us something along the lines of *A-B-A¹-C-A-D-D/A*. This slide-rule account can't begin to explain the allure of the song, although one can see how the repetition of those extended notes in the *A* pay off.

As for the Bloom-Mercer team, this was not their only song standard: the next year brought forth "Fools Rush In (Where Angels Fear to Tread)." Their collaboration, though, began poorly with an underfunded West End edition of Lew Leslie's *Blackbirds* series. The 1928 edition, with songs by Jimmy McHugh and Dorothy Fields ("I Can't Give You Anything But Love" [page 60]) had been wildly successful. Not so *Blackbirds of 1936*, or—when Leslie finally arranged funds for the trans-Atlantic transfer—*Blackbirds of 1939*. This edition shuttered after a week on Broadway, marking the end of all things "blackbird."

DON'T GET AROUND MUCH ANYMORE

music by Duke Ellington, lyric by Bob Russell
non-production song (1942)

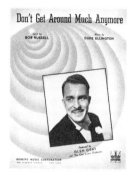

The five-note pickup provided by Duke Ellington, stepping down the scale a full octave, provides the hook upon which **Don't Get Around Much Anymore** is built. And what a hook, leading into whole notes in bars 1 and 3 of the *A* (of *A-A-B-A*). "Missed the Saturday / dance" is cannily constructed, starting with a quarter note on the half beat, which gives the effect of halting on the ledge prior to descent:

Going into bar 5, Ellington adds a sixth note, a final eighth; but for the final cadence of the *A*, he converts to an ascending seven-note pickup:

This makes the song. Every time we hear that five-note pickup, we momentarily hesitate on the ledge as if we're on a roller coaster; every time we get to the end of the *A*, we bump upward in the rush of the title phrase. As was the case with other big band numbers, this started as a recorded-but-unpublished 1940 instrumental under the title "Never No Lament." Two years later, pop lyricist Bob Russell provided a lyric, and the already-popular tune, now in song form, took off.

EARLY AUTUMN

music by Ralph Burns and Woody Herman, lyric by Johnny Mercer

non-production song (1952)

This gem was created circuitously through the big band route. Burns—a pianist/arranger who was to become a top orchestrator for stage and screen—wrote a three-part "Summer Sequence" for Woody Herman and His Orchestra, introduced at a 1946 Carnegie Hall concert. The following year, Burns came up with "Summer Sequence Part 4," which featured Herman on alto sax as well as twenty-year-old Stan Getz on tenor. Burns then took his "Part 4"—with the jazz improvisations therein—and developed it into a new piece, the 1949 instrumental **Early Autumn**.

As a onetime band singer, Mercer had an easy rapport with jazz tunes and built a sideline transforming them into pop hits. This was not incidental; as cofounder/co-owner of Capitol Records, he was ever on the prowl for lucrative material. Capitol, in fact, had a major hit with the 1949 "Early Autumn." Mercer finally put words to it in 1952, coming up with what quickly became a standard. (At this point, for reasons unknown, Herman's name was added as cocomposer; did the germ of the melody come from his sax improvisation in "Summer Sequence Part 4"?)

The song version, which fits into a neat thirty-two-bar *A-A-B-A* form, is built upon what sounds like—and in fact, was—a sax riff. The first bar, after a chromatically ascending pickup, features a descending arpeggio of eighth notes capped with an upward figure of eighth notes in the second ("when an early / autumn walks the land, and chills the breeze"). This two-bar sequence is repeated down a step, in bars 3–4; down a step further in 5–6; and resolved in bar 7. The contrasting bridge ("that spring of ours that started") leisurely grazes along until it builds to a startling chromatic two-bar modulation back to the *A*.

As for Mercer, he clearly recognized that his assignment was to write a lyric to fit the instrumental's existing title ("Early Autumn") and did so with apparent ease. "There's a dance pavilion in the rain, all shuttered down," he muses in the second *A* section, and we are swept by that chill early autumn freeze.

EAST OF THE SUN (AND WEST OF THE MOON)

music and lyric by Brooks Bowman
from the musical *Stags at Bay* (1934; published 1935)

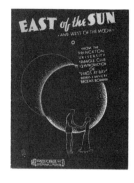

Here's a tale of one of those Ivy League chaps who spends his campus years writing songs for college musicals. Not Cole Porter, Yale '13, but a fellow you've likely never heard of named Brooks Bowman, Princeton '36. Unlike Porter, whose early fame was restricted to the New Haven campus, Bowman scored an immediate success with **East of the Sun (and West of the Moon)**※. Written when he was twenty and included that December in the 1934 Triangle Club musical *Stags at Bay*, this was apparently the first "college song" to be issued independently by a commercial publisher. By August 1935, it was number one on the Hit Parade; it was followed, as it happens, by Fred Astaire's recording of Irving Berlin's "Cheek to Cheek" [page 26]).

After graduation, Bowman went for a brief studio stint in Hollywood with minimal results, returning east in October 1937 and securing a publishing contract with Jack Robbins of Robbins Music. The next afternoon he attended the Yale/Army football game in New Haven; on the way back, four days before his twenty-fourth birthday, he was killed in an automobile accident. All of this would make an interesting enough anecdote on its own, but it turns out that "East of the Sun (and West of the Moon)" is an exceptional song.

Bowman builds his melody on the triplets suggested by the title phrase:

Those triplets recur constantly: three sets in each of the first three eight-bar sections (of *A-B-A¹-C/A*), twelve sets in all. The strong melody is enhanced by colorful and at times surprising harmonies—for example, the drop of a major sixth at the end of the *A*, from *c* to a surprising *e♭* (in the key of G). The song climaxes with a restatement of the title phrase instantly diminished by an errant *d♭* (over an E♭-7 chord), followed by a second restatement of the title phrase in a four-bar coda. "East of the Sun (and West of the Moon)" belongs in company with two other uncannily effective gossamer-wing ballads: the 1939 "How High the Moon" [page 57] and the 1954 "Fly Me to the Moon" [page 41]. All three, as can be surmised from the titles, are evocative ballads bathed in moonglow. Each came from a one-hit composer. Morgan Lewis (of the former) and Bart Howard (of the latter) both had extended, if less-than-stellar, careers. Poor Brooks Bowman, though, never got a chance.

EVERYTHING I HAVE IS YOURS

music by Burton Lane, lyric by Harold Adamson
from the motion picture *Dancing Lady* (1933)

What a difference a note makes; especially when it's a Gershwin-esque blue note, direct from a twenty-one-year-old Gershwin protégé. **Everything I Have Is Yours**⸓ is a perfect sentiment for a white-tie-and-tails nightclub ballad for dancing couples, which is the purely ornamental spot it was designed to fill in thirty-two bars.

Lane chooses to turn the romantic affirmation of the title phrase into a question: working in the key of C, he starts the *A* (after a quarter rest) with six eighth notes—*g–a–b–d–c–b*—that naturally resolve with another *a*:

Lane, instead, lands on a jarringly mellow *b♭*; given that this accompanies the word "yours," the music is clearly suggesting that "everything I have" is not *exactly* yours. Lane's errant *b♭* (over an A♭7 chord) recurs five times throughout the *A-B-A¹-C/A* song, resulting in that slight, and delicious, jolt every time. Try whistling the title phrase without the *b♭*, and yes—it works. But then you'd have just another ordinary fox-trot, which "Everything I Have Is Yours" decidedly isn't.

As for Lane, he started as a teenaged song plugger at Remick's, the same Tin Pan Alley publisher that had launched Gershwin a dozen years earlier. But Lane had neither Gershwin's drive nor ego; and the stock market crash sent him wandering to Hollywood. A chance encounter allowed him to place the fresh-off-the-piano-bench "Everything I Have Is Yours" in the new Joan Crawford–Clark Gable–Fred Astaire film, and a career was born.

EV'RY TIME

music and lyrics by Hugh Martin (credited to Hugh Martin and Ralph Blane)
from the musical *Best Foot Forward* (1941)

Hugh Martin had, since 1938, singlehandedly propelled the sound of Broadway vocal arrangements into the modern era by becoming arranger of choice for composers Rodgers, Porter, Duke, Berlin, and more. Approached with the opportunity to audition as composer of a proposed musical comedy, Martin wrote what was more or less his first "real" song. Producers George Abbott and Richard Rodgers heard **Ev'ry Time** and instantly gave him and partner Ralph Blane the job (retaining the right to replace the tyro songwriters at will, which turned out to be unnecessary.)

An unrequited love song in something of the Lorenz Hart "Little Girl Blue"/"Glad to Be Unhappy" vein, the melancholy lyric is set to a straightforward melody featuring numerous repeated notes (in the *A* sections) and descending scales in the *B* sections (of *A-B-A¹-B¹*). The song raises eyebrows, though, with the chromatic harmony under the melody in bars 2 and 6 of the *A*s. No wonder Rodgers was entranced. Let it be added that Martin—who had his pulse on the Broadway of the day—slyly worked the titles of two of the prior season's hit musicals, *Cabin in the Sky* and *Lady in the Dark*, into his lyric.

With respect to authorship: The songs for *Best Foot Forward, Meet Me in St. Louis*, and miscellaneous other projects were jointly credited to Martin and Blane but most always written independently. The officially credited Martin/Blane songs included in this book ("The Boy Next Door" [page 19], "Ev'ry Time," "Have Yourself a Merry Little Christmas" [page 50], and "You Are for Loving [page 198]," as well as the not-included "Trolley Song") were written solely by Martin. He was always careful to stress that the pair's first massive commercial song hit, the jointly credited "Buckle Down, Winsocki" from *Best Foot Forward*, was written entirely by Blane, albeit with one change. "Buckle down, Tioga," it went. The show's producer, Richard Rodgers, thought the name of the college lacked punch. That producer—Richard Rodgers—had previously written another college musical, *Too Many Girls*, in which the school had been named Pottawatomie, after a Native American tribe. Rodgers and Larry Hart even included a song called "Pottawatomie." "The name of the school is nothing," Rodgers is said to have said when he heard the song. "It should have *sock!*"

FASCINATING RHYTHM

music by George Gershwin, lyric by Ira Gershwin
from the musical *Lady, Be Good!* (1924)

Although this was nowhere near George Gershwin's biggest hit thus far—the 1919 "Swanee" [page 165] was a blockbuster, while "I'll Build a Stairway to Paradise" (1922) and "Somebody Loves Me" (1924) were surely stronger sellers—I contend that **Fascinating Rhythm** was the first song that *sounds* like Gershwin. (*Rhapsody in Blue*—which assuredly *does* sound like Gershwin—was first performed on Valentine's Day of 1924, but it could only be heard in the concert hall that year. Gershwin made a truncated recording, on two sides of a 78 platter, which was released in June and thus in circulation before "Fascinating Rhythm" was introduced in November.)

The success of the song comes from the main figure, taking up half of the eight-bar *A* (of *A-B-A-B/A*). The title is set to six eighth notes followed by an eighth-note rest. This is then repeated twice, starting immediately (as opposed to at the beginning of the next bar). Thus, those two emphatic final notes (initially accompanying the word "rhythm") come a half beat earlier on each hearing, altering expectations and making a fascinating rhythm indeed:

The latter half of the *A* repeats this pattern. The bridge starts out more calmly, with four quarter notes, but that fascinating rhythm intrudes with a bar of eighth notes (with the lyric, literally printed in parentheses, commenting "start a-hopping, never stopping"). As for that "fascinating rhythm [beat]" figure, it recurs in thirteen of the thirty-two bars. The refrain is preceded by a driving misterioso sixteen-bar verse propelled by a pounding bass accompaniment, as if that little rhythm is so darn persistent that it'll drive you insane (to borrow Ira's word image). You may note George's use of accented triplets linking bars 4–5 and 12–13, and how the verse is linked to the refrain by a syncopated seven-note chromatically ascending scale. Talk about music that *sounds* like Gershwin.

FLY ME TO THE MOON

music and lyric by Bart Howard
non-production song (1954)

Bart Howard, master of ceremonies and accompanist at the swank Blue Angel Supper Club on the Upper East Side, wrote a song called "In Other Words" in 1954 and had little-known singer Felicia Sanders introduce it at the club. At the same time, singer/comedienne Kaye Ballard was just scoring her first major success in the off-Broadway musical *The Golden Apple*. With that show preparing a quick transfer to Broadway, Ballard recorded a single of her big song, "Lazy Afternoon" [page 100]. Someone or other determined that on the flip side she should record "In Other Words." Both songs achieved instant renown and remain jazz favorites into the new century.

After eight years and dozens of recordings, music and record sellers—weary of explaining to patrons asking for **Fly Me to the Moon** that there *was* no "Fly Me to the Moon" and the song they were looking for was "In Other Words"— prevailed on the publishers to just change the title. "Fly me to the moon and let me play among the stars" the song begins. Those famous first words are only heard once in the song, whereas the original title "in other words" is repeated four times. The song—"slowly and tenderly" is the tempo marking—is a gentle waltz, or it was until Frank Sinatra recorded it in 1964. Determining with arranger Quincy Jones that this was no gentle waltz but a swinging rhythm number, Sinatra plunged and made a compelling case of it, to the extent that the 3/4 version is rarely employed. But "Fly Me to the Moon"—or "In Other Words," or whatever you call it—is a favorite by any name, in any tempo.

THE FOLKS WHO LIVE ON THE HILL

music by Jerome Kern, lyric by Oscar Hammerstein 2nd
from the motion picture *High, Wide and Handsome* (1937)

Since their last Broadway collaboration in 1932, Kern had kept busy (and successful)—notably with the score for the Astaire-Rogers *Swing Time* (1936)—while Hammerstein had met with a string of failures with other composers, a string that would not end until 1943, with *Oklahoma!* Kern and Hammerstein reunited during this period for one Hollywood musical, unsuccessfully so, but bringing forth **The Folks Who Live on the Hill**.

This lovely, bucolic song is more artful and complex than it might seem. This can first be heard in the hymnlike verse, which—in bar 15 (of sixteen)—hits an unexpected blue note ($e\flat$, in the key of C)—signaling that Kern is in an adventurous mood. How adventurous? The form is a standard *A-A-B-A¹*. But the *A*s are twelve bars, with the gentle pace—suggesting a horse-drawn carriage, as the film took place in 1860 rural Pennsylvania—briefly disrupted in the fifth bar by an accented quarter note on the fourth beat. The bridge changes pace, with a series of dotted eighths and sixteenths, lasting a shortened six bars. At that point Kern uses a series of eighth notes ("and when the kids grow up and")—pivoting between *g* and *a* with different chords beneath—to thrust us back into the key of C for the final restatement, which is extended to fourteen bars to allow a most satisfying conclusion. If the film that contained it, *High, Wide and Handsome*, was roundly lambasted, it did serve to introduce Hammerstein to director Rouben Mamoulian—who would stage both *Oklahoma!* and *Carousel*.

GEORGIA ON MY MIND

music by Hoagy Carmichael, lyric by Stuart Gorrell
non-production song (1930)

The lazily laconic **Georgia on My Mind** was an early affirmation that the folksy composer of "Star Dust" [page 162] was not just another one-hit wonder. The A-A^1-B-A^2 refrain is marked by the spare opening two bars ("Georgia, Georgia"); the harmonically adventurous accompaniment that follows, and the use of the title in an odd parenthetical, fill in the final bar of that first A (which is, indeed, printed in parentheses in the sheet music).

Gorrell, a college friend from Indiana University, was one of Carmichael's New York roommates in the winter of 1930. He pitched in on the lyric, his first and only attempt at songwriting. "Georgia on My Mind" has long served as the official song of the Peachtree State, but the question—which appears to have been dodged purposely by both Carmichael and Gorrell—is whether the Georgia is the state or some mythical sweetheart. The lyric can be taken either way, not that it matters. Let it be said that the verse does indeed sound like someone sittin' on some Georgia porch strummin' a lazy geetar. Let it also be said that although Carmichael had at that point driven through Georgia en route to his short-lived job as a Miami lawyer, he had never lived in the state in question.

GET HAPPY

music by Harold Arlen, lyric by Ted Koehler
from the stage revue *Ruth Selwyn's 9:15 Revue* (1930)

How do you become a legendary songwriter, anyway? Harold Arlen did so inadvertently, without even trying. A singer by trade, he was cast in a small role in the 1929 Vincent Youmans musical *Great Day!* (a score that included "More Than You Know" [page 123]). When the tryout went through an extended salvage period—people started calling it "Great Delay"—Arlen was drafted to help out as an extra pianist for dance rehearsals. As the work interminably ground on, Arlen tired of the traditional introductory pickup notes ("ba ba ba dum-bum-bum") and came up with his own catchy variation:

A songwriter friend from Brooklyn, the pre-Hollywood Harry Warren, passed through and suggested that the riff had the makings of a song. Harry sent Harold to a staff lyricist at his publisher, a diligent craftsman named Ted Koehler. Koehler came up with words to match Arlen's catchy improvisational phrase ("sing hallelujah, come on, **Get Happy**"⁕), and song—and songwriter— were born. Koehler's publisher, Remick, bought the song, and Koehler took it to Ruth Etting, who had made an enormous hit singing "Love Me or Leave Me" [page 107] in *Whoopee!* Etting had several years earlier been pulled out of the chorus on the recommendation of Koehler, so she was glad to insert "Get Happy" into the new show she was headlining, and there you are.

Ruth Selwyn's 9:15 Revue opened on a Tuesday and was forcibly closed that Saturday, never having paid the week's $9,000 worth of salaries. It was a seven-performance flop, despite interpolations from the likes of Gershwin, Youmans, Victor Herbert, and Rudolf Friml (in most cases "trunk" songs discarded from earlier musicals) along with new songs by Kay Swift. But "Get Happy" attracted immediate attention and enough writing assignments to convince singer Arlen to switch to a new career. His decision turned out pretty well.

GOOD-BYE TO ALL THAT

music by Arthur Schwartz, lyric by Ira Gershwin
from the musical *Park Avenue* (1946)

Park Avenue—a "smart set" musical comedy about marriage and divorce among the upper crust—turned out to be not so smart in a Manhattan recalibrated following the end of the war. The gilt-edged creators were lyricist Ira Gershwin and composer Arthur Schwartz under the direction of George S. Kaufman, who had earlier fashioned *Of Thee I Sing* with the former and *The Band Wagon* with the latter. Nothing about *Park Avenue* worked, although the songwriters came up with two very good songs, "There's No Holding Me" [page 175] and **Good-bye to All That**. For Schwartz, this is the last of what we might consider his "penthouse reveries" ("Dancing in the Dark" [page 31], "I See Your Face Before Me" [page 75])—although the view from the postwar Upper East Side turned out to be irrevocably different from that of an Art Deco penthouse.

The main phrase of the *A-B-A¹-B¹* song stretches over four casually paced bars: "the things we / planned" / "good-bye to all / that"). Schwartz builds his melodically restrained *A* on a descending pattern: bars 1 and 2 start and end on *a* (*a–g–g/a*, in the key of C), bars 3 and 4 on *g* (*g–g–f–a/g*). The rest of the *A* continues on a descending line that—in the case of this song, at least—suggests a deflation of hope leading to resigned acceptance of the inevitable. Schwartz varies this in the bridge, giving us an ascending scale building to a high *c*, only to fall off the cliff, if you will, with a drop to *eb*. In the final section, when Gershwin talks of "the paradise we could have known," comes an even larger drop, a full octave, as the lyric ends with the title phrase of farewell. All along, mind you, Schwartz supports his lovely, if melancholic, melody with the colorful harmonics present in his earlier penthouse songs, most notably in the latter halves of the *A* sections.

The forty-nine-year-old Ira—still in mourning for younger brother, George, who had died in 1937—seems to have taken the quick failure of *Park Avenue* as a signal that enough was enough. He retreated to his house in Beverly Hills, where he wrote a few more film scores with composers Harry Warren, Burton Lane, and Harold Arlen (see "The Man That Got Away" [page 118]) before more or less retiring his pencil in 1954. But attempt another Broadway tryout, after the consecutive rapid-fire failures of *The Firebrand of Florence* (1945, with Kurt Weill) and *Park Avenue*? As Ira might have said, "but not for me." Or, as he did write on this very occasion: "good-bye to all that."

GUESS WHO I SAW TODAY

music by Murray Grand, lyric by Elisse Boyd
from the stage revue *New Faces of 1952* (1952)

New Faces of 1952 was the standout edition of producer Leonard Sillman's occasional series of annuals, produced whenever he could scrape together enough cash. (It was in this edition that Sillman introduced a young sketch writer, one Melvin J. Brooks, who contributed a still-funny takeoff on *Death of a Salesman*. Brooks was to later pattern the immortal Max Bialystock on the diminutive but no less flavorful Sillman.) The edition in question contained an array of interesting songs, including the excellent (albeit too specialized for inclusion herein) "Boston Beguine," with music and lyrics by young Sheldon Harnick.

Altogether worthy of our list, and something of a cabaret standard, is **Guess Who I Saw Today** by Murray Grand (a nightclub stalwart of the era) and Elisse Boyd (of whom I can find little trace). This is a story song—an exceptional one, and unlike any I can think of. Starting with an intrinsic verse in beguine tempo, the writers go forty-three bars before—with one word in the final bar—answering the question the title raises. Yes, there are comedy songs that offer *supposedly* surprising switches (like the Berlin song that proceeds to say I hate this about you, I hate this, I hate that—but "Outside of That I Love You"). "Guess Who I Saw Today," though, is a poignant, moodily resigned piece that holds the listener through to that twist on the very final, dissonant note. The form is also unusual, in that the *A* (of *A-A¹-B-A²*) is only six bars. A^1 is enlarged to eight, with the title phrase added at the end. Apologies if this description skirts describing just where the song leads; I wouldn't dream of spoiling it for you.

HAND IN HAND

music by Jerome Kern, lyric by Oscar Hammerstein 2nd
from the London musical *Three Sisters* (1934)

Those of us who spend years digging through the unsung songs of favorite songwriters are bound, on occasion, to find something astonishing. Thus, I offer **Hand in Hand**, written by Kern and Hammerstein for a big—in size, and in failure—pseudo-English extravaganza produced at Drury Lane, London. Here we have Kern at his purest, demonstrating all of the skill of his later years without feeling the need to insert the playful twists or harmonic sophistication that allowed him to keep up with Gershwin, Porter, and Berlin. Although eschewing sophistication, the song is certainly not simple. It is an anthem-like hymn, yes; in actuality, *two* anthem-like hymns intertwined. As such, it doesn't handily separate into verse and refrain. (Kern presumably recognized this; he chose not to label the "burthen" in the published music.)

Instead, we'll map the fifty-nine bars as *A-A¹-A/B-C-B/A*. The *A* ("I have but one heart to give") starts with a straightforward two bars centering on *g* (in E♭) but continues with a two-bar descending scale figure repeated in bars 3–4, 5–6, and 7–8. The *A¹* takes this up a third, with each descending figure starting a step lower. The next *A* section is identical to the first, although the melody of the first two bars is played but not sung. The first half of the song ends with an extra three-bar vamp that anticipates the melody of *B*. The second anthem ("hand in hand we'll walk together") is even more glorious than the first. Kern works his way up the E♭ scale, an octave and a fourth (from low *b♭* to high *e♭*), over five quarter notes and then gradually steps his way down. This is the Kern of "I've Told Ev'ry Little Star," a thoroughly winning 1932 song from *Music in the Air*, which is omitted from this book because we simply can't include everything. The glint in the composer's eye that inhabits "Ev'ry Little Star" is here replaced by what Hammerstein herein terms "twilight's delicate shading." Rather than giving us a climactic ending, Kern returns to the initial *A* for a most gentle finish.

HAPPY DAYS ARE HERE AGAIN

music by Milton Ager, lyric by Jack Yellen
from the motion picture *Chasing Rainbows* (1930; published 1929)

Certain songs become so familiar, through repetition and cultural appropriation, that one can't help but think of them generically: as if they are not songs devised by some Tin Pan Alley peddlers but just always existed. Such is the case with Milton Ager and Jack Yellen's **Happy Days Are Here Again**.⁑ This song more or less stood as melodic promise of soon-to-arrive better times through the Great Depression, and then World War II, and various crises that have arisen over the course of time: things may be bad, but here—at least—is an antidote in thirty-two bars. All of that is somewhat ironic, in that the song was not intended as a Depression-era rouser; it was written in the summer of 1929, three months before anyone anticipated that Wall Street would soon come tumbling down. After a couple of dismal years, a fellow named Franklin Delano Roosevelt in 1932 ran against President Herbert Hoover and his hollow pledge that "prosperity is just around the corner" with a promise that vote for FDR and—presto—"happy days are here again." The song is bright and simple seeming:

So bright and simple that we overlook the craft.

Ager bases the first half of his sixteen-bar *A* atop a C chord, which pounds its way along while the melody starts on middle *c* and works its way—restricting itself only to *c*, *e*, and *g*—up to high *e* and back down. Hidden beneath the brightness are two threateningly bluesy tones (*d#* in the key of C) found in the harmony of bars 2 and 6. Maybe days aren't quite so happy, not just yet. All through this, lyricist Yellen—who with longtime partner Ager and later collaborators wrote hundreds of songs with usually clever lyrics (most notably, "Ain't She Sweet")—does his job so well that we overlook how succinctly to the point this song is. In 1962—by which time "Happy Days Are Here Again" was seen in some circles as something of a cliché—a twenty-year-old Barbra Streisand recast it as a sardonic dirge to great effect. Did this bring new meaning to the song? Maybe not. It was always there, in those bluesy colors Ager hid in the harmony.

HAVE YOU MET MISS JONES?

music by Richard Rodgers, lyric by Lorenz Hart
from the musical *I'd Rather Be Right* (1937)

Here is one of Rodgers and Hart's more straight-forward love songs, although R&H rarely cared to write anything straightforward. **Have You Met Miss Jones?** starts with a conversational twelve-bar verse. But Rodgers startles us a bit with an unexpected $a\flat$ (in the key of F) in the very first bar ("it happened, i FELT it happen"). The $a\flat$ reappears in bar 5, this time beneath a fermata (hold mark), again on the word "felt," which suggests that the notion of feelings will be at issue. The refrain, marked "gracefully and not fast," is a thorough delight but with a twist. The strongly romantic *A* begins with a drop of a fifth ("HAVE YOU met Miss Jones"), countered by an ascending scale in bars 3–4; then comes a second drop of a fifth/ascending scale, without a blue note in sight—until we get to the bridge (of *A-A¹-B-A²*), that is. Rodgers leads into it with three pickup notes—repeated high *d*s ("AND ALL AT / once I lost my / breath")—which are intrinsic to the song. That is to say, pickup notes are often ornamental; here, we can't imagine this particular bridge having been devised without them. In bar 3 of the bridge, Rodgers not only returns to that errant $a\flat$ from the verse; he repeats it five times, causing a detour through foreign keys (D♭, G♭) en route to a return to F. In *A²*, Hart's singer tells how the girl had no effect on his equilibrium whatsoever until "all at once I lost my breath" and was scared to death, which wraps up the story of Miss Jones very nicely indeed.

HAVE YOURSELF A MERRY LITTLE CHRISTMAS

music and lyrics by Hugh Martin (credited to Hugh Martin and Ralph Blane)
from the motion picture *Meet Me in St. Louis* (1944)

The hymnlike **Have Yourself a Merry Little Christmas**※ is a hardy perennial, thanks to its holiday topicality. The lyric is less happily nostalgic than you might think; the talk of "all our troubles," the absence of "faithful friends who are dear to us" and everyone being together someday soon "if the fates allow" illustrate that Martin was writing in the depths of World War II. (He enlisted in the army immediately after finishing his work on the film.) Martin's original lyric went "have yourself a merry little Christmas, it may be your last." Judy Garland, who was to introduce the song in the film, complained: "If I sing that lyric to little Margaret O'Brien" (playing her sister), "the audience will think I'm a monster."

The song is a simple A-A^1-B-A^2, with the title phrase tagged onto the final section to take us to thirty-six bars. The title phrase, starting in bar 1 with quarter notes of c–e–g–c (in the key of C), is simplicity itself; the second bar has an eighth-note run from g down to c. The bridge starts high, with three repeated quarter notes ("ONCE A-GAIN as in olden days"). The hopefully hesitant (or hesitantly hopeful) nature of the song is cemented by the start of the tag with a drop of a major seventh, on "so HAVE YOUR-self a merry little Christmas now." Martin makes it all seem as simple as a breath o' holiday pine. Although the song is credited to Martin and Blane, it was written by Martin, who was quick to add that it wouldn't exist without Blane. According to Martin, they were struggling to come up with a song for the slot; Blane suggested, "What about that little music box–like tune you sometimes play, it sounds like a madrigal"; and that was enough to point the way. (See authorship note on page 39.)

THE HEATHER ON THE HILL

music by Frederick Loewe, lyric by Alan Jay Lerner
from the musical *Brigadoon* (1947)

Lerner and Loewe's one-hit musical among their first four attempts, *Brigadoon*, featured a score so strong that the Broadway crowd needn't have been surprised when the pair later turned out the record-smashing *My Fair Lady* (1956). *Brigadoon* has at least a handful of exceptional songs, including "There But for You Go I" [page 174]. **The Heather on the Hill**,⸓ which has the hallmarks of a first-rate pop song, develops in a manner that leaves us marveling at Loewe's craft.

The *A* (of *A-A¹-B-A²*) trips along like a schottische— or more specifically, per Lerner, as if we are roamin' through the mornin' dew (which ties into the mystical highlands locale of the plot.) Loewe constructs his *A*—following a lushly romantic verse ("can't we two go walking together")—with ascending patterns of dotted eighths and sixteenths ("the mist of May is in the gloaming") starting on a *b♭* (in the key of E♭):

The figure builds to *a♭* in bar 2, *c* in bar 4, and *e♭* in bar 6 before resolving on *g* (or, in the *A¹*, an *e♭*). And then! The three pickup notes from *A¹* to *B* stay on *e♭*, as does the first note of the bridge ("THERE MAY BE OTH-er days as rich and rare"). But that fourth *e♭* (accompanying the syllable "oth-") is now a *d#* in the new key. Loewe somehow transmogrifies from E♭ to E-minor to E-major to a B7 chord over the first two bars and positively startles us with abrupt but delicious changes as he melds from G#-minor to C#7 to B♭-minor (while the singer sings "there may be other springs as full and fair"). After that he magically finds his way back to E♭ for *A²*. If that sounds complicated in description, forget it and just listen to the music. The enchantment is more like sleight of hand, although Loewe makes it seem effortless.

HERE I'LL STAY

music by Kurt Weill, lyric by Alan Jay Lerner
from the musical *Love Life* (1948)

Kurt Weill's most frequent musical comedy collaborator, Ira Gershwin, had withdrawn from the partnership in 1945 following the twin failures of the team's
stage musical *The Firebrand of Florence* and film
musical *Where Do We Go from Here?* This followed
the significant success of their initial show, the 1941
Lady in the Dark. Alan Jay Lerner, meanwhile, had
parted ways with Frederick Loewe after their third
work, the 1947 hit *Brigadoon*. Cheryl Crawford, who
produced both Weill's 1943 *One Touch of Venus* (see
"Speak Low" [page 158]) and *Brigadoon*, matched
Kurt and Alan for *Love Life*, an early exploration of what would come to be
known as the "concept musical." The show, which was termed a musical vaudeville and took place across the centuries, was more ambitious than inviting. It
did, though, give us the deceptively haunting **Here I'll Stay**.

The *A* section ("there's a far land I'm told") is built on a rising-and-
descending stepwise progression, with two pickup quarter notes leading us
to *e♭* (in the key of B♭) in bar 1; *f* in bar 3; *g* in bar 5; and then high *c* before
resolving back to *f* in bar 7. The bridge (of *A-B-A-C-A¹*) starts with that same
pattern (leading to a high *b♭* in the first bar) before going on a different path.
There follows a repeat of the initial *A* section, after which Weill introduces a *C*
section ("for that land is a sandy illusion") that starts with four repeated high *d*s,
the highest melodic tone thus far. This section is set to a bass line of chromatic
whole notes, starting on *a♭* and moving to *e♭* before going back to *g* to take us
into the final section. Here, Weill builds to a climactic high *e♭* ("and so HERE
I'll stay") before descending for the final note not to the expected *b♭* but to an
uncanny and eerily effective *c*—at first, anyway; the sheet music provides a second ending with the expected *b♭*. The results are a romantic but restless ballad
of longing repressed in favor of matrimony, which expressed the theme of *Love
Life* considerably better than other elements of the musical.

HERE'S THAT RAINY DAY

music by James Van Heusen, lyric by Johnny Burke
from the musical *Carnival in Flanders* (1953)

 The award-winning and hit-generating collaboration of Jimmy Van Heusen and Johnny Burke ran aground, after a dozen years, when they embarked on their second and final Broadway musical together. If the 1946 *Nellie Bly* was a considerable disaster, *Carnival in Flanders* (1953) was one of the debacles of its era. The show went through four book writers during its extended tryout, winding up with Hollywood's Preston Sturges and culminating in a six-performance Broadway run. Even so, it contained one of Burke and Van Heusen's—or anybody's—supreme ballads of lost love, **Here's That Rainy Day**.❋

The composer contrasts the lyricist's melancholic melodic line of the *A* ("maybe I should have saved those left-over dreams") with the clarion-clear plaint of the title phrase in the bridge (of *A-B-A-B/A*). Meanwhile, he drives the song, from first to last, with an insistently pulsing rhythm:

Van Heusen is stingy with anything less than quarter notes, along with a mere two dotted quarters and eighths and otherwise only one set of eighth notes. Trivial to point out, perhaps, but it might help explain how effectively the emotional music washes over you in this marvelously poignant song, although not, apparently, as presented onstage.

Although the thirty-two-bar published version is nonpareil, the song was devised as something of an extended solo cantata to fill the holes in the plot and just kill time. ("What do lonely people do on a rainy day?" starts the long interlude. "I'll sit down and write a book!") This was something of a Rodgers and Hammerstein-like soliloquy, only without Rodgers or Hammerstein, and serves as a fairly strong example of the difference between Hollywood pop writers and Broadway masters. Word has it that while the show was wallowing on the road, star Dolores Gray would speed through this oversized "Rainy Day" at breakneck speed—daring conductor Hal Hastings to keep up—in hopes of getting fired, as was costar William Gaxton (top-billed leading man of *Of Thee*

I Sing and *Anything Goes*). It didn't work, but Gray knew enough to restrain herself for the Broadway opening and remains the only person to win the Best Actress Tony Award with a run of less than a week. As for Burke and Van Heusen, who served as coproducers of *Carnival in Flanders*, the debacle was more than enough to sever their song hit-strewn partnership then and there.

HONEYSUCKLE ROSE

music by Thomas Waller, lyric by Andy Razaf
from the stage revue *Load of Coal* (1929)

A more or less direct follow-up to "Ain't Misbehavin'" [page 3], **Honeysuckle Rose**⸭ is irrepressibly enjoyable. "Ev'ry honeybee / fills with jealousy / when they see you out with me." The first three bars start on *c* (in the key of F) and end on *a*, with a dotted eighth-and-sixteenth detour down to *d* in between:

This eminently whistleable figure leads, inevitably, to the *f* on which it lands in both bars 5 and 7. The bridge marks a significant change from all those dotted eighths and sixteenths in the *A*. Waller fills the first two bars with half notes—*f*-*g* / *g*#-*a*—each of which is punctuated by a low *c* on the offbeat ("don't [slam] buy [slam] / sug- [slam] / -ar [slam]"). Two slightly syncopated bars follow, after which he repeats it all, up a step.

Note that if you compare Waller's two 1929 hits, you'll find that both are distinguished by bridges that temporarily change the direction of the songs with cannily conceived melodic figures: "Ain't Misbehavin'" with a series of repeated thirds, "Honeysuckle Rose" with those rising half notes. Razaf's lyric, meanwhile, suggests something far naughtier than those jealous honeybees and droopin' flowers might indicate. No matter; the whole thing comes across innocent and as sweet as—well—honeysuckle, which is the point.

HOW ABOUT YOU?

music by Burton Lane, lyric by Ralph Freed
from motion picture *Babes on Broadway* (1941)

Burton Lane and occasional Hollywood collaborator Ralph Freed wrote the score for this vehicle for
Mickey Rooney and Judy Garland, who had already
teamed for MGM's quasi-adaptations of the Broadway musicals *Babes in Arms* and *Strike Up the Band*.
How About You? is not a romantic ballad, mind
you; it's an ebullient charm song humorously inves-
tigating what you might call like (as opposed to love)
at first glance.

The music for this list song is irresistibly appeal-
ing, as is the lyric. "I like New York in June, how
about you?" The title comes as a response—at the end of each musical phrase—
to each successive statement, usually jumping a fifth between "-bout" and "you."
(When they sing "I like a Gershwin tune," Lane—who as a teenager was men-
tored by George himself—throws in a suitable B-minor-7 chord.) The bridge (of
A-B-A¹-B/A) starts by copying the pattern of the *A*; diverts into a string of repeated
eighths and sixteenths ("I like potato chips, moonlight and motor trips"); and
ends with the title phrase starting on an ear-raising *d#* (in the key of G):

Those repeated notes return at the start of the final section, the song niftily
wrapping up after thirty-two deft bars.

Lyricist Freed wrote hundreds of songs, few of note and without a modicum
of the success of his older brother: Arthur Freed, whose songs included "Singin' in the Rain" and who—as head of the MGM musical unit—produced *Babes
on Broadway*. No matter; Ralph's lyric for "How About You?" is excellent and,
with those potato chips and motor trips, ever memorable.

HOW ARE THINGS IN GLOCCA MORRA?

music by Burton Lane, lyric by E. Y. Harburg
from the musical *Finian's Rainbow* (1947; published 1946)

Tasked with the need to write a most unusual song to serve as the thematic hook for a most unusual musical, Burton Lane and Yip Harburg came up with **How Are Things in Glocca Morra,**⁎ a compellingly authentic-like Irish folk song mixing nostalgic sentiment with irresistible charm. (*Finian's Rainbow* told of a crotchety old Irishman who steals a leprechaun's pot of gold and flees to a mythical stand-in for Fort Knox, figuring that if the U.S. government grows its gold there, he should, too. Subplots deal with the leprechaun-in-pursuit, who loses his powers as he falls for a mere mortal lass, and a bigoted U.S. senator who turns—well, let's just say that the satirical plot was unusual.)

"I told Burt to write an Irish tune," Harburg recounted to Max Wilk in the latter's illuminating set of songwriter interviews, *They're Playing Our Song*, "but to make it his *own* Irish tune." This Lane did: "Danny Boy" as distilled through mid-century Manhattan. Harburg suggested the phrase "there's a glen in Glocca Morra"; Lane eventually came back with a distinctive melodic phrase built upon six eighth-note pickups, so distinctive that Lane uses it three times in the *A* section, albeit with slight melodic alterations:

In *A¹* (of *A-A¹-B-A²*), he interrupts the flow midway with an extra two-bar phrase ("does that laddie with the twinklin' eye come whistlin' by"); this in direct response to Harburg's whimsical observation that "the Irish always add a little bit." After giving us those six pickup notes six times over the first twelve bars, Lane is canny enough to thenceforth omit them. The final *A* section is only four bars, as opposed to eight in the first and ten in the second: just a simple revision of the title phrase, replacing all those eighth notes with a string of contemplative quarter notes. The melody crests on the song's high note, an *f* (in the key of F), asking "how are things"—with a melancholy hold on that note—"in Glocca Morra this fine day?"

For what it's worth, note that contemplative ten-bar verse: "I hear a bird—a Glocca Morra bird." It well may be that Harburg built his entire song on the notion of that Glocca Morra bird (which he made up), stumbling on the realization that his Irish heroine might as well come from a village called Glocca Morra (which he made up). But no: in the original printings of the song, she hears "a *Londonderry* bird." This is the sort of last-minute refinement a perceptive lyricist might make during the Philadelphia tryout, and isn't it perfect?

HOW HIGH THE MOON

music by Morgan Lewis, lyric by Nancy Hamilton
from the stage revue *Two for the Show* (1940)

This jazz standard hails from an all-but-unknown composer and an all-but-forgotten Broadway revue. Yet, **How High the Moon** was instantly signaled out and recorded—and recorded and recorded. The popularity of the song is understandable, starting with the expressive opening statement ("Somewhere there's music, how faint the tune") that ends not on the expected b♮ (in the key of G) but an unsettling b♭ (on the word "tune"). The initial figure is then repeated, a full step lower over a shifting harmony.

In the bridge (of *A-B-A-B¹*), Lewis—having switched the underlying chord to E♭—lands on the expected b♭ whole note in bar 3 but moves in bar 5 to a most unsettling b♮. (The lyric at this point, with the whole notes in question capitalized: "there is no moon above when love is far away TOO, till it comes TRUE.")

But attempting to describe musical moondust in words is unprofitable. "Buddy" Lewis and his collaborator, Nancy Hamilton, wrote three intimate revues—with *One for the Money* (1939) and *Three to Make Ready* (1946) on either side of *Two for the Show*; the final edition included at least one charming song, "The Old Soft Shoe." Lewis also served as dance music arranger for *Oklahoma!* (1943) but remains remembered almost solely for the imperishable "How High the Moon."

HOW LONG HAS THIS BEEN GOING ON?

music by George Gershwin, lyric by Ira Gershwin
from the musical *Funny Face* (1927)

The Gershwins start **How Long Has This Been Going On?** so intriguingly—George with a bluesy one-tone interval, Ira with "I could cry / salty tears"—that it grabs our attention and never lets up. The *A* (of *A-A¹-B-A¹*) begins with three or four notes per bar, mostly on the beat, before resolving neatly with the syncopated title phrase:

The bridge ("oh, I feel that I could melt"), too, is built around a trick rhythm:

George presents this four-bar phrase twice, the second a minor third above the first, with Ira rhyming away (melt/felt, hurled/world, and in the second refrain creep/sleep and rendezvous/true). The twenty-four-bar verse is not always used but worth searching out for those deliciously mellow instrumental pickup notes George uses to lead into the refrain. Ira, meanwhile, shows his erudite mettle by citing both Gilbert and Sullivan *and* Dante's inferno in adjacent lines. Also of note, in the final *A* of the second refrain is the lyric "Kiss me twice / then once more / that makes thrice / let's make it four!"

Although this was literally an Astaire song, it was introduced by Adele rather than brother Fred. They couldn't quite have the siblings sing a duet about kissing, could they? In any case, the song was cut during the tryout—at which point *Funny Face* was still titled *Smarty*—and resurfaced seven weeks later in the next Gershwin musical to reach Broadway, *Rosalie*.

I CAN'T GET STARTED

music by Vernon Duke, lyric by Ira Gershwin
from the stage revue *Ziegfeld Follies of 1936* (published 1935)

This jazz standard is perfectly formed by Messrs. Duke and Gershwin, working together after Harburg left the former to work with Arlen while George was otherwise engaged with the music-heavy *Porgy and Bess*. The lightly syncopated *A* (of *A-A-B-A*) is carefully constructed along the lines of: I can do *this* (specifically, "I've flown around the world in a plane") / I can do *this* / I can do *that*, but **I Can't Get Started** with you. The bridge ("you're so supreme, lyrics I write of you") turns this around, with bars 1 (after three pickup notes), *3*, and *5* consisting of a whole note *a♮* (in the key of C). This then descends in gentle rhythm:

The music insouciantly breezes along with little evidence of Duke's often adventurous harmonies—except, maybe, where he inserts an unexpected *a♭* in the title phrase ("can't get START-ed with you"). The song owes much of its success to Gershwin's characteristically charming prosody, or does it? It attracted little initial attention despite being introduced by a thirty-something comedian soon to decamp to Hollywood (which is to say, Bob Hope) who in the course of the revue scene couldn't "get started" with another film-bound thespian, Eve Arden. The song found belated fame the following year via a recording by Bunny Berigan and his Orchestra, with Berigan wailing away on trumpet and providing the vocal as well.

I CAN'T GIVE YOU ANYTHING BUT LOVE

music by Jimmy McHugh, lyric by Dorothy Fields
from the stage revue *Lew Leslie's Blackbirds of 1928* (1928)

The team of Jimmy McHugh and Dorothy Fields got off to a rousing start with this charmer, introduced in tandem with several equally catchy (if not quite so exceptional songs) in a hit Broadway revue transplanted from Harlem. **I Can't Give You Anything but Love** is launched by the title phrase in step-patterned quarter notes, with "love" given a whole note, after which they add a surprising "ba-ay-by":

The three-syllable figure—two eighth notes leading to a dotted half, at half-tone intervals—is repeated on subsequent uses of "baby" but also in four of the eight bars of the bridge (in *A-B-A¹-B¹*). The line "diamond bracelets Woolworth doesn't sell" seems to have instantly signaled that Fields—one of the not-very-many women songwriters heard on Broadway until then—was, to quote one of her later lyrics, "top-drawer, first-rate." This can be heard from the very start of the verse: "Gee, but it's tough to be broke, kid, it's not a joke, kid, it's a curse."

Rumor has long circulated that the music for "I Can't Give You Anything But Love" was written by Thomas "Fats" Waller and sold to McHugh for a song (or maybe a hamburger). There seems to be no merit behind this tale, and Waller himself never appears to have made such a claim. Given the hundreds of varied and tuneful songs McHugh turned out over a long career—including two abundantly joyful additional *Blackbirds* numbers, "Diga Diga Doo" and "Doin' the New Lowdown"—we have no reason to expect that he didn't write this one.

I COVER THE WATERFRONT

music by John W. Green, lyric by Edward Heyman
from the motion picture *I Cover the Waterfront* (1933)

Going into this survey with Johnny Green's *Body and Soul* [page 17] as one of the incontrovertible entries, I imagined that he must have at some point written a suitable follow-up. Green spent much of his career as an in-demand bandleader and then as a Hollywood musical director, where he shared in Oscars for four movie musicals featuring Broadway songs he didn't write (*Easter Parade, An American in Paris, West Side Story*, and *Oliver!*). I quite enjoy some Green songs—"I'm Yours," "Easy Come, Easy Go," "The Steam Is on the Beam"—but it took me a while to come across something worthy of standing beside "Body and Soul": **I Cover the Waterfront.** Inspired (as they say on the music cover) by the 1933 murder-melodrama of the same name, it was used as theme music.

If Ed Heyman's lyric is a bit unwieldy due to that title phrase, the song is marvelous. The two-bar title phrase—marked by half-note triplets ("I CO-VER-THE / waterfront") is immediately followed by another two-bar phrase ("I'm WATCH-ING-THE / sea") that is somehow rhapsodic:

The final note of that phrase, mind you, is an unexpected *f#* (in the key of G). After repeating the first eight bars (the song is *A-A¹-B-A¹*), Green contrasts those initial triplets—which start on the third beat—with six sets of triplets, all starting on the downbeat. He also contrasts his *A*—filled with phrases of consecutive notes—with a bridge marked by repeated notes and severe intervals: an octave drop going into bar 2, a leap of a minor seventh into bar 3, another octave drop into 4, and more. The overall effect is evocative and, yes, rhapsodic.

I DON'T WANT TO WALK WITHOUT YOU

music by Jule Styne, lyric by Frank Loesser
from the motion picture *Sweater Girl* (1942; published 1941)

Neophyte composer Jule Styne, on the staff of the "poverty row" studio Republic Pictures, convinced his boss—a fellow named Cy Feuer, but that's a story for a different book—to "borrow" the up-and-coming Frank Loesser from Paramount for the hayseed comedy *Sis Hopkins*. Loesser, infuriated at being forced into the downgrade assignment with a "cowboy song" composer, sullenly sat down to work with Styne. Jule played a melody he had floating in his head. "Stop!" Frank shouted, "don't play that here! We'll write that song at Paramount!" **I Don't Want to Walk Without You**, indeed, demonstrates the skills that would take both Styne (with that pure and straightforward melody) and Loesser (with playfully colloquial lyrics) to ASCAP's highest earning classification.

The title phrase—with the word "baby" amended—is strung across the first four bars:

The bridge ("I thought the day you left me behind") proceeds as might be expected until bar 6, when Styne introduces a C#-diminished chord (in the key of E♭) en route to a cadence that leads into the restated *A* (of *A-B-A-B/A*) with an errant *d♭*. And, mind you, he makes it sound simple. The final section starts with the repeated-note figure from the original bridge, builds to a climax midway, and then gently repeats the title phrase. At this point Loesser adds the coup de grâce by appending, in place of "baby," a colloquial "no sirree." Let it be added that the song's message of walking without your sweetheart had special resonance when the first hit recording was released—seven months before the film—within weeks of the attack at Pearl Harbor. And for those interested in such matters, the Styne-Loesser score for Republic Pictures's *Sis Hopkins* (1941) included "Cracker Barrel County" and "That Ain't Hay."

I FOUND A MILLION DOLLAR BABY
(IN A FIVE AND TEN CENT STORE)

music by Harry Warren, lyric by Billy Rose and Mort Dixon
from the stage revue *Billy Rose's Crazy Quilt* (1931)

Composer Harry Warren spent a decade trodding the lanes of Tin Pan Alley prior to find his particular niche in movie musical world in 1933 with *42nd Street*. This transcontinental migration was instigated in part by his 1931 song hit, **I Found a Million Dollar Baby (in a Five and Ten Cent Store)**. A thoroughly delightful story song, the title phrase more or less entered the lexicon. (If dot.com readers don't understand the concept of the local five-and-dime, they can do a search for Woolworth's or simply ignore it.)

The four-bar title phrase falls at the end of the three *A* sections (of *A-A-B-A*). The song, though, is structured on the casually syncopated first half of that phrase ("I found a million dollar baby"), a dotted-eighth-and-sixteenth figure that Warren uses nine times throughout. He inserts into the accompaniment a mini-vamp of dotted eighths and sixteenths ($c–c\#$ / $d–d\flat–c\natural$) that plays a prominent place when selectively repeated. Warren also demonstrates his canny use of pickup notes, with a chromatic four-note lead-in to the bridge ("SHE WAS SELL-ING / chi—na—") and even more so with a parenthetically casual "in-ci-dent'ly" prefacing the final *A*.

Billy Rose—who produced the eponymous *Crazy Quilt*, which starred his then-wife, Fannie Brice—took the lead lyricist credit, as was his habit. One imagines that the skillfully sketched thirty-two-bar saga of chance meeting (in that April shower) through courtship, to wedded bliss, came from Mort Dixon. A journeyman writer, his numerous catchy titles include "Bye Bye Blackbird" and "I'm Looking over a Four Leaf Clover."

I GET A KICK OUT OF YOU

music and lyric by Cole Porter
from the musical *Anything Goes* (1934)

Porter's finest and most durable musical—with the exception, on both counts, of *Kiss Me, Kate* (1948)—contained this sterling ballad. **I Get a Kick Out of You**⅋ might not be his best-known song, but it is among the very finest. (Although it was introduced in *Anything Goes*, it was written three years earlier for the unproduced musical *Star Dust*—and thus predates Porter's 1932 "Night and Day" [page 127]. In fact, three of the *Star Dust* songs were used in *Gay Divorce*.) Porter takes the standard form so prevalent among the musical comedy kings at Harms and turns it on its ear.

The delightfully rhythmic *A* (of *A-A¹-B-A²*, each with sixteen bars) is straightforward enough, pushed along by the frequent use of half-note triplets; that is, three notes evenly spread over four beats:

The first three bars offer an ascending figure, from *c* to *b♭* (in the key of E♭). This figure recurs starting in bar 5; then again in the first and fifth bars of *A¹* and *A²*. It also appears twice in *B*, accommodating a key change by starting on *e♭*. Where Porter plays tricks—and while the song flows ever so naturally, he might well have consciously contrived this sleight of hand—is in the restated *A*s, specifically starting in bar 7 of the sixteen-bar sections. The melody in *A*, accompanying the words "mere alcohol doesn't thrill me at all," ascends to *b♭*. In *A¹* ("I'm sure that if I took E-VEN-ONE-SNIFF") he continues with additional triplets, peaking on *c*. *A²* is even more enhanced ("flying too high with one GUY-IN-THE-SKY") and travels—somewhat rapturously—up to an *f*. In all three cases, Porter ends the sections identically, coming down to earth with the title phrase. Note that the "guy in the sky" phrase continues with "is my idea of nothing to do." So Cole effortlessly spreads, like fresh-churned butter, a six-pointed rhyme (fly/high/guy/sky/my/i[-dea]) over a mere nineteen beats. The sixty-four-bar refrain is preceded by a marvelous verse. Without going into detail, let us note that when the "totally cold" singer suddenly finds an exception to her boredom, midway through, the key sweetens; we get a bright *b*♮ when she's "out on a quiet spree," which almost immediately reverts to the expected *b*♭ at the return of "the old ennui."

I GET ALONG WITHOUT YOU VERY WELL (EXCEPT SOMETIMES)

music and lyric by Hoagy Carmichael
non-production song (1939)

Mixed in with so many well-known wonderful Hoagy Carmichael songs is the relatively obscure but equally special **I Get Along Without You Very Well (Except Sometimes)**. The longish title phrase is set mostly to quarter notes ranging over the first three bars:

This sets the pattern for the initial *A* section, which extends to an ungainly but inevitable twenty bars. This is due to a number of repeated phrases that are more or less necessary to accomplish the needs of the lyric. The *A* then repeats in a shortened fourteen-bar version, with one of the ascending runs of quarter notes removed. The eight-bar bridge is built around whole notes; it, too, is repeated, before moving on. So, we have *A* (twenty bars)-*A¹* (fourteen bars)-*B* (eight)-*B* (eight)-*A²* (fourteen). Mixed into the ascending phrases of the *A* are full scales of quarter notes. So, yes, this is a decidedly unusual song of sixty-four bars but touching, tender, and musically intriguing.

The backstory is unusual as well. Finding an initialed-but-unsigned poem he had long since clipped from a forgotten magazine, the song was initially published with the legend "words inspired by a poem by J. B.?" Following the immediate popularity of the song, the poet was identified as the recently deceased Jane Brown Thompson.

I GOT RHYTHM

music by George Gershwin, lyric by Ira Gershwin
from the musical *Girl Crazy* (1930)

Working out themes for one of his several 1928 musicals, George Gershwin came up with what brother Ira described as a slow melody based on the pentatonic scale. (That is, a scale based on five tones, rather than the seven we are accustomed to. You can easily play it on your piano by starting on the *f*#/*g*♭ and moving up the black keys.) Not finding a use for the tune, George filed it away. He later pulled it out of his notebook, speeded it up, and voilà: **I Got Rhythm**.✵

The refrain is indeed thoroughly pentatonic save for two accidentals, in bar 6 of the *A* sections (on the first word of the phrase "WHO could ask for anything more") and in bar 2 of the *B* ("old man troub-LE"). Ira, who loved to rhyme so much that he even wrote a song called "I Love to Rhyme," came up with a highly unconventional rhyme scheme for George's spare melody, which offers little more than a measly two notes a bar:

That's to say, seventy-five notes over thirty-four bars: no rhymes—or, rather, one rhyme, hidden in the bridge (of *A-A-B-A¹*). Ira avoids rhymes in both of the ascending, two-note phrases found in bars 1 and 2 of the *A*, as well as in the descending phrases of 3 and 4. The rest of the *A* consists of a phrase ("I got my man, who could ask for anything more?") that is repeated verbatim at the end of the second *A* and twice in the culminating *A¹*. A tacked-on verse in revivalist mode is, indeed, rhyme-filled. The song was slotted into *Girl Crazy* as the roof-raising first-act finale, an instant classic as delivered by then-newcomer Ethel Merman. But it's fair to say that "I Got Rhythm" did more for Merman than Merman did for "I Got Rhythm." At least, the song has been altogether rousing in all guises, no matter who is singing or playing it, and is likely to remain so.

I GOTTA RIGHT TO SING THE BLUES

music by Harold Arlen, lyric by Ted Koehler
from the stage revue *Earl Carroll's Vanities, Tenth Edition* (1932)

Arlen first established himself a master of the blues—or at least the Broadway/Tin Pan Alley version of the blues—just two years into his career with **I Gotta Right to Sing the Blues**,§ demonstrating for all time that he, indeed, had the right not only to sing but to *write* the blues. These included, soon thereafter, "Stormy Weather" [page 163] and eventually "Blues in the Night" [page 16].

The sixteen-bar verse establishes this from the outset, giving the vocalist a series of wailing blues cries followed by percussive chords: "I don't" [ba-dum] "care who" [ba-dum] "knows I" [ba-dum] "am blue." And that's just the start. The title phrase at the top of the refrain rings out like a clarion call, with the last word of the phrase ("blues") held for four beats over two bars:

Arlen ends *A¹* (of *A-A¹-A-B/A*) with seven half notes in a chromatic scale, to Koehler's lyric "(all I) see—in— / me—is— / mis—e— / -ry—." Arlen didn't create the piano arrangements used for his sheet music, but the fills here—in both refrain and verse—dynamically reflect his musicianship.

I GUESS I'LL HAVE TO CHANGE MY PLAN
(THE BLUE PAJAMA SONG)

music by Arthur Schwartz, lyric by Howard Dietz
from the stage revue *The Little Show* (1929)

I Guess I'll Have to Change My Plan was what we might call an inadvertent hit. Wrapping up the score for what was to become their first Broadway success, Schwartz and Dietz were asked by leading man Clifton Webb for a black-tie-and-tails solo expressing "suave romantic frustration" (as Dietz later recalled). Rushing back to the stereotypically stale hotel room, Schwartz played through a bunch of his unpublished and available-for-use past creations. Coming upon a gently stylish, schottische-like tune that clambered up and down the scale in a vaguely pentatonic fashion, Dietz grabbed it, and there was "I Guess I'll Have to Change My Plan."

This had been written in the summer of 1920, when Schwartz and Larry Hart were resident at Brant Lake Camp in the Adirondacks; the musical they wrote was called *Dream Boy*, with the title character singing "I love to lie awake in bed, right after taps I lift the flaps above my head" to that lazy tune. (My son informs me that in 2015, his last summer at Brant Lake Camp, they were *still* singing "I Love to Lie Awake in Bed.") The Schwartz/Dietz version kept the theme of lying awake in bed, you might say, but with a significantly more mature drift: "I told her how she'd fit into my dream of what bliss is," goes the verse, "then the blow came, when she gave her name as missus." The rarely performed complete version goes on to conclude that "forbidden fruit" is, in fact, better to taste. The song did well enough within *The Little Show*, and that was that—until it resurfaced in the hands of London nightclub duo Delys and Clark with such success, due to the lyric's risqué praise of the allure of extramarital sex—that it was republished in 1932 prominently subtitled "The Blue Pajama Song." Delys and Clark imported the song to America with such instant notoriety that it was recorded over a six-day stretch, that August, by three competing labels, Columbia (with Rudy Vallee), Brunswick (Guy Lombardo), and Victor (Paul Whiteman). "Why did I buy those blue pajamas," the lyric muses, "before the big affair began?"

I HAD A LOVE ONCE

music and lyric by Harold Arlen, from the unproduced television musical
Clippety Clop and Clementine (1973; published 1985)

Following an astoundingly creative quarter century—from 1929 ("Get Happy"
[page 44]) to 1954 ("A Sleepin' Bee" [page 147])—in which he more or less
defined his own musical world, the magic of Harold Arlen (1905–1986) faded.
He wrote two additional musicals—*Jamaica* (1957) with Harburg and *Saratoga* (1959) with Mercer. His final major project was the animated film *Gay
Purr-ee* (1962), which reunited him with both Harburg and Judy Garland, but
with nary a song of interest in any of them. After that, the new work of Arlen
went mostly unheard. His final project, a counterculture television musical
written with an off-off-Broadway playwright, couldn't find a producer and was
abandoned. The composer, struggling with the loss of his wife in 1970 and
beginning to feel the effects of the Parkinson's disease to which he ultimately
succumbed, stopped writing.

His final song, according to friend and biographer Ed Jablonski, was the
astonishing **I Had a Love Once** (written in 1973, unpublished until 1985, and
initially recorded in 1988). This is something of an elegy to Arlen's lost life, his
lost wife, and just general "loss." Typical of Arlen at his most introspective, it
forges its own thirty-five-bar path in what the composer described as "a pensive
mood." Although a standard *A-B-A-A* type labeling doesn't quite work in this
case, what we will call the six-bar *A* section consists of two initial instrumental
bars of a pulsing C-major-7 chord; the one-bar title phrase; another nonvocal
C-7 bar; the title phrase; and then a final bar of that pulsing chord. Then comes
an eight-bar bridge ("roll on you rivers") and a four-bar *C* ("one moment 'twas
good"), which is reminiscent of the flavor of Arlen's score for the 1946 musical
St. Louis Woman ("Come Rain or Come Shine" [page 28] and "I Wonder What
Became of Me" [page 79]). Then comes a four-bar variation of the *A*, led by
those pulsing chords, and a *D* section that peaks and then falls with a remarkable
series of off-kilter five-note octave descents ("touched by a silver stream"). The
song ends with a final variation of the bridge, with the song dying out ("gone is
my loved one") and dwindling to a final two bars of those C-7 pulses. It's the
last of Arlen; pure, undistilled, exquisite Arlen at that.

I LEFT MY HEART AT THE STAGE DOOR CANTEEN

music and lyric by Irving Berlin
from the "All-Soldier Show" *This Is the Army* (1942)

Readers who suspect me of underappreciating the work of Irving Berlin within these pages will be confounded by the inclusion of **I Left My Heart at the Stage Door Canteen.**⸸ I can't help it. It is Berlin at his most straightforward; sweet and gentle, with an enormous tug at the lost heart in question. The keenly patriotic composer, who at thirty had famously entertained the troops during World War I (bringing forth the 1918 "Oh, How I Hate to Get Up in the Morning"), now pushed aside his booming songwriting/publishing career to write and perform, worldwide, in his very own World War II Soldier Show. (Promotional material was emblazoned with the legend "The Army Emergency Relief Fund receives all the net proceeds.") The song is decidedly old-fashioned in form, which was not a detriment in 1942 but something of a strength.

Berlin starts with a spare, chord-based sixteen-bar verse that is intrinsic to the whole, telling us the who and what in the simplest of terms. The title phrase spans the first four bars of the *A*, preceded by three significant quarter notes. Berlin demonstrates, too, his technical skill; after "I left my heart at—" he writes in an eighth-note rest, making the listener wait *just a moment* to ponder where the heart was left. (He uses this 'hesitation rest' four times throughout the refrain, always serving to enhance the words that follow.) Once the full title is delivered, we know the gist of the entirety; the saga of a forlorn soldier boy ("Old Mister Absentminded" he calls himself) who leaves his heart at the Stage Door Canteen can proceed in only one direction. That said, Berlin fills the song with unexpected images; most notably the soldier sitting there dunking all the doughnuts the hostess can possibly serve up.

The music appears as simple as can be, though you might note that in the gently descending bridge (of *A-B-A-C/A*) the first bar starts on a high *d* (in the key of F); the second on *c*; the next on *b♭* and on down to *f*. We might not understand why this is so very effective, but Berlin surely knew precisely what he was doing. The *C* swerves abruptly into sentimental pathos of the sort that Berlin and every Tin Pan hack used to conjure, the better to sell song sheets. Here, though, as Irving writes about "a soldier boy without a heart," it is an altogether perfect mix of song and sentiment.

I LOVE A PIANO

music and lyric by Irving Berlin
from the musical *Stop! Look! Listen!* (1915)

Irving Berlin burst upon the scene and shook up American popular music in 1911 with "Alexander's Ragtime Band." As much as I admire "Alexander," I can't drum up high enthusiasm for it, perhaps due to overfamiliarity. I greatly prefer the jaunty explosion of musicality called **I Love a Piano**.§ If I am by this point equally familiar with both, the latter and later song—after innumerable hearings—never fails to provide a jolt. Written in ragtime, or what we might more accurately term "Tin Pan Alley ragtime," Berlin has something of a pianistic field day:

"I know a fine way to treat a Steinway," we are told; what's more, "you can keep your fiddle and your bow, Give me a P-I-A-N-O, oh, oh!" This was from an already prodigious tunesmith who at that time had likely not come within miles of a Steinway and would forever favor a tricked-up transposing piano he came to call his "Buick." No matter. "I Love a Piano" is robust and rambunctious enough to make anyone want to—well, love a piano.

I MAY BE WRONG BUT I THINK YOU'RE WONDERFUL!

music by Henry Sullivan, lyric by Harry Ruskin
from the "revusical comedy" *Murray Anderson's Almanac* (1929)

A charmingly disarming lyric, matched to sprightly music with built-in surprises, makes **I May Be Wrong But I Think You're Wonderful!** a durable song hit. Even now, generations later, it retains that charm. Coming from a pair of songwriters who were all but unknown, then and now, the song is irrepressibly refreshing.

Harry Ruskin's title phrase tells us precisely where we're going, while Henry Sullivan sets it to quarter notes and halves, with a kicker at the end:

That initial rest on the first beat recurs in bars 1, 3, 5, and 7 of the *A* sections (of *A-A-B-A¹*), twelve times in all. This propels the song until it is offset by the contrasting bridge, which starts on the beat and is braced by triplets. It also gives the lyric a chance to explain itself ("if dear in you I've picked rightly, it's the very first time"). The refrain is preceded by a relatively dense verse that sets up the situation, the singer explaining that "I have been a loser all my life"; a second verse and refrain accentuate various character defects. This leads one to wonder: is he or she wrong yet again? Is she or he not, in reality, so wonderful?

I ONLY HAVE EYES FOR YOU

music by Harry Warren, lyric by Al Dubin
from the motion picture *Dames* (1934)

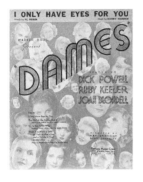

Harry Warren and Al Dubin—who in their three Hollywood years (since *42nd Street* in 1932) had displayed a proclivity for large-scale production numbers—demonstrated that they could just as easily, and just as effectively, wax poetic. **I Only Have Eyes for You**⅗ is a keenly romantic ballad, with a richly embracing melody hidden beneath which are some crafty touches from Warren.

The *A* section ("are the stars out tonight") presents a long-lined phrase extending over six bars. The title phrase culminates with a whole note in bar 7; but rather than simply holding it through the cadence, Warren goes down a half step (while Dubin appends "dear") to lead us onward. The next section (of *A-A¹-B-A²*) proceeds identically until that last note of the title phrase. Instead of dropping a half step as before, he raises it a half step ("for YOU") to a foreign-sounding *c#* (in the key of C). The song, thus far, has featured ten sets of quarter-note triplets ("I don't / KNOW-IF-IT'S CLOUD-Y-OR / bright"). Here, Warren gives us two figures of descending quarter notes, the first ending with half notes, the second with a whole note *g*. After that—just like at the end of the first *A*—he surprises us with a *b♭* ("a crowded avenue, YOU are here"). But none of that return-to-the-original-*A* for Warren. Instead of going from *c* to *b♭* (like the first time) or *c#* (the second), here he travels up to high *e* ("all dis-ap-pear / from / VIEW"). He then raises it to *f* for a climactic restatement of the title phrase over a four-bar tag.

I REMEMBER YOU

music by Victor Schertzinger, lyric by Johnny Mercer
from the motion picture *The Fleet's In* (1942)

Mercer and composer Victor Schertzinger give us a thoroughly engaging ballad of love at first sight. The lyricist once again found a perfect title phrase—**I Remember You**—which not only works as a lyric but is perfectly set by the composer in a simple step-wise pattern introduced in the first bar. The figure is repeated in bar 3 and copied in the other two *A* sections (of *A-A-B-A¹*). A slow descent is built into the *A* sections: the first three bars start on f#, after which Schertzinger moves bar by bar to *f♮*, *e*, *e♭*, and finally *d*. That same step-patterned title phrase, up a fourth, begins the bridge section as well. The *A¹* develops into something rather different. Unlike the eight-bar sections in the rest of the song, the composer expands it to twelve bars by interrupting it, midway, with four lyrical bars before returning to the initial pattern from the title phrase.

Schertzinger was better known for his long and successful career as a film director, starting in the silent era. (He received an Oscar nomination for directing the 1934 *One Night of Love*, losing to Frank Capra for *It Happened One Night*. That same year, he won for the new category of Best Original Score, beating out *Gay Divorcee*.) For Schertzinger—who also directed *The Fleet's In*—it was the end of the line; he died of a heart attack before the film was released. If this short-circuited what might have been a successful partnership for Mercer—their score included not only "I Remember You" but "Not Mine" [page 128], "Tangerine," and "Arthur Murray Taught Me Dancing in a Hurry"—Johnny had months earlier entered into what would turn out to be his most important, if occasional, collaboration: with Harold Arlen.

I SEE YOUR FACE BEFORE ME

music by Arthur Schwartz, lyric by Howard Dietz
from the musical *Between the Devil* (1937)

The initially successful collaboration of Schwartz and Dietz proved problematic as they attempted the move from revues to book musicals. Dietz's day job as head of publicity and (eventually) vice president at MGM—he's the man who came up with Leo the Lion—took understandable precedence. The team reunited several times over the decades, without their earlier success. That said, **I See Your Face Before Me** belongs atop the Schwartz and Dietz list alongside "Dancing in the Dark" [page 31] and "Alone Together" [page 7].

After a conversationally contemplative verse, Schwartz moves into his so-very-expressive refrain. The *A* section (of *A-B-A-C/A*) is built on repeated notes; within the eight bars, eleven consecutive plaintive-but-insistent *g*s and ten *f*s (in the key of E♭):

♩ ♫♩. ♪│♩ ♩.│♩ ♫♩. ♪│ 𝅝 │♩ ♫♩. ♪│♩ ♩.│♩ ♫♩. ♪│ 𝅝

The first two bars contain the seven-note title phrase, with bars 3–4 containing another four *g*s before stepping up to *b♭*. The balance of the *A* section repeats this pattern, one step lower. The bridge copies the rhythm of the first bar (i.e., the repeated notes accompanying the phrase "I see your face be-") in the first and fifth bars. The *C* starts with this same five-note pattern—using different notes—before resolving with that initial repeated note pattern. Thus, over the thirty-two bars, we have the rhythmic pulse of the title phrase no fewer than eleven times. This might sound like a tad too much repetition in description, but just listen to how exquisitely it works.

I THOUGHT ABOUT YOU

music by James Van Heusen, lyric by Johnny Mercer
non-production song (1939)

"I took a trip on a train, and **I Thought About You**" starts the refrain. Van Heusen provides a leisurely syncopated theme:

This, joined to Mercer's lyric of romantic longing, makes the song indestructible from the start. A typical Tin Pan Alley songwriter anecdote, from Mercer: Johnny embarked to Chicago—for a radio appearance, singing with Benny Goodman's Orchestra—direct from a session with Jimmy, the just-completed melody threading through his mind. How to set it? He literally devised "I took a trip on a train," he said, while dozing on the 20th Century Limited. Or perhaps not; the lyricist has *also* been quoted as saying that he wrote the lyric first—on the 20th Century Limited—and subsequently handed it off to the composer. No matter.

Van Heusen, meanwhile, demonstrated his expert use of instrumental "fills," with dynamic syncopated figures following each melodic phrase. The bridge (of *A-B-A¹-B/A*) is leisurely, in a whistling sort of manner; and the final section neatly ties the two themes together. Mercer, for his part, gives us a most interesting rhyme scheme. The *A* sections feature a mere two rhymes each ("train/lane," "you/blue"). The *B*, though, is overloaded with color: "two or three cars parked under the stars"; and then, "a winding stream" that leads to "and / with each beam / same old dream." The refrain is preceded by a simple eight-bar verse that perfectly sets up that trip on a train. Van Heusen and Mercer—who worked on three songs in New York before heading west, where they teamed (respectively) with Johnny Burke on the one hand and Harold Arlen on the other—make it look, and sound, easy.

I WANT TO BE WITH YOU

music by Vincent Youmans, lyric by B. G. DeSylva
from the musical *Take a Chance* (1932)

Buddy DeSylva was one of those highly ambitious entertainment-world figures who molded powerful careers forged on their own considerable creative talents. He came to Tin Pan Alley in 1919 with a string of Jolson hits (including "April Showers" and "California, Here I Come!"); was an early collaborator of Kern ("Look for the Silver Lining") and George Gershwin's best and strongest lyricist ("Somebody Loves Me") until Ira was seasoned enough to take over. Then came the fabled DeSylva, Brown, and Henderson partnership ("The Birth of the Blues" [page 14]). When the trio went to Hollywood during the Depression, DeSylva—a hometown boy—became the producer at Fox responsible for Shirley Temple's greatest hits. After returning to Broadway to produce Porter's *DuBarry Was a Lady* and Berlin's *Louisiana Purchase*, he became executive producer of Paramount Pictures in 1941. And in his spare time, he and Johnny Mercer started their own record label, Capitol.

Stepping back to 1932, the first DeSylva-produced Broadway musical expired after a week in Pittsburgh. Rather than folding, he kept the star (Ethel Merman); retained some of the songs (including "Eadie Was a Lady") he had written with Richard A. Whiting and Nacio Herb Brown; wrote a new book; and brought in composer Vincent Youmans to supplement the score. *Take a Chance*, as they retitled the former *Humpty-Dumpty*, was a hit, at least by Depression standards.

I Want to Be with You[§] was cut and perhaps never even performed onstage. One of those "smoky penthouse" songs, it is as richly chromatic as Youmans's finest. The *A* (of *A-A-B-A*) is leisurely, marked by an intriguing title phrase that shows up not at the start or the end but in bars 3 (with a stark drop of a fifth) and 5 (with an even more severe drop of a sixth). The bridge is altogether astonishing, with severe intervals and chromatics on a level with "Body and Soul" [page 17]. The intense Youmans accompaniment features rhapsodic chords that more than live up to the tempo marking, "poco appassionato."

I WISH I DIDN'T LOVE YOU SO

music and lyric by Frank Loesser
from the motion picture *The Perils of Pauline* (1947)

Among the numerous songwriters included in this book are several exceptional composer-lyricists, notably Messrs. Berlin and Porter; several composers who provided lyrics now and then, including Rodgers, Arlen, and Carmichael; and even a lyricist who was suitably adept at writing music when the occasion warranted, namely Mercer. But we have only one top-rank lyricist who, after a decade of picking tunes from the pianos of various top-rank composers (Styne, Carmichael, Schwartz, Lane)—and turning said tunes into hits—suddenly started writing his own. Music, that is.

Frank Loesser grew into a composer/lyricist on a level with the aforementioned fellows, plus a musical-theatre showman in a way that few of his peers could equal. How that alchemy was transmuted isn't within the scope of our discussion. Let's just say that Frank, like Johnny, recognized a good tune when he heard one, and grabbed it, to the extent that he started to hear them even *without* Jule or Hoagy sitting alongside the piano bench. (As discussed in the introduction, songs from Loesser's classic musicals—*Guys and Dolls*, *The Most Happy Fella*—aren't within the scope of this book.) He seems to have started writing music in earnest during the war, with a massive 1942 hit, "Praise the Lord and Pass the Ammunition"; but it wasn't until 1947 that **I Wish I Didn't Love You So** proclaimed Loesser as not merely some lyricist who plunked out tunes on the side.

This is what you might consider a "simple" thirty-two-bar ballad in simple *A-A-B-A* form, with a standard pop-romantic lyric, but the music is anything but simple. The melody starts with a whole note: a high *e♭* (in the key of E♭), the highest tone in the song. Strings of descending notes take him to rest on whole notes in bars 3 (*b♭*), 5 (*g*), and 7 (*e♭*):

He throws in an *e♭* octave drop along the way, on the second and third notes of bar 4. After a repeated *A*, he starts the bridge with three pickup *e♭*s that jump not the octave but a discordant minor seventh, to *d♭*. As a final fillip—and it's a supremely effective one—he finishes the final *A* with a restatement of the title phrase, but he starts it *a beat late*, as if the lovelorn singer has an uncontrollable throb:

And this I suppose you can pinpoint as the start of a greater Loesser.

I WONDER WHAT BECAME OF ME

music by Harold Arlen, lyric by Johnny Mercer
from the musical *St. Louis Woman* (1946)

A great Arlen-Mercer art song, with mood and lyric specific to its dramatic origins (even though the song was cut during the tryout), seems difficult to fit into a study of the "great American songbook." But **I Wonder What Became of Me** is inarguably great, American, and fitting for any old songbook. So here we have it.

This is one of Arlen's tapeworms; the *A* (of what can be described as *A-A¹-B-A²-C*) is twelve bars at first, eight bars when we next hear it, and ten the last time through. As Arlen might suggest, we follow the rules when we can, man, but that's impossible when you're somewhere over the rainbow. The lament is informed by the sound of "pianos making music all the night"; whether Arlen wrote this to fit Mercer's word image or the other way around, the songwriters place their song in a precise milieu with that piano in the foreground (and in the musical accompaniment). The *A* is marked by sustained tones, with ten of the twelve bars starting with notes held three or more beats. The bridge ("life's sweet as honey") turns plaintive, with a throbbing pulse driven by triplets. Arlen uses three pickup notes while taking us from *eb* to *db*, the highest tone in the song thus far. (He continues on to *fb* and *g*.) When he returns for *A²*, it is now up a fourth, starting on high *c* instead of the *g* at the start. After ten bars, he abruptly shifts to new material in the *C* based on a five-note figure ("and I / can't ex- / -plain") that is musically repeated, verbatim—but against different chords—three times before the song ends with a restatement of the title phrase.

As for Mercer, he was the acknowledged king of evocative word phrases from "jeepers creepers" to "hooray for Hollywood," from "accentuate the positive" to "my huckleberry friend." But I don't know if ever he came up with something so impressionistically gossamer as that feeling you can't analyze, "like when a baby sees a bubble burst before its eyes."

IF I LOVE AGAIN

music by Ben Oakland, lyric by J. P. Murray
from the musical *Hold Your Horses* (1933; published 1932)

The only distinctive note about this thoroughly undistinguished musical—a Shubertian Winter Garden extravaganza starring madcap comedian Joe Cook as a New York hansom cab driver who becomes mayor—was that the top-billed composer of the occasion was "Russell Bennett," better known as orchestrator Robert Russell Bennett (who surely made far more on this occasion from his arranging efforts). *Hold Your Horses*, which opened in the depths of the Depression and was one of only three musicals—and eleven productions, overall—running on Broadway that week, quickly capsized, and Bennett's work hasn't been heard since.

One of the interpolated songs added during the tryout, though, stands out: **If I Love Again,** by the little-known Ben Oakland and the altogether unknown J. P. Murray. (Not altogether unknown, it turns out: under the name John Murray, he was coauthor of the hit stage and screen farce *Room Service*.) The driving verse is built on scale-like passages with alternating bars of repeated notes. In bar 12 (of fourteen), Oakland—who has been moving along between F and D-minor chords (in the key of F)—suddenly throws in a jarring B♭ chord—before returning to key for the refrain. The *A* starts melodically, with a pattern of four quarter notes (in bars 1-3-5-7) leading to whole notes (in bars 2-4-6-8). The bridge (of *A-B-A¹-B/A*) starts on *d* (over a D-minor chord) and takes us, in five steps, up to a high *f*. This pattern is then repeated a tone lower. In the final section, he accentuates the aforementioned high *f* ("love")—now a whole note—and immediately drops it an octave ("you"); as if to acknowledge that although the singer might someday *say* he or she loves someone else, "my heart will not be true, I'll be loving you."

Broadway record keeping being enigmatic, I have reason to suspect that this song was initially performed late in the run of the preceding season's Shubert revue *Americana*, itself notable for (a) the initial collaboration of Arlen with both Harburg and Mercer, and (b) the inclusion of the immortal "Brother, Can You Spare a Dime?" [page 20]. It was introduced on that occasion by a long-forgotten actor named Rex Weber, who introduced "If I Love Again" in *Hold Your Horses*. And in between these two frivolous entertainments, Weber played the role of Peachum in the twelve-performance flop *The Threepenny Opera* ("Mack the Knife" [page 112]).

ILL WIND (YOU'RE BLOWIN' ME NO GOOD)

music by Harold Arlen, lyric by Ted Koehler
from the stage revue *Cotton Club Parade*, 24th edition (1934)

Another atmospheric blues ballad from Arlen and Koehler, following the prior year's "Stormy Weather" [page 163]. **Ill Wind** is marked by the use of plaintive whole notes mixed in with Arlen's usually note-heavy melodies, notably in the first and third bars of the *A* sections:

The ten-bar *A* sections (of *A-A-B-A¹*) feature extended final cadences, accentuating the mournful nature of the song by amending Koehler's phrase "you're blowin' me no good" with a repeated "no good." The final *A* is twelve bars, with yet another double reiteration of "no good." The eight-bar bridge features no fewer than eight downward octave jumps landing on the offbeat. Arlen uses a three-note phrase—high *c#* going up to *d* and then down that octave—eight times within bars 1–2, over altering chords, and does it again in bars 5–6.

Having examined many thousands of pieces of commercial sheet music over the years, "Ill Wind" is one of only two pieces I recall that includes a second, full arrangement of the song. Labeled "Optional Piano Accompaniment Suggested by the Authors," it is mostly accompaniment—leaving the melodic line to the singer—and moodily dazzling enough to leave us grateful to "The Authors" for the suggestion. The other case, for the record, is Kern and Hammerstein's "Reckless," from the 1935 Jean Harlow film of that title. "Blues—Arranged by Roger Edens and Jerome Kern"—it states, demonstrating that this was not quite Kern's natural métier.

I'M ALL SMILES

music by Michael Leonard, lyric by Herbert Martin
from the musical *The Yearling* (1965; published 1964)

It was not all that uncommon in the forties or fifties or sixties for a flop musical, even a dire failure, to have at least one song or two worth notice. Legions of hapless investors over the years—angels, they used to call them—sat at a backer's audition and thought "this sounds like a hit" (or, more accurately, "this sounds like a *hit!*"). *The Yearling* is a case in point, a surefire catastrophe that barely staggered to town and closed the next night.

The impetus for the adaptation was clear: it was based on Marjorie Kinnan Rawlings's Pulitzer-winning 1938 novel and MGM's 1946 film version starring Gregory Peck. But a Broadway musical about a boy and his pet deer in the Florida woods, culminating with the lad shooting his beloved critter? Songs from such an effort, no matter how intriguing, are likely to disappear even before the curtain falls; the *Yearling* cast recording session was swiftly, and understandably, canceled. But composer Michael Leonard—who like many aspiring Broadwayites supported himself at the piano—coached a singer named Streisand, who long before the show reached the stage saw fit to record not one but four *Yearling* songs.

I'm All Smiles is a waltz, or what we might call a jazz waltz; Leonard drives what appears to be a friendly, unsophisticated charm number with constantly shifting harmonics—starting with an $f\natural$ over a D major chord (the song being in D major)—into something instantly and swingingly attractive. The A section (of A-A^1-B-A^2-C) wends its path back to D major, while A^1 leads to the $g\flat$ chord that starts the bridge, eventually working its way to D major and those shifting harmonies in A^2. The waltz culminates in a grand eighteen-bar ending that builds and builds and builds—seventy-eight joyously driving bars in all, mired in the first act of this unsophisticated, bathetic, backwoods three-performance flop.

I'M AN OLD COWHAND (FROM THE RIO GRANDE)

music and lyric by Johnny Mercer
from the motion picture *Rhythm on the Range* (1936)

The pop music audience has been enamored of the novelty song since time immemorial, or at least since poor old Yankee Doodle ate his macaroni. The late Stephen Sondheim once wrote to great effect that "you gotta get a gimmick"; Johnny Mercer's **I'm an Old Cowhand**⸹ has a handful of gimmicks, nifty ones. Given that he wrote the song with no composer in sight—while driving across the Texas prairies, on a six-day trek from Hollywood to his hometown of Savannah, Georgia—the music is exceedingly basic, contrived as a skeleton upon which to hang myriad lyric jokes. Even so, the jingle-like tune is so catchy that you likely cannot un-catch it.

Here is a pop song with a refrain of a mere twenty bars. The eight-bar *A* puts the humorous title rhyme up front:

The construction is simple, with whole notes in bars 1, 3, 5, and 7, each launched by four pickup notes. The *B* section is five notes to a bar to something of a tom-tom beat, consisting of four flavorful jokes in rapid succession. (The slant is Mercer's observation that modern-day Texas cowboys "ride the range in a Ford V8" and "never roped a steer 'cause I don't know how.") The song ends with a four-bar tag that is a gimmick in itself, to that immortal lyric "Yippy-I-O-Ki-Ay, Yippy-I-O-Ki-Ay." That's the whole thing. The title phrase and the yippys take up seven of the twenty bars, with myriad gag lines in between. (The song also has a rarely sung verse of nineteen bars.)

The original sheet music printing includes four lyric refrains; at least another four are in print, and Mercer—who delighted in the acclaim he got while singing his songs—seems to have improvised numerous others. But first, he managed to get this unusual ditty to then newly established crooner Bing Crosby—who, like Mercer, had been a singer with Paul Whiteman's Band and not incidentally was a former boyfriend of Mercer's wife. Crosby inserted it into his next film, the song quickly overtook the airwaves, and Mercer's stock as a songwriter moved into high V8 gear.

I'M BEGINNING TO SEE THE LIGHT

"words and music" by Harry James, Duke Ellington,
Johnny Hodges, and Don George
non-production song (1944)

I'm Beginning to See the Light is a marvel of simplicity, in thirty-two bars. The *A* (of *A-A-B-A*) consists of a two-bar phrase (accompanying "I never cared much for moonlit skies") that is restated three times. The first, in bar 2 ("moonlit skies") is on *b* (moon) and *e* (-lit skies). Bar 3 stays on the original notes; bar 4 is lowered to *b♭* and *e♭*. Bar 6 stays on the original pitch, and the section ends with the title phrase. That's the pattern for the three identical *A* sections, the melody interrupted by those flatted tones in bar 4. The bridge, meanwhile, is exceptional: a two-bar melody ("used to ramble in the park") on a B7 chord that is then reconfigured to B♭7 and finally A7, with the section resolving on E♭7. Then it's back to the *A*, verbatim. It all works delightfully, which suggests that there is something to be said for formula when it's so well formulated.

Although this is most usually considered a "Duke Ellington song," the music came jointly—as per the copyright registration—from bandleader/trumpeter Harry James, Ellington, and alto sax player Johnny Hodges, with the lyric by frequent Ellington collaborator Don George.

I'M IN THE MOOD FOR LOVE

music by Jimmy McHugh, lyric by Dorothy Fields
from the motion picture *Every Night at Eight* (1935)

The success of "I Can't Give You Anything but Love" [page 60], "On the Sunny Side of the Street," and other rhythmic songs took the new team of McHugh and Fields to Hollywood. "Songdom's Most Illustrious Partnership," a 1934 full-page ad heralds them, "Writers of Songs You Love to Sing." They responded with more hits, capped by the languorously rhapsodic **I'm in the Mood for Love**.

The song is craftily constructed, built on that title phrase in the first bar that is set to quarter-note triplets. This figure reappears fifteen times over thirty-two bars—or so it seems; a close examination shows that McHugh varies the rhythm ever so slightly:

Bars 1 and 3 of the *A* sections (of *A-A¹-B-A¹*) spread those three triplets over two beats; bars 5 and 7, though, substitute an eighth note/quarter/eighth, which is so close that I suppose many performers just stick to the triplets. The alteration does provide an extra, inner spring to the song. What's more, McHugh uses that eighth/quarter/eighth figure—with an altered melody—three times within the bridge. This, along with the whole notes he uses in bars 2 and 8 of the A sections (contrasting to the quarter/dotted half in bars 4 and 6) presumably contributes to the feeling you get, or at least I get, of drifting along aimlessly in a rowboat with a ukulele. Not that I've every drifted along aimlessly in a rowboat with a ukulele.

Digging through the uncollected film songs of McHugh and Fields, one might be surprised to discover that the eight-bar verse to "Dinner at Eight"—the title song of the 1933 MGM comedy classic—is built on the very same musical phrase as "I'm in the mood for love," in the earlier case set as the less-than-deathless "in your appointment book." Too good to waste, eh?

After the instant success of "I'm in the Mood for Love," the honeymoon—and the partnership—suddenly disrupted. The producers of the 1935 film version of Jerome Kern's *Roberta* determined, as they were going before the cameras, that they needed words to fit the instrumental accompaniment of a fashion sequence. Fields, who was in the right place at the right time, was drafted and came up with the lyric for what she called "Lovely to Look At." Kern—unaware of what happened until after the filming—was delighted to have an unexpected song hit, without any excess labor no less—so much so that he requested Fields for his next assignment. And when musical patriarch Kern spoke, what could McHugh do but acquiesce? McHugh nevertheless—due to his contractual agreement with Fields—shared the "Lovely to Look At" Oscar nomination, even though he didn't work on the song. And he shared the significant royalties, too.

I'M OLD FASHIONED

music by Jerome Kern, lyric by Johnny Mercer
from the motion picture *You Were Never Lovelier* (1942)

Mercer—six months after "Blues in the Night" [page 16] marked the beginning of his collaboration with Harold Arlen—was honored by an invitation to collaborate with the great Jerome Kern on the newest Fred Astaire movie musical. *You Were Never Lovelier* was less than memorable, but the score included one of Kern's final song classics, **I'm Old Fashioned.** This is a near-perfect combination of music and words. Kern is in the same melodic mind-set as in his somewhat more grandiose "All the Things You Are" [page 5].

The music travels in an unconventional manner. After a lovely *A* and a colorfully developed bridge, the first half of Kern's *C* precisely mimics the rhythm of the *A* but with a significantly different melody. He follows this by a four-bar down-and-up climb ("sighing signs, holding hands," etc.) to take us back to the *A*. Except we only get four bars of the *A*, leading to eight bars of new material; thus, *A-B-C-A/D*. The refrain (or burthen, as Kern termed it) is preceded by a tender verse, the harmony in the second half built around an ascending "thumb line."

The cleverly colloquial Mercer, meanwhile, is suitably and gently deferential to the great master but as distinctive as ever, with the "old-fashioned things" he favors including "the sound of rain upon a window pane." I admit to preferring rain on the pane even above raindrops on roses, although I can't confess to having ever *heard* raindrops on roses. And don't get me started on kitten whiskers.

ISN'T IT A PITY?

music by George Gershwin, lyric by Ira Gershwin
from the musical *Pardon My English* (1933; published 1932)

Following two of their most substantial Broadway successes—*Girl Crazy* (1930) and *Of Thee I Sing* (1931)—the Gershwins hit a rough stretch. The year 1933 saw two dire failures; George's only subsequent musical, *Porgy and Bess* (1935), was also a short-lived disappointment, albeit one that was to establish itself (to say the least) following the composer's death in 1937. *Pardon My English* was, more or less, a bad idea poorly done; but it did bring forth the exceptional **Isn't It a Pity?**[*] The pity is that these mighty happy lovers "never met before"; thus, a happy ballad with just a bit of half-rapturous uncertainty.

George begins his *A* (of *A-A^1-B-A^2*) with an upward scale pattern, from *e* to *b* (in the key of C); has a triplet leading to a half-note figure in bars 2 (ending on an *a*), 3 (ending on *g*), 4 (ending on *f*), and only reaches a somewhat settled pitch (*g*) at the end of the section:

♩. ♫ ♩ | ♪ ♫ ♩ | ♪ ♫ ♩ | ♪ ♫ ♩ | ♫ ♫ ♪ | ♪ ♫ ♩ ♩ | ♩.

The descending triplets are offset, in George's sheet music accompaniment, by ascending triplet fills. The brothers lead into the bridge with an intriguing, syncopated phrase ("just think of all the") during which George throws in an *f#* to lead us from the key of C to E minor. We are back in C for *A^2*, with a somewhat grand final cadence.

Ira, meanwhile, is in his most happily playful mood; the hero reads Heine in China while his erstwhile heroine confesses that "my nights were sour, spent with Schopenhauer." The lyric also demonstrates his craftsmanship: the eight-bar *A* sections contain only one simple rhyme (ending bars 2 and 4: "I look at you"/"I never knew"), with the bridges containing six (such as "neighbors/labors," "salmon/backgammon"). The jolly Germanic *Pardon My English* took place in Dresden, opening within days of Hitler and his Nazi Party seizing power as the world uneasily watched. Sour nights, indeed.

ISN'T IT ROMANTIC?

music by Richard Rodgers, lyric by Lorenz Hart
from the motion picture *Love Me Tonight* (1932)

Since their initial breakthrough in 1925, the team had written a string of song hits: some snappily upbeat ("Manhattan"), some earnestly romantic ("With a Song in My Heart" [page 196]), some heartbreakingly unrequited ("A Ship Without a Sail" [page 145]). **Isn't It Romantic?** marked the beginning of what might be called the mature Rodgers and Hart.

The verse ("I've never met you, yet never doubt dear") is built on four repeated notes, three of them pickups: twelve sets of them over sixteen bars! What's more, Rodgers clinically lowers the tone: g (in the key of E♭) leading into bar 1, f into bar 2, $e♭$ into the next, then d. The refrain is built on the title phrase, consisting of four pickup notes (d–$e♭$–c–d) leading to a pair of $e♭$s. Most unusually, he immediately repeats that same figure—on the beat, not as a pickup—to start bar 2 and goes on from there:

We get that figure four times within the A (of A-B-A-B^1) as well as in the final phrase of the song. Rodgers also works in some of his very right-sounding wrong notes. For example, he ends the first half of the bridge with the harmonically melodic $e♭$–$e♭$–g–g–$e♭$ ("in the trees above"). After repeating the first two bars, though, he moves to $e♭$–$e♭$–c–c–$d♭$ ("you were meant for love"). That sour $d♭$—on the word "love," no less—makes the *perfect* wrong note. Let it be added that the published version is an extreme reduction of the lyric; the song was used in the film within an extended sequence including numerous characters and locales.

"Isn't it romantic, soon I will have found some girl that I adore," the conceited, as-yet unenlightened leading man Maurice Chevalier sings. "Isn't it romantic, while I sit around my love can scrub the floor!" They don't write them like that anymore, and no wonder.

IT HAD TO BE YOU

music by Isham Jones, lyric by Gus Kahn
non-production song (1924)

This standard, written and recorded by popular bandleader Isham Jones, demonstrates the power of melodic simplicity: the rhythm of the phrase **It Had to Be You**—consisting of five pickup notes held over to the next bar—is heard five times in the eight-bar *A* (of *A-B-A-C*), four times in the bridge, and more in the *C* (that ends with three repetitions of the title):

That it works so well is testament to that warmly mellow five-note figure.

The lyric is memorable in that this love song gently acknowledges that the beloved might sometimes "be cross, or try to be boss"; even so, "with all your faults, I love you still." This comes from the reliable if relatively overlooked Gus Kahn, whose impressive catalog includes the likes of "Pretty Baby," "Ain't We Got Fun?" "Carolina in the Morning [page 24]," "Liza" (with George and Ira), plus "Love Me or Leave Me" [page 107] and "Makin' Whoopee" [page 116]. He enhances the simplicity of the song and doubles down on the theme (that "it had to be you") by using "you" or relevant rhymes ("who," "true," "blue," "do") ten times over thirty-two bars. Although Kahn is long forgotten, he was honored with a posthumous pseudo-biopic from Warner Bros.: *I'll See You in My Dreams*, the title borrowed from another 1924 collaboration with Jones.

IT NEVER ENTERED MY MIND

music by Richard Rodgers, lyric by Lorenz Hart
from the musical *Higher and Higher* (1940)

Rodgers provides one of his simpler musical settings for his most sardonic ballad of love lost, **It Never Entered My Mind**. The poignant melody is set to a slight rocking accompaniment, gently alternating between F and A minor chords (in the key of F). The *A* section (of *A-A¹-B-A²*) starts with four repeated quarter-notes followed by five bars in a mostly descending pattern; this is counteracted by the abrupt appearance of the ascending title phrase in bar 7, followed by an instrumental fill. The bridge breaks from the rocking pattern, for eight bars anyway. It begins with a drop of a major sixth—from high *d* (the highest note thus far)—and then builds through a series of stepwise repeated notes up to *e*, which becomes the highest note of the song. This is as the singer bemoans in frustration that "now I even have to scratch my back myself." The final section takes us through the first five bars of the *A*, after which it culminates in an extended five-bar ending, the better to allow Hart room for a final triple rhyme. The verse offers a perfect setup for this song of despair, built on repeated notes: the first five bars consist of *f* repeated no fewer than *twenty-seven* times; the next three bars have *g* repeated thirteen times. Hart has the singer complain about having to sit alone at solitaire, having to "order orange juice for one," and to "wish that you were there again to get into my hair again."

IT'S A MOST UNUSUAL DAY

music by Jimmy McHugh, lyric by Harold Adamson
from the motion picture *A Date with Judy* (1948)

One of the lesser offerings from the MGM musical factory was the teenagers-do-a-show saga *A Date with Judy*, starring not MGM's own Judy but Jane Powell. Jimmy McHugh and Harold Adamson's **It's a Most Unusual Day** is an unusual song (albeit not a *most* unusual song), in that it's a lengthy (ninety-six-bar), sweeping waltz with something of the exuberance of Rodgers and Hart's "Lover" [page 109]. The allure is simply described: the title phrase consists of quarter notes (starting with two pickups) interrupted by a half note:

The rest of the *A* (of *A-A¹-B-A²*) consists of quarter notes until culminating with the title phrase, this time with "most" written not as a two-beat note but as a quarter followed by a rest, which then drops an octave for the first syllable of "unusual."

Harold Adamson—an experienced lyricist whose occasional collaborations with the likes of Youmans, Carmichael, and Lane brought forth "Time on My Hands" [page 182] and "Everything I Have Is Yours" [page 38]—uses that three-syllable "unusual" from the title phrase eight times over the course of the song, which is enough to warm the heart of an old-time Tin Pan Alley song plugger such as McHugh. Adamson also offers some not-quite rhymes ("an old na-tive BORN Ca-li-FORN-ian would say") that fly by at such a clip that they work splendidly. For the composer, there was to be a career-capping resurgence—posthumously, when he couldn't much enjoy it—with the Broadway revue *Sugar Babies* (1979), with songs pulled from the McHugh catalog.

IT'S ONLY A PAPER MOON

music by Harold Arlen, lyric by Billy Rose and E. Y. Harburg
from the play *The Great Magoo* (1932; published 1933)

The participation of Billy Rose gives us an opportunity to discuss those occasional collaborators who appear to have contributed little, or nothing, to the songs copyrighted in their names. As producer of what turned out to be a negligible Ben Hecht-Gene Fowler-George Abbott tale of sideshow denizens of the Coney Island boardwalk, Rose saw that an incidental song was indicated. He called on Harburg, who—eager to annex Arlen as a full-time collaborator—took the assignment. The producer—whose contribution most likely was providing the job, describing the song slot, and asking Harburg for something cynically cockeyed—not only claimed a full share of credit but decreed that his name be listed first. Although Arlen's music had begun to attract attention, he had not yet written "Stormy Weather" [page 163]; as for Harburg, he was all but unknown at the time and thus unable to turn down the assignment.

Within about three months he coined not only that "paper moon" and its "Barnum & Bailey world," but also the "chestnuts in Autumn" of "April in Paris" [page 9] and that theme song of the era, "Brother, Can You Spare a Dime" [page 20]. *The Great Magoo* lasted eleven performances; Brooks Atkinson of the *New York Times* remarked that "it is all rather stale and malodorous." The song in question, "If You Believe in Me" (as it was originally titled), went unpublished, unrecorded, and forgotten—an altogether valueless song, in most such cases.

But because Rose recognized its worth—or maybe mostly because he had a full ownership share—he inserted it into his next production, *Billy Rose's Crazy Quilt of 1933*. (*Billy Rose's Crazy Quilt*, starring his wife, Fannie Brice, had a Broadway run in 1931 and included "I Found a Million Dollar Baby (in a Five and Ten Cent Store)" [page 63]—with music by Harry Warren and lyrics, in order of billing, by Billy Rose and Mort Dixon.) The 1933 edition was not for Broadway; it was booked as a stage revue to accompany motion pictures in major movie palaces, for a six-month tour starting July 1933. Rose retitled the song **It's Only a Paper Moon**;[*] arranged for the initial publication and the first of well over three hundred recordings that September; and inserted it in that

November's *Take a Chance*, a film version of the 1932 Broadway musical (see "I Want to Be with You" [page 77]).

Harburg in later years was known to complain about Rose's commandeered share of "It's Only a Paper Moon," which by my estimate has generated hundreds of thousands of dollars. But . . . if Billy Rose hadn't truly believed in "If You Believe in Me," and if he hadn't stood to earn a veritable fortune from his slice of the authorship, would the unsung/unpublished/unrecorded song ever have resurfaced? So perhaps Rose's authorship share was, indeed, worth it to the Arlen/Harburg bank accounts.

IT'S THE GOING HOME TOGETHER

music by Jerome Moross, lyric by John Latouche
from the musical *The Golden Apple* (1954)

The avant-garde Jerome Moross and the esoteric elitist John Latouche—both of whom were sitting on the blacklist—joined for this highly unconventional musical transplanting Homer's Ulysses and Helen of Troy to Mount Olympus; the one in Washington State, USA. The experimental *Golden Apple* caused enough excitement and received such laudatory notices to warrant a quick Broadway transfer, although it proved way too specialized for success. Although "Lazy Afternoon" [page 100] was the enduring hit of *The Golden Apple*, **It's the Going Home Together** is equally worthy. Much of Moross's writing has a spare, Copland-esque feeling to, in *The Golden Apple* and his various film scores (*The Big Country*, *The Proud Rebel*, *The Cardinal*). Moross, in fact, earlier had served as orchestrator on Copland's films *Our Town* and *The North Star*. After a harmonically sparse verse that is gentle despite being crammed with words and sixteenth notes, Moross leads us into a refrain marked "slowly with expression." It *needs* to be performed slowly: the poetry of the lyric and the musical structure demand it.

Here Moross creates an unusual texture, shifting—bar by bar—from eighth notes to quarter notes:

The form, in eight-bar sections, is most unusual; or we might say unique in an open Americana way: *A-A-A¹*, with the final section restating the melody over an A♭ chord (rather than the E♭ in the earlier sections) and proceeding to a rhapsodic end. That's twenty-four bars, filled with more notes than you can count; I get 155. The song never feels rushed, though; it's a hymnlike anthem to noble values, albeit from a complex score that mined and at times poked a finger in the eye, or ear, of various American song styles.

I'VE ALWAYS LOVED YOU

music by James Mundy, lyric by John Latouche
from the musical *The Vamp* (1955)

In conscientiously and doggedly burrowing through songs by the thousands, known and unknown, it was inevitable that I should stumble across at least one or two obscure items that—as I soldiered through—all but screamed out for attention. **I've Always Loved You**⁑ might be the most obscure of the bunch: an all-but-unknown song from an all-but unknown musical by a virtually unknown composer. But if you bother to seek it out—and if you are able to find it—I imagine it will have a similar effect.

Jimmy Mundy was a jazz man, saxophonist, and arranger. (He has one fairly known song to his credit, the 1942 "Trav'lin Light" written with Trummy Young and Johnny Mercer.) As far as I can tell, he was only the second of three black composers to write the entire score for substantially "white" Broadway musicals; the first was Thomas "Fats" Waller of the 1943 *Early to Bed*, the other Duke Ellington of the 1966 *Pousse-Café*. (There might be others, but I can't think of one.)

Mundy's presence on Broadway was altogether accidental. The plan was to produce an Americanized version of Saint-Saëns's 1877 opera *Samson et Dalila*, to follow in the tracks of the highly successful *Carmen Jones* (Bizet, 1943) and the less successful *Helen Goes to Troy* (Offenbach, 1944) and *My Darlin' Aida* (Verdi, 1952). Mundy was hired to jazzify the music for what they initially called *Samson and Lila Dee*, with the adaptation by John Latouche; the latter had written lyrics for Duke's *Cabin in the Sky* (with a black cast) and the other Duke's *Beggar's Holiday* (with an integrated cast). Ultimately, Saint-Saëns was jettisoned, as was the biblical theme; and when the producers were unable to line up Lena Horne (or the equivalent), the action was moved to silent-movie Hollywood with the femme fatale transmuted into Carol Channing. (The tryout title, *Delilah*, was ultimately changed to *The Vamp* as some tryout audiences are said to have expected a Bible story.) In any case, Mundy—who was already on board as arranger—became the composer as well.

"I've Always Loved You" is a wonderfully jazzy ballad, despite an unusual and unsuccessful verse. The *A* (of *A-A¹-B-A²-C/A*) is marked by repeated notes that end with minor third jumps, resulting in minor key tonalities. The bridge, though, leaps into striking chords beginning with E-major-7 (straying from the original key of C) and working its way through F#-minor-7 to G-major-7 to D-minor-7 on its way back to where it started. Why the song didn't work its way into jazz circles, I can't imagine, although almost no vestige of *The Vamp* has survived.

I'VE GOT THE WORLD ON A STRING

music by Harold Arlen, lyric by Ted Koehler
from the stage revue *Cotton Club Parade*, 21st Edition (1932)

Songwriters Harold Arlen and Ted Koehler—with "Get Happy" [page 44] and "I Gotta Right to Sing the Blues" [page 67] to their immediate credit—were wafted uptown to the mob-backed Cotton Club in Harlem for a string of popular revues that brought forth a handful of immortal song classics. First among them was the lighter-than-air, how-can-I-possibly-express-how-happy-I-feel charmer **I've Got the World on a String**.⸘

Arlen provides a jauntily whistleable title phrase that in the second bar leaps from a high *b♭* (in the key of F) to an even higher *f* (which is marked with a fermata, indicating that it should be held):

The *A* section (in *A-A-B-A¹*) jumps along the scale before comfortably resolving. Arlen contrasts this in the bridge with alternate bars featuring an *a* repeated seven times ("LIFE IS A BEAUTIFUL thing") over contrasting chords. The workmanlike Koehler provides a suitably gentle lyric, with numerous simple rhymes—including countering "sittin' on a rainbow" with "I can make the rain go"; thus, the one syllable "rainbow" with the two-word "rain go." Rather unusually, A^1 features a radical revision of the final section of the melody (at "what a world, what a life") while Koehler keeps the original lyric intact. Ted was soon thereafter displaced from Harold's side by the flashier Yip Harburg and then the altogether dazzling Johnny Mercer, with occasional visits from Ira Gershwin; but the half dozen Arlen-Koehler standards—capped by "Stormy Weather" [page 163]—remain quite as impressive as they must have sounded originally.

JEEPERS CREEPERS

music by Harry Warren, lyric by Johnny Mercer
from the motion picture *Going Places* (1938)

Given the increasing alcoholism of Harry Warren's longtime lyricist (Al Dubin) along with the sudden death of Johnny Mercer's composer-at-the-time (Richard A. Whiting), Warren and Mercer were briefly united in the Hollywood game of musical collaborator chairs. The temporary team quickly came up with the charming "You Must Have Been a Beautiful Baby" (for the November 1938 Dick Powell release, *Hard to Get*) and the even better **Jeepers Creepers** (for the December Dick Powell release, *Going Places*). Given that this was a racetrack movie, and that the song was sung by Louis Armstrong to a *horse*, I guess you could say that the song comes out of the gate like a shot.

Warren starts his verse with eleven rapidly repeated *f*s over the first two bars, and in due time repeats them. The refrain swings along, starting with the title phrase that consists of four whole notes. After an eighth rest comes a conversely syncopated "where'd you get those peepers":

Ac-Cent-Tchu-Ate the Positive
Harold Arlen–Johnny Mercer
(page 1)

Ain't Misbehavin'
Thomas Waller–Harry Brooks–Andy Razaf
(page 3)

All the Things You Are
Jerome Kern–Oscar Hammerstein 2nd
(page 5)

Alone Together
Arthur Schwartz–Howard Dietz
(page 7)

April in Paris
Vernon Duke–E. Y. Harburg
(page 9)

The Ballad of the Sad Young Men
Tommy Wolf–Fran Landesman
(page 12)

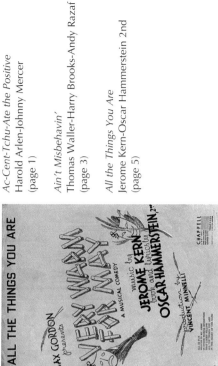

The Birth of the Blues
B. G. DeSylva-Lew Brown-Ray Henderson
(page 14)

Blues in the Night
(My Mama Done Tol' Me)
Harold Arlen-Johnny Mercer
(page 16)

Body and Soul
Johnny Green-Edward Heyman-Robert
Sour-Frank Eyton
(page 17)

Brother, Can You Spare a Dime?
Jay Gorney-E. Y. Harburg
(page 20)

Can This Be Love?
Kay Swift-Paul James
(page 21)

Carolina in the Morning
Walter Donaldson-Gus Kahn
(page 24)

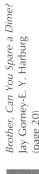

Charleston
Cecil Mack-Jimmy Johnson
(page 25)

Come Rain or Come Shine
Harold Arlen-Johnny Mercer
(page 28)

The Continental
Con Conrad-Herb Magidson
(page 29)

Dancing in the Dark
Arthur Schwartz-Howard Dietz
(page 31)

Darn That Dream
James Van Heusen-Eddie De Lange
(page 32)

East of the Sun (and West of the Moon)
Brooks Bowman
(page 37)

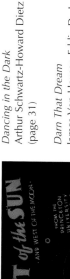

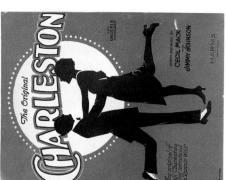

Everything I Have Is Yours
Burton Lane–Harold Adamson
(page 38)

Get Happy
Harold Arlen–Ted Koehler
(page 44)

Happy Days Are Here Again
Milton Ager–Jack Yellen
(page 48)

Have Yourself a Merry Little Christmas
Hugh Martin–Ralph Blane
(page 50)

The Heather on the Hill
Frederick Loewe–Alan Jay Lerner
(page 51)

Here's That Rainy Day
James Van Heusen–Johnny Burke
(page 53)

Honeysuckle Rose
Thomas Waller–Andy Razaf
(page 54)

How About You?
Burton Lane–Ralph Freed
(page 55)

How Are Things in Glocca Morra?
Burton Lane–E. Y. Harburg
(page 56)

I Can't Get Started
Vernon Duke–Ira Gershwin
(page 59)

I Can't Give You Anything But Love
Jimmy McHugh–Dorothy Fields
(page 60)

I Get a Kick Out of You
Cole Porter
(page 64)

I Got Rhythm
George Gershwin-Ira Gershwin
(page 66)

I Gotta Right to Sing the Blues
Harold Arlen-Ted Koehler
(page 67)

I Left My Heart at the Stage Door Canteen-Irving Berlin
(page 70)

I Love a Piano
Irving Berlin
(page 71)

I Only Have Eyes for You
Harry Warren-Al Dubin
(page 73)

I See Your Face Before Me
Arthur Schwartz-Howard Dietz
(page 75)

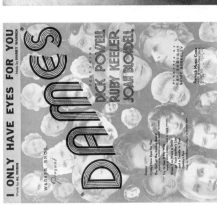

I Want to Be with You
Vincent Youmans-B. G. DeSylva
(page 77)

If I Love Again
Ben Oakland-J. P. Murray
(page 80)

Ill Wind (You're Blowin' Me No Good)
Harold Arlen-Ted Koehler
(page 81)

I'm an Old Cowhand
Johnny Mercer
(page 83)

Isn't It a Pity?
George Gershwin-Ira Gershwin
(page 87)

Isn't It Romantic?
Richard Rodgers-Lorenz Hart
(page 88)

It's Only a Paper Moon
Harold Arlen-Billy Rose-E. Y. Harburg
(page 92)

I've Always Loved You
James Mundy-John Latouche
(page 94)

I've Got the World on a String
Harold Arlen-Ted Koehler
(page 95)

Lazy Afternoon
Jerome Moross-John Latouche
(page 100)

Lazy River
Hoagy Carmichael-Sidney Arodin
(page 100)

Let's Do It
Cole Porter
(page 103)

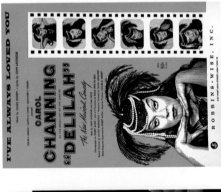

The bridge ("golly gee, when you turn those heaters on") features intervals of a third—a break from the *A* (of *A-A-B-A*), which is entirely constructed of adjacent notes. Then it's back to the initial statement, with a snappy two-bar coda ("where'd ya get those eyes"). The unforgettable title phrase was not coined by Mercer; he recalled hearing Henry Fonda use it repeatedly, as a folksy bowdlerized oath, in the 1935 film *The Farmer Takes a Wife*. But it was Mercer who, in conjunction with those four half notes from Warren, launched the phrase into the vernacular.

JUST IN TIME

music by Jule Styne, lyric by Betty Comden and Adolph Green
from the musical *Bells Are Ringing* (1956)

Faced with a leading man who was incredibly handsome, incredibly charismatic, and incredibly unable to croak out a tune, Jule Styne—who had started his career coaching non-singing stars at the Hollywood studios—came up with a canny solution: a surefire showstopper based mostly on two notes: d–$c\#$–d | $c\#$–d–$c\#$ | d–$c\#$–d | $c\#$–d–$c\#$. Repeat indefinitely—or for the entire *A* and half of the *A¹* (of *A/A¹/B/A²*), with the exception of one *g* for effect. Add appropriate harmonic shifts in the accompaniment, thus avoiding monotony, and you have **Just in Time**. Sydney Chaplin, son of Charles, did it so well that Styne wrote starring roles for him in two additional musicals. And he *still* couldn't sing, although that wasn't detrimental when his leading ladies were Judy Holliday and Barbra Streisand.

KEEPIN' MYSELF FOR YOU

music by Vincent Youmans, lyric by Sidney Clare
from the motion picture *Hit the Deck* (1930; published 1929)

Vincent Youmans wrote his third hit Broadway musical in 1927, the nautical-flavored *Hit the Deck*. This gave him two musicals at the time that had run longer than anything by his one-day-older rival, Gershwin. (This likely didn't mean much to George, who by that point had *Rhapsody in Blue* and *Concerto in F* to his credit; but it surely meant a lot to the talented-but-insecure Youmans.)

Hit the Deck had lyrics by occasional Kern-collaborator Clifford Grey and newcomer Leo Robin; the latter later wrote "Thanks for the Memory" [page 172] and the musical *Gentlemen Prefer Blondes*. *Hit the Deck* included two significant hits, "Hallelujah!" and "Sometimes I'm Happy." By the time the show was filmed two years later, Youmans had progressed from intriguingly snappy rhythmic numbers ("Tea for Two" [page 171]) to intricately moody masterworks ("More Than You Know" [page 123]). Thus, Youmans added **Keepin' Myself for You**, a colorfully moody torch song. The lyrics, by Sidney Clare (of "Ma, She's Making Eyes at Me!" and "On the Good Ship Lollipop"), are inferior but workable. As was not uncommon with Youmans, the melody is built on a simple two-bar figure that recurs repeatedly:

As always, though, Youmans makes slight but distinctive alterations. Bars 1–2 are built around a perfectly respectable, and expectable, interval drop of a fourth. In bars 3–4, the drop becomes an almost unearthly major sixth. That uncanny *d♭* half note in bar 3 (in the key of E♭) sounds altogether wrong, doubled by a repeated appearance in bar 4 and compounded by *c♭* in bar 5; when the sequence comes around in the second *A* (of *A-A¹-B-A¹*), it sounds strange but somehow right. When we hear it once more in the final eight, we look forward to the dissonance.

This explains, in part, what make Youmans's songs—and there are six included in this book—so alluring: he comes up with an intriguing figure and repeats it, with sly melodic or rhythmic alterations that leave us anticipating what we'd found unsettling twenty bars earlier. Youmans provides two additional treats in this song. He enters the bridge with an uncanny cadence, with the $e\flat$ in the melody transformed into $d\#$. That's the same note, of course; but he changes the underlying chord from $E\flat$—through B7—to E major 7th. (Apologies: this is far simpler to hear than explain in words.) You also might want to look for the way he incorporates the opening figure he uses in the verse—which can be described as repeated eighth notes against a chromatically descending inner harmony line—into the refrain accompaniment, indicating that this was not some random matching of verse and refrain.

LAURA

music by David Raksin, lyric by Johnny Mercer
from the motion picture *Laura* (1944; published 1945)

Hollywood composer Raksin's "theme melody" for Otto Preminger's film noir classic *Laura* (released in 1944) was so very evocative that Raksin's music publisher—noting the demand for the piano solo version of the theme—went looking for a lyric, but not to Mercer, as it happens. He appears to have been third choice. (The first was the post-*Oklahoma!* Oscar Hammerstein; his representatives insisted on a share of the publishing rights, which was nonnegotiable.) No matter; Mercer fashioned words that perfectly suited the mood ("**Laura** is the face in the misty night"). With a new verse created for the pop song release, the Raksin/ Mercer version was published in 1945 and remains a songbook standard long after the film itself faded from view. Listeners who love Rodgers-esque wrong notes will find a lovely one midway through the bridge (of *A-B-A-C*) in bar 13, the $A\flat$ (in the key of C) within Mercer's phrase "you never QUITE recall."

LAZY AFTERNOON

music by Jerome Moross, lyric by John Latouche
from the musical *The Golden Apple* (1954)

This stunning seduction-in-song from *The Golden Apple* [see page 93] is more languid than lazy. Moross and Latouche spread their seven-syllable title phrase ("It's a **Lazy Afternoon**ˢ") over two full bars. This is followed by twenty-two cascading eighth notes—capped by a set of lovely triplets—over the next three bars. This *A* section is then repeated, starting on an *a* (in the key of C) instead of the *e* heard the first time. After all those leisurely eighth notes laced through the *A* sections, the bridge is built mostly on descending quarter notes with Latouche providing a delectable word picture ("a fat pink cloud hangs over the hill, unfoldin' like a rose"). Moross inserts an extra, ninth bar at the end of the bridge, simply to add a languid pause in the melody. The final *A* is truncated to six bars, followed by a four-bar tag. That's forty-five bars, every one just right.

LAZY RIVER

music and lyric by Hoagy Carmichael and Sidney Arodin
non-production song (1931)

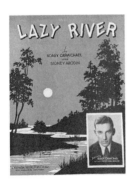

If this comfortably casual song—about throwing away your troubles and loafing along with blue skies up above—sounds melodically like something a clarinetist might use to warm up his chops, there is a reason for that. A fellow out of New Orleans, one Sidney Arodin, devised this decidedly catchy melody. Carmichael, in the first rush of success following "Star Dust" [page 100] and "Georgia on My Mind" [page 43], heard Arodin warming up and suggested they join to convert the strain into a pop song. They did, with Hoagy apparently altering the refrain, adding the verse, and writing the lyric for **Lazy River**.ˢ For Arodin, this seems to have been his one and only composition; but here we are remembering and talking about this otherwise anonymous sideman more than seventy years after his death.

LET YOURSELF GO

music and lyric by Irving Berlin
from the motion picture *Follow the Fleet* (1936)

If Irving Berlin's breakneck compositional pace was dampened by the Depression on Broadway and Tin Pan Alley, he found employment and—it seems—new inspiration on the other coast. This can be seen in "Cheek to Cheek" [page 26], from the 1935 *Top Hat*, and two equally stunning songs in the next year's *Follow the Fleet*: "Let's Face the Music and Dance" [page 104] and **Let Yourself Go**. Given that Berlin immediately copyrighted everything he wrote—sometimes years before the songs were published or performed—it appears that these three were written more or less concurrently.

The song is built around a marked pivot between minor and major; the first six bars of the *A* (of *A-A-B-A*)—starting with a whole note over the first bar ("COME— / get together")—are restrained until the title phrase in the final two bars, which transmutes the key from the original G minor to G major, as if to say: go onto the dance floor, slip out of that minor key mood, and—hell, just let yourself go. (Note that the sixteen-bar verse—"as you listen to the band don't you get a bubble," which pivots between B♭7 and E♭7 chords—anticipates the refrain but is entirely in the major.) The bridge begins with the title phrase, now ascending as opposed to the descent in the *A*. Relax, "the night is cold but the music's hot." Hot music, indeed.

An analytical coda: after comparison of the three above-mentioned exceptional songs, I couldn't help noticing an intrinsic difference. The first two seem to be fitted, almost step-by-rhythmic-step, to Astaire. "Let Yourself Go," despite its creative bravura, doesn't quite seem like it was created to order for him. It turns out that although he launched it to fame, prior to the release of the film, with a recording—"Sung by Fred Astaire, Tap Dancing by Fred Astaire" says the label—it wasn't performed in the film by Astaire, but by Ginger Rogers.

LET'S CALL IT A DAY

music by Ray Henderson, lyric by Lew Brown
from the musical *Strike Me Pink* (1933)

With DeSylva—of DeSylva, Brown, and Henderson—having deserted the notably successful trio of hitmakers ("Birth of the Blues" [page 14], "The Varsity Drag" [page 186]) for Hollywood, Brown and Henderson found a notorious bootlegger with a yen for show business: Waxey Gordon. The racketeer backed the songwriter/producers to the tune of a reported 150,000 Depression dollars for *Forward March*, which quickly collapsed on the road.

With the same songs, a new script, a new star (Jimmy Durante), and that limitless budget, the newly dubbed *Strike Me Pink* reached Broadway as a hit. The score included the colorfully moody, end-of-the-affair ballad **Let's Call It a Day**. This moves along at a steady pace, propelled by triplet pickup notes. The *A* sections are an unusual twelve bars: a four-bar phrase (incorporating the title) leads to six bars against chromatically descending whole notes and culminates in a two-bar repeat of the title. The eight-bar bridge (of *A-A-B-A*) features repeated notes in the melody set against a series of half notes, in octaves: *e* and low *e* (in the key of F) in the first bar, *e♭* and low *e♭* in the second, stepping down ultimately to *a♮* before returning for to those pickup triplets for the final section.

Just how sentimentally romantic the song was on Broadway is questionable, as by that point it had been taken over by Durante himself. *Strike Me Pink* went on to be filmed with great success by Samuel Goldwyn, starring Eddie Cantor and Ethel Merman. Not that it did Waxey much good. Even before the show closed, he had started a seven-year-run at Leavenworth. Gordon later made the front page of the *Times*—when he died at Alcatraz, in 1952. That's show business.

LET'S DO IT (LET'S FALL IN LOVE)

music and lyric by Cole Porter
from the musical *Paris* (1928)

Cole Porter first stormed Broadway in 1916, at the age of twenty-four, with a vanity production so vain that he headed off in shame to join the French Foreign Legion—or so far-from-accurate legend has it. In any case, he spent more than a dozen years mostly on the Continent as a dilettante, occasionally sending "promising" songs for use in London and Broadway revues. Living in palatial splendor in Paris and Venice, Porter's talent was recognized by various visitors from Shubert Alley—including one named Gershwin and two named Rodgers and Hart—so much so that Porter had a home at Harms for the songs he wrote for a 1928 "play with songs" called *Paris*.

Let's Do It✻ was so good—and so instantly popular—that within the year Porter was a thirty-eight-year-old overnight sensation. And no wonder. "Let's Do It" is pure delight, with a saucily sophisticated wink in the eye. (The song is subtitled "Let's Fall in Love," although the original music cover misprinted it as "Let's Make Love.")

The main figure is built on a quarter note (g, in the key of E♭) followed by a quarter note rest, $g♭$, and then f ("birds [beat] do it / bees [beat] do it"). That figure is used in four of the eight bars in A (of A-A^1-B-A^2):

♩ 𝄽 ♫♩ | ♩ 𝄽 ♫♩ | 𝄽 ♫.♫♫. | ♩ 𝄽 ♫♩

The bridge ("the Dutch in old Amsterdam do it") features repeated notes in a chromatic descending fashion bar by bar. As for the lyric, Porter wrote at least six refrains full of people and animals who "do it." The birds and bees quoted above are not the original; the first refrain, in 1928 (and in early printings of the sheet music), cited ethnic groups in sometimes derogatory fashion and were altered, apparently in the mid-'40s, by the author.

LET'S FACE THE MUSIC AND DANCE

music and lyric by Irving Berlin
from the motion picture *Follow the Fleet* (1936)

Irving Berlin, who with an eye on mass sheet music sales was not always the most adventurous of songwriters, could on occasion keep up with the Joneses. Or—more to the point—the Gershwins, Kerns, and Porters. **Let's Face the Music and Dance**, for Berlin's second consecutive Fred Astaire-Ginger Rogers film, *Follow the Fleet*, is astoundingly good. It's almost as if he considered his own excellent "Cheek to Cheek," from their prior showcase, and thought: *I can do better than that.* (Or did he think, "anything I can do, *I* can do better"?) Coming in the depths of the Depression, the melancholy message—"there may be trouble ahead," "there may be teardrops to shed," the fiddlers will "ask us to pay the bill"—was surely clear to all listeners. But just keep on dancing, Berlin says, and we'll get through. Of course, if you dance like Astaire, look like Rogers, or have a bank account like Berlin, prospects are relatively cheery.

The composer seems to be trying to stick to a standard—and easy to hum—*A-A¹-B-A* form but can't help breaking away again and again. The initial *A* is fourteen bars: a typical eight-bar *A* with a two-bar extension (for "music and love and romance") followed by the four-bar title phrase. In *A¹*, he gives us the identical first four and final four but an altogether different inner eight ("before they ask us to pay the bill"). The bridge is a standard eight, and a nice one built on whole notes and two sets of quarter-note triplets. He then reprises the first *A*, or at least the first ten bars before restating the four-bar minor-key title phrase—our third hearing of it—and then turning it triumphantly major. Thus: *A*(fourteen)-*A¹*(sixteen)-*B*(eight)-*A²*(eighteen), and every last one of those fifty-six bars sounds precisely right. It was not so populist, from someone who prided himself on being a simplistic tunesmith of the people.

LET'S GO

music by Milton Schafer, lyric by Ira Levin
from the musical *Drat! The Cat!* (1965)

The 1965 musical *Drat! The Cat!* was a thoroughly unworkable nineteenth-century melodramatic mystery musical spoof, with the cat of the title being a nubile cat burglar and the hero a bumbling patrolman. You get the picture. It has several interesting songs, including one ballad ("She Touched Me") that achieved a certain amount of popularity, although I find it to be a bit too synthetic; and a misterioso comic duet ("Holmes and Watson") with grand music but a lyric that is incoherent when separated from that convoluted plot. **Let's Go** is perhaps not quite so adventurous but makes it to our list because it works so delightfully.

Composer Milton Schafer builds his melody on triplets, with four sets in his three *A* sections; the song is made, for me, by the use of cascading triplets built on descending notes over changing harmonies in three consecutive bars at the end of the sections:

These triplets result in highly unusual seven-bar *A* sections, but it's the results that matter. The lyric is by Ira Levin, better known as the author of the play *Deathtrap* and the novel *Rosemary's Baby*, in his only attempt at a Broadway musical. His work on *Drat! The Cat!* is promising, but he clearly realized that more money was to be made in other endeavors. Let it be added that the sheet music includes an extended second ending that I find unconvincing, so I simply ignore it.

LITTLE GIRL BLUE

music by Richard Rodgers, lyric by Lorenz Hart
from the musical *Jumbo* (1935)

Rodgers demonstrates his delight in the unexpected in the gentle **Little Girl Blue**, set to a Hart lyric of supremely unrequited love. After building the first three bars on multiple repeated notes he leaps from f (in the key of F) up a major sixth to d at the start of bar 4 ("what can YOU DO"); then a major fifth (f to c) at the start of bar 5; and then a major fourth (f to $b\flat$) at the start of bar 8. The intervals are enhanced, in each case, by repeated notes before each jump. (The first two A sections—in this A-A-B-A^1 song— are an unusual twelve bars, the B is eight, and the final A is only four.) Rodgers leads into the bridge with a downward octave jump—and then gives us another in the next bar ("NO USE old girl, YOU MAY as well surrender"). To further mark this lovely bridge: After a bar of alternating as and cs, he repeats the figure but throws in a couple of $c\sharp$s before niftily wafting his way back into F major.

Hart, meanwhile, effortlessly tosses off a quadruple rhyme: surrender/slender/send a/tender. The verseless song has what might seem like an enigmatic waltz interlude, with a lyric referring to the circus ring; the musical in question featured a full-grown circus. This was the one in which Jimmy Durante had a crossover in which he tried to sneak Jumbo—this is the only musical in memory with a real, live, straw-chewing elephant playing the title role—off the premises. When the sheriff asked, "Where are you going with that elephant?" Durante got one of the bigger stage laughs on record by replying innocently, "What elephant?"

LORNA'S HERE

music by Charles Strouse, lyric by Lee Adams
from the musical *Golden Boy* (1964)

Composer Charles Strouse, who through his long career concentrated on up-beat musical comedies (most successfully with *Bye Bye Birdie* and *Annie*), was in a musically melancholic mood while writing the Sammy Davis Jr. vehicle *Golden Boy*. The show—based on Clifford Odets's celebrated 1937 play about a young fellow torn between the violin and the boxing ring, only updated to deal with the racial climate of the times—was excessively troubled. But the score might be considered Strouse's most adventurous work. **Lorna's Here,**⸸ one of the songs not written for the character that Davis played, is a bluesy and somewhat masochistic ballad redolent of stale whiskey and stagnant cigarette smoke.

What seems headed for a standard thirty-two bars takes an unexpected turn three quarters of the way through. Thus: *A*(eight)-*B*(eight)-*A*(eight)-*C*(four)-*D*(seven), followed by a repeat of the *C* and *D* (the latter extended to eight bars). Strouse and his seriously underrated original collaborator, Lee Adams, leave plenty of room for intrinsic instrumental fills, the results being exceedingly lovely and exceedingly sad.

LOVE ME OR LEAVE ME

music by Walter Donaldson, lyric by Gus Kahn
from the musical *Whoopee!* (1928)

Broadway enjoyed a parade of torch songs as the twenties stopped roaring and moved into the Depression: "Why Was I Born" [page 193], "More Than You Know" [page 123], "A Ship Without a Sail" [page 145], "Body and Soul" [page 17], and more. **Love Me or Leave Me** was the first and, for a while, one of the more popular. It threatens to be overly dramatic: the florid verse begins, "the suspense is killing me." But then Donaldson gets down to his refrain.

The melody is built on the rhythmic pattern of the first two bars:

This figure reappears, sometimes slightly varied, over six (of the eight) bars of the *A* (of *A-A-B-A*). The composer changes this up in the bridge ("there'll be no-one unless that someone is you"), significantly altering the beat:

Lyricist Kahn, meanwhile, gives us a lesson in alliteration. "Love me or leave me and let me be lonely" starts the song. The next *A* features "ight" words: "you might find the night time the right time for kissing." And although we've seen all too many rhymes for "kissing" over all too many songs, how often has anyone thought to rhyme it with "reminiscing"? The results are altogether stunning, dramatically wrenching, and would likely retain its prominence after nearly a century if the composer's name were Gershwin, Rodgers, or Porter rather than Donaldson.

LOVE TURNED THE LIGHT OUT

music by Vernon Duke, lyric by John Latouche
from the musical *Cabin in the Sky* (1940)

With Ethel Waters to write for—at the height of her fame, seven years after introducing "Stormy Weather" and in her first and only book musical appearance—Vernon Duke and John Latouche lavished her with dynamic material. These included the glorious folklike hymn that served as the title song of *Cabin in the Sky*; the giddy, roof-raising charm song "Taking a Chance on Love" [page 170]; and **Love Turned the Light Out**, a searing torch song. (They also gave her a fourth showpiece, "Savannah," which allowed her to dress up fancy and out-vamp the sultry rival for her man's affections.)

"Love Turned the Light Out" starts with an overly dramatic sixteen-bar vamp in C-minor; rubato, filled with accidentals and exaggerated arpeggios. After that Duke sets a relaxing rhythm—marked "slowly (with feeling)"—and shifts to C-major for the refrain. Not C-major exactly; rather, C-major with a flatted seventh (*b*♭). This is a not uncommon blues mode, with a name from the Greeks: Mixolydian. Duke counters the leisurely two-bar title phrase with three sets of quarter-note triplets:

Said triplets are introduced by an earlier set of highly chromatic triplets in the accompaniment, in the latter half of bar 2; these serve to punctuate the song, practically stopping it in its tracks in the second bar of each *A* (of *A-A¹-B-A¹*). The bridge ("last night the moon was shining for joy") starts in E-minor, for the first four bars; moves to E-major, in recognition of that moon shining for joy; and then works its way back to the Mixolydian at the moment when "Mister Love turned the light out."

LOVER

music by Richard Rodgers, lyric by Lorenz Hart
from the motion picture *Love Me Tonight* (1932; published 1933)

Love Me Tonight, which turned out to be the supreme movie musical accomplishment of the team of Rodgers and Hart, was not conducive to pop hits: the interweaving of story, music, and photography called for songs that served purposes other than offering the stars an opportunity to stand in front of the camera and sing. (The director was Armenian-born Rouben Mamoulian, who would later revolutionize the Broadway musical with *Porgy and Bess*, *Oklahoma!*, and *Carousel*.) This fantastical romantic fantasy of a Parisian tailor and a glamorous princess called for a brief section of song wherein the latter—dreaming of meeting the so-called man of her dreams while driving a horse cart—keeps interrupting her simple *A-A-B-A¹* song at the cadences by yelling to her steed, in rhyme, "whoa" and "not too fast." Music publishers being what they are, it was determined that this sweeping waltz could and should stand on its own, so they summoned the authors to excise that horse and suitably convert it. Thus came, in 1933, the glorious all-purpose version of **Lover**.

This might be as sweeping a waltz as Rodgers ever propelled into ¾ time. The melody (in the key of C) features tones gently descending in chromatic manner: "lover, when I'm / near you, and I / hear you" is set to *c–c–b–c/b–b–b♭–b♮/b♭–b♭* and on. The bridge ("all of my future is in you") changes this with a pattern of quarter notes: *g#–a–g#–a–g#–a/b-b.* A gloriously entrancing sixty-four bars, preceded by a thirty-two-bar verse—written for the pop-song release—accentuates the operetta-like nature of the refrain but ends with a tongue-in-cheek joke, to wit: "when you are away it's awful, and when you are with me it's worse."

Bruce Pomahac recalled a conversation he had with the aged Yip Harburg, who explained that "waltzes are really hard to write. There are only two wonderful waltzes." The first was, yes, Rodgers and Hart's "Lover." The other one, I suppose we should record for posterity, was a pleasing-enough waltz that nobody is likely to place on any wonderful, great, or favorite list: "Let's See What Happens" (music by Jule Styne) from the cranky Harburg's failed swan song, *Darling of the Day.*

LOVER, COME BACK TO ME!

music by Sigmund Romberg, lyric by Oscar Hammerstein 2nd
from the musical *The New Moon* (1928)

When first I began to plumb the depths of Broadway music for my 1985 book *Show Tunes*, I quickly set aside operetta kings Victor Herbert, Rudolf Friml, and Sigmund Romberg as being too antiquarian for my taste. (Also too antiquarian, let it be added, was the brashly all-American George M. Cohan.) Not a question of age, mind you, as Romberg kept turning out hits into the mid-1940s while Friml lived until 1972; rather, age of musical style. In compiling this book, I have dutifully played through every one of the hundreds of these fellows' song sheets residing in deep recesses of my cellars and found that they remain too antiquarian for my taste, every last song with one exception: the very fine **Lover, Come Back to Me!** (Note that my issue is not the actual age of these songs; this one is from the 1928 operetta *The New Moon*, with lyrics by a post-*Show Boat* Oscar Hammerstein.)

The *A* section ("the sky was blue, and high above") is built on a series of tentative four-note ascending phrases, preceded by an eighth rest:

♪ ♫♩ | ♪ ♫♩ | ♪ ♫♩ | ♪ ♫♩ | ♪ ♫♫ | ♩ ♩ | ♫♩ ♩ ♩ | ♩.

Romberg doesn't start a phrase on the initial beat until he introduces the title phrase in bar 7. Each bar of the bridge (of *A-A-B-A¹*), conversely, does start on the beat. This section is quite different, suddenly in the minor mode and beginning with a long-lined phrase over the first two bars ("I remember ev'ry little / thing you used to do") consisting of twelve eighth notes. He then starts to restate the *A* but after three bars inserts an astonishing G#-diminished chord. This leads to the climactic end, complete with an operetta-worthy high *g*.

LULLABY OF BROADWAY

music by Harry Warren, lyric by Al Dubin
from the motion picture *Golddiggers of 1935* (1935)

Despite writing a number of popular songs over a decade on and around Tin Pan Alley (including "I Found a Million Dollar Baby [in a Five and Ten Cent Store]" [page 63]), Harry Warren couldn't quite get a foothold in theater land. This son of Italian immigrants—born in Brooklyn as Salvatore Antonio Guaragna—didn't fit in with the Broadway club of melting pot composers such as Berlin, Kern, Gershwin, and Rodgers. Are you beginning to see a pattern? Warren had to go to Hollywood to find fame and constant employment, which he did with two major song hits about: Broadway, of course. "Forty-Second Street," written for the 1932 movie of that title, started his string of West Coast hits, and it was followed by the equally iconic **Lullaby of Broadway**.⸸ In both cases, he had lyricist Al Dubin—a Russian/Jewish immigrant, as it happens—providing the toothsome and memorable lyrics.

"Lullaby of Broadway," in the key of D, starts out like a shot with six repeated *f*#s ("come on along and listen to") that go up to *g* in bar 2; followed by six repeated *e*s falling to *d* over the next two bars:

♪. ♫ ♩ ♩ | ♪♪ ♩♩ | ♪. ♫ ♩ ♩ | ♩ ♩.

This sequence is then repeated to complete the section. A^1 is a variation start-ing on b (against a G chord); then comes a third variation, which uses the first six bars of the original A before switching to ascending quarter notes ("un-til the / dawn") leading to the cadence. Thus, over the course of A-A^1-A^2, we have heard that initial pattern ten times. Never underestimate, I guess, the clarion power of syncopated repeated notes, at least not in Warren's hands. Great craftsman that he was, he came up with an altogether different but complemen-tary bridge ("good- / night / ba- / -by") constructed of six whole notes followed by a bar of quarters leading to a final whole note. After a thorough repeat of the bridge, Warren—at least in the original six-page sheet music edition—goes through the entire thing again, with a climactic ascending phrase ("let's call it a day") leading to a five-bar coda saluting "old Broadway." And how! Ten eight-bar sections (A-A^1-A^2-B-B-A-A^1-A^2-B-B) plus the coda, an eighty-five-bar lullaby. Warren got his first of eleven Oscar nominations, taking home the statuette over the other two nominees: Mr. Berlin (for "Cheek to Cheek" [page 26]) and Mr. Kern (for "Lovely to Look At").

MACK THE KNIFE

music by Kurt Weill, "English Words by Marc Blitzstein
(Original German Words by Bert Brecht)"
from the musical *The Threepenny Opera* (1955)

It seems, by definition, that there's no place for **Mack the Knife**⸸—which was written in 1928, in Berlin, for the musical *Die Driegroschenoper*—within the *Great American Songbook*. At the same time, "Mack the Knife" not only belongs, but in some ways defines, the *Great American Songbook*. So here we are.

Weill and Brecht's "Moritat," which translates to "murder ballad," achieved something of an international success when it was introduced. But the song and the musical were targeted by the Nazi regime, with "Kultur Bolshevist" Weill fleeing Germany in 1933. That same year, there was an indifferent Broadway adaptation called *The Threepenny Opera* that quickly disappeared; the estimable Percy Hammond of the *Herald*

Tribune called it "a mummy grinning on a dung hill." (Initial press releases gave the title as *The Three-Pence Opera*.) As war approached, American tolerance for all things German,—including musical comedy ballads—diminished.

Weill is known worldwide as the composer of "Mack the Knife," yes; but when he died in 1950, the obituaries I've located identify him as the composer of "Speak Low" [page 158] and "September Song" [page 144] with no mention of what is now considered his masterwork—because in 1950, "Mack the Knife" didn't exist. The popularity of the song as we know it stems from Marc Blitzstein's wonderfully American-slang recast of the antihero, who until that time was known as Macheath or Mackie Messer. Mack the Knife is as American as Billy the Kid, or even Minnie the Moocher. Blitzstein's colorful translation, first heard in concert in 1952 (under the baton of L. Bernstein) and published in 1955, propelled the "Moritat"—which is, after all, about a brutal murderer—into a pop chart sensation.

Weill's music is conceptually simplistic: a street crier's cautionary tale in the form of a sixteen-bar hurdy-gurdy ballad. This is insidiously and insinuously repeated, again and again, with Weill's original arrangement and orchestration serving the song remarkably. The numerous best-selling recordings of the song don't bother with Weill's arrangement, but they have done so well that the song—and, indeed, the composer—is far more famous today than when Weill was alive. So yes, "Mack the Knife" does indeed demand a prime slot in the *Great American Songbook*. And given our hypothesis that Blitzstein's word image is wholly responsible for the enduring strength of the song, let us note the number of times the name "Mack the Knife" appears in the many refrains (eleven, apparently) Blitzstein wrote for "Mack the Knife." Once and only once; but that, with the title, was enough to transform the thoroughly excellent but languishing "Moritat" into an enduring sensation.

MAGIC MOMENT

music by Arthur Schwartz, lyric by Howard Dietz
from the musical *The Gay Life* (1961)

Arthur Schwartz and Howard Dietz—who created some of the most remarkable ballads of the 1930s (including "Dancing in the Dark" [page 31] and "I See Your Face Before Me" [page 75])—drifted apart after ten years. Dietz concentrated on his career heading the publicity department at MGM, with occasional songwriting forays including three extreme failures with Vernon Duke. Schwartz continued writing, working with his pick of top-string lyricists (Loesser, Fields, Hammerstein, Gershwin, Mercer) on lesser-string efforts. Following Dietz's retirement from MGM, the aging pair reunited in an unsuccessful attempt to find their former magic.

The Gay Life was something of a frothy Viennese counterpart to Lerner and Loewe's *Gigi*, one of those charming-roué-discovers-that-the-sweet-little-girl-he's-toyed-with-for-years-is-suddenly-sexually-pleasing sagas. (Such tales, hopefully, have been retired for all time.) Schwartz and Dietz's renewed collaboration did bring forth three fine songs led by **Magic Moment**, which would likely rank high among their catalog if it had been introduced in a more melodically friendly era. The song is a mere twenty-two bars—slowly wistful bars, in an unusual form of A-A^1-A^2-B-B^1 with a two-bar coda. The initial phrase is constructed of two alternating tones (*g* and *a♭*, in the key of E♭) that are heard four times—two sets of quarter notes followed by four eighth notes ("I've been wait-ing / for-the-mag-ic mo-ment / you'll say you love / me")—before moving to quarter notes of *b♭* and *c*:

The second A^1 moves this pattern down a tone. A^2 starts on the original tones but moves up to a high *e♭* leading to the first bridge, which features a series of repeated eighth notes ("YOU AND I BE-LONG to- / geth-er"). The song was preceded, on stage at least, by a twenty-six-bar verse that is so plot-related as to be unusable for our—or anyone's—purposes. But *Magic Moment* is exquisite songwriting.

MAKE SOMEONE HAPPY

music by Jule Styne, lyric by Betty Comden and Adolph Green
from the musical *Do Re Mi* (1960)

Jule Styne was one of the many Hollywood composers who tried to transplant themselves to Broadway, and just about the only one who managed a sustained and celebrated stage career. (For reasons explained in the introduction, we have excluded songs from excellent musicals including Styne's *Gypsy* from this book.) **Make Someone Happy**, from one of his less-than-successful musicals, offers one of Styne's many immensely pleasing melodies.

It is built on a catchy two-bar title phrase. The song starts with a *g*, in the key of E♭ ("make")—held for a full measure and a quarter—followed by descending eighths ("someone") and quarters ("happy"):

This figure, starting on various tones—with the first bar consisting of either whole notes or repeated quarters—is repeated no fewer than fourteen times within the forty-bar refrain. The song promises to be a standard thirty-two affair, but after a traditional *A-B-A* Styne cuts short his second *B* ("Love is the answer") after only four bars and moves into a rangy four-bar *C* ("Once you've found him"). He only then concludes with a euphoric restatement of the initial theme. Thus: *A-B-A-B¹-C-A¹*. Along the way, Styne surprises us with an errant *c♭* (in the key of E♭) in the third bar of the *B* sections; and uses the *C* section to build up to a high *e♭* to start the final *A¹*.

Comden and Green, for their part, don't simply provide pretty words for this lovely tune: they craft a lyric that builds off the title phrase, qualifying it by adding that you should "make just *one*—someone happy." After that they expand on the word one: "one heart," "one smile," "one face." There is also a fourteen-bar verse that is rarely used, and even in the context of the show sounded tacked on to justify the baritone breaking out into a suitable-for-the-charts ballad.

MAKIN' WHOOPEE!

music by Walter Donaldson, lyric by Gus Kahn
from the musical *Whoopee!* (1928)

There's something wonderful about a great comedy number. **Makin' Whoopee!**⚹ was written to order for the star of *Whoopee!*, Eddie Cantor. At the time second only to Jolson in Broadway world, Cantor specialized in this sort of raised-eyebrow number, his round-faced innocence countering sometimes suggestive lyrics. It is also a case where a popular phrase became a widely known euphemism that retains its meaning nearly a century later. Composer Walter Donaldson and lyricist Gus Kahn were both established popular songwriters with more than a few standards together—"Carolina in the Morning" [page 24]—and apart (Walter's "My Blue Heaven" [page 124], Gus's "It Had to Be You" [page 89]).

Donaldson builds his *A* ("another bride, another June, another sunny honey-moon") on altered intervals: his three pickup notes—*d–e–d* (in the key of G) jump to *b* in bar 1; *c* in bar 2; and then a full octave to *d* in bar 3: "another bride, another June, another sunny honeymoon." Note the wordplay; Kahn avoids that already clichéd June/moon rhyme by inserting sunny/honey(-moon) *within* it! These multiple rhymes over the first four bars are followed by two-syllable rhymes in the next two bars ("another season, another reason"). Kahn does a masterful job of building a comedy lyric about a poor soul who so enjoys makin' whoopee that he gets married; philanders around; and after two refrains winds up nearly in jail. "You'd better keep her," the judge advises, "I think it's cheaper / than makin' whoopee."

THE MAN I LOVE

music by George Gershwin, lyric by Ira Gershwin
from the musical *Lady, Be Good!* (1924)

This earliest of George Gershwin's evergreens had a checkered history, which is somewhat beside the point. **The Man I Love**⁑ was what might be considered his first great song, although it was preceded, by several months, by the instantly acclaimed *Rhapsody in Blue*. You might profitably compare "The Man I Love" to the so-called Love Theme (Andantino Moderato) of the *Rhapsody*, but that is beside *our* point. This "molto semplice e dolce" (very simple and sweet) melody, which by now is so well known—or should be—might well have sounded surprising on first hearings.

The initial two-bar phrase of the *A* (in standard thirty-two-bar *A-A¹-B-A²*) is that syncopated strain matching Ira's words "Someday he'll come along, the man I love," with the first notes of each bar alternating between *bb* and *c* (in the key of Eb) and ending on *db*. The third bar is the same; thereafter the notes are lowered a step at a time. Significantly, bar 4 ends on *c*, bar 5 on *cb*, bar 6 on *ab* leading to the cadence on *g*:

$$\text{♪ ♩♪♩ | ♪ ♪♩ | ♪♩♪♩ | ♪ ♪♩ | ♪ ♩♪♩ | ♪ ♪♩ | ♩ ♩ | ○}$$

All the while, Gershwin alters the harmony on us. He starts on an Eb chord, moves to Eb-minor, Bb-minor, C7, and on. (The so-called thumb line, on the original sheet music arrangement, features whole notes descending by half steps from *g* to *c*.) *A¹* ends with a distinctive cadence leading into C-minor for the bridge ("maybe I shall meet him"), with severe chromatics leading us through a rainbow of intense colors and back to *A²*. The refrain is preceded by a sixteen-bar verse with alternate bars of whole notes is followed by ascending dotted eights and sixteenths, which takes us to a curiosity.

George, who wrote *four* full-scale musicals in 1924 (plus that little "Rhapsody"!) devised the *A* section as the verse for an already written refrain of an altogether different song. Too good to waste, he realized, hence it was saved to be used as a song of its own. "The Man I Love" was included in his December musical that year—introduced by star Adele Astaire, sister of that dancing fellow—but tossed out after two weeks of the tryout. The song resurfaced in the 1927 tryout of *Strike Up the Band*, which folded altogether; and then was added to, and cut from, the 1928 musical *Rosalie*. In the meanwhile, "The Man I Love" had been popularized in England and on recordings, to the extent that when the revised version of *Strike Up the Band* successfully opened in 1930, the song had in a round-about manner become too familiar to include as a "new" song—and thus was never used on Broadway while George was alive.

THE MAN THAT GOT AWAY

music by Harold Arlen, lyric by Ira Gershwin
from the motion picture *A Star Is Born* (1954)

Arlen's assignment: write a "dive song," to order, for his "Over the Rainbow" girl, Judy Garland, who was at the time altogether down and out. Arlen—who knew a thing or three about boozy torch songs—and Ira Gershwin came up with a lacerating plaint about "a one-man woman looking for **The Man That Got Away.**⁂"

Set to a slow but insistent beat, this is one of Arlen's so-called tapeworms, working its way through sixty-one bars. He starts out with a typical A-B-A^1-B^1 of eight bars each, only at the end of the second bridge it is surprisingly extended—with "good riddance, goodbye"—into an unexpected C, followed by a repeated A^1 (winding to a wailing "livelong night and day"). The song ends with a final B^2 plus a five-bar tag.

Gershwin, writing what turned out to be his final major song, is with Arlen every step of the way, from "the night is bitter" onward; a perfect match of words and music, which makes it all the more remarkable to note that Arlen's music had been written a dozen years earlier to a lyric by none less than Johnny Mercer. "I Can't Believe My Eyes" was one of the team's initial songs, written for *Blues in the Night* (1941) along with "Blues in the Night" [page 16] and "This Time the Dream's on Me" [page 179]. "I've seen Sequoia, it's really very pretty" it starts. Which shows just how much words can contribute to a song, even if they come from a master who coined "my mama done tol' me" that same month. To illustrate this last remark, as Mercer might say, here's Arlen in a 1972 interview with writer Max Wilk: "Sometimes a lyric depletes a melody, just as a poor melody can deplete a good lyric." (Arlen was careful not to name the song or the writers, making clear that both were close friends of his and excellent lyricists. Mercer's words have subsequently been published.) "The second lyric made that melody sound like the Rock of Gibraltar! The first lyric made my melody sound so puny, it was unbelievable . . . With one man's words the song was enormous in its strength, and with the other's it was puny. One lyric made life glorious, the other deadened it."

MAYBE IT'S TIME FOR ME

music by Laurence Rosenthal, lyric by James Lipton
from the musical *Sherry!* (1967)

File this among the more harmonically arresting—and unusual—ballads of the Broadway musical. Composer Laurence Rosenthal expresses the character's romantic ambivalence by rooting his melody on notes out of key: the first three bars of the printed sheet music, in the key of F, begin not on *c* (as reasonably expected) but on *c#* (preceded by a *c♮* pickup); the fourth bar starts with *f#*. Following three eight-bar sections (*A-A-B*), he gives us an abbreviated *A* of four bars followed by a twelve-bar tag. Unconventional, but **Maybe It's Time for Me** works marvelously. The musical for which it was written, James Lipton's adaptation of the Kaufman-Hart comedy *The Man Who Came to Dinner*, was poor in all elements; and a live recording demonstrates that the song was ineffectively performed. But standing on its own—which is, after all, how a song should be judged—it is striking.

♦

MEMPHIS IN JUNE

music by Hoagy Carmichael, lyric by Paul Francis Webster
from the motion picture *Johnny Angel* (1945)

Hoagy Carmichael kept turning out occasional song hits into his fifties, the final pair being Oscar-nominee "Ole Buttermilk Sky" (in 1946) and Oscar-winner "In the Cool, Cool, Cool of the Evening" (in 1951). The final Carmichael tune on my personal piano rack, though, is **Memphis in June**, a gloriously lazy reverie reminiscent of the early songs written while he was still one of the boys playing in the band (such as "Rockin' Chair," "Georgia on My Mind" [page 43], and "Lazy River" [page 100]). This one, with evocative lyrics by Paul Francis Webster about sittin' on "a shady veranda" and cousin Amanda "makin' a rhubarb pie," smells of honeysuckle and "sweet oleander"—some of which phrases might well have come from Carmichael, who tended to make such suggestions to his collaborators.

Webster, whose first collaboration with Carmichael had been "Baltimore Oriole" (1942), went on to win not one but three Best Song Oscars (one of which was for "Love Is a Many-Splendored Thing," another for "The Shadow of Your Smile"). "Memphis in June" was introduced, in an ineffective 1945 film noir, by Carmichael himself. Launched by his appearance as a barroom piano player—playing the Carmichael/Mercer "How Little We Know?" in the 1944 Bogart-Bacall *To Have and Have Not*—Hoagy became a familiar Hollywood face for the next decade, usually sitting at a battered upright. So much so that British writer Ian Fleming, in his first novel, *Casino Royale* (1953), describes James Bond as looking rather like Hoagy Carmichael.

MISTY

music by Errol Garner, lyric by Johnny Burke
non-production song (1955)

Misty is yet another Songbook favorite initially devised as an instrumental. Jazz pianist Errol Garner conjured it, reportedly while gazing through an airplane window following a storm or some such thing. He recorded it in late 1954 with such success that a Johnny Burke lyric was soon added, and a pop standard was born. (Unlike in other cases, the song version was published just seven weeks after the instrumental.) The music—a standard thirty-two-bars in *A-A¹-B-A¹* form—is instantly identifiable from the dotted half note in the first bar, preceded by two eighth-note pickups and followed by a pianistic string of eighth notes ("look at me—I'm as / helpless as a kitten up a / tree"):

Garner makes use of frequent arpeggiated chords followed by repeated notes, along with a couple of severe interval jumps to dynamic effect: leaping a major seventh in bar 2 ("I'm as / HELP-LESS") and dropping a minor sixth in bar 6 ("I get / MIS-TY"). The *B* begins with an ascending string of five triplets up to an unexpected *d♭* (in the key of E♭), which in the next bar goes to a high *f♭*. In the second half of this section, the same triplet string leads to *d♮* and *f♮*.

As for lyricist Burke, history—or at least anecdotal history—relates that after providing Bing Crosby with twenty-odd film scores and numerous staggeringly successful hit songs (including "Pennies from Heaven" [page 137] and "Swinging on a Star" [page 168]), Crosby determined that Burke was drinking too much for comfort—for Bing's comfort, that is. Given the ultimatum, Van Heusen chose to stick with Bing. (Crosby and Van Heusen were noted for their own drinking, but never mind.) Thus, the fabled team of Burke and Van Heusen was terminated, the composer moving on to Sammy Cahn for a second string of song hits devised not only for Crosby but Frank Sinatra as well. This transpired, apparently, during the extended tryout of the 1953 Burke and Van Heusen Broadway debacle *Carnival in Flanders*, a musical that nevertheless resulted in the immortal "Here's That Rainy Day" [page 53].

Thus, the lyricist was stranded alone in New York when the "Misty" assignment came along. Drinking or not, Burke came up with an inarguably superb lyric. What makes this account somewhat questionable is that Burke went on, in 1961, to write the Broadway musical *Donnybrook!*—not only the lyrics but music as well. Although the show was unsuccessful, Burke's score is charming and admirable, far superior to the several stage musicals turned out over the years by Burke and Van Heusen and Cahn and Van Heusen. Burke died in 1964, at the age of fifty-five—with "Misty" being his final hit.

MOONGLOW

music and lyric by Will Hudson, Eddie De Lange, and Irving Mills
non-production song (1934)

"It must have been **Moonglow**,"✻ we are told. This remarkably evocative stardust song—not "Star Dust," but a similar jazz band instrumental-turned-pop song from the same publishing house—is surprising in several ways.

Here we have a song in which the *A* section (of *A-A-B-A*) is built on three notes, and three notes only. That's right; three notes presented in varying order throughout twenty-four of the thirty-two bars. Bars 1, 3, and 5 consist of alternating *e* and *g* (in the key of G); 2, 4, and 6 include only *b*. Bars 7–8 consist of *g* repeated six times. Is that the formula for a great song? Apparently so. Composer Will Hudson shifts the underlying harmonies to the extent that we might not realize, or care about, the limited range. The bridge, on the other hand, starts with a descending chromatic scale with even more felicitous chord play. And then it's back where we started, with that three-tone *A*.

Eddie De Lange was one of the rare bandleaders who wrote lyrics rather than music. Irving Mills not only published but also managed many bands of the era, as a result of which he was able to claim an authorship share of more than a few notable songs including Ellington's "Sophisticated Lady" [page 157], "Mood Indigo," "It Don't Mean a Thing (If It Ain't Got That Swing)," and the Ellington-De Lange "Solitude."

MORE THAN YOU KNOW

music by Vincent Youmans, lyric by William Rose and Edward Eliscu
from the musical *Great Day!* (1929)

Nearing the end of his all-too-brief, dozen-year career, Youmans transcended his early style built on smart rhythmic numbers (such as "Tea for Two") by developing a string of remarkable ballads with melodies so strong that they are practically unearthly. The first of these was **More Than You Know**, which offers such emotional heft that it is almost florid; the composer seemingly senses just how much he can get away with. Youmans spent most of his career in a losing battle to compete with the one-day-older George Gershwin, but "More Than You Know" seems like a case of trying to top the musical emotionality of Kern's *Show Boat*.

Following an overwrought but effective verse befitting this desperately unrequited love song, Youmans builds his thirty-two-bar refrain on quarter-note triplets:

He uses five sets of these triplets in each of the three *A* sections. This is contrasted by the bridge, built on descending scale runs. And lest anyone should be confused by the lyricist credit, Youmans—who, in response to an ever-expanding chip on his shoulder due to the increasing popularity of George and other Harms tunesmiths, broke away to start his own publishing firm—determined that his lyricist's name was too informal for such a high-tone enterprise. Thus, he decreed that the billing read "William Rose" in lieu of the more plebeian "Billy."

MY BLUE HEAVEN

music by Walter Donaldson, lyric by George Whiting
non-production song (1927)

Walter Donaldson, a Tin Pan Alley composer with a knack for catchy melodies ("Carolina in the Morning" [page 24], "Makin' Whoopee" [page 116]), turned out one of the quintessential fox-trots of the roaring twenties. The *A* is built around a four-note pickup leading to a whole note, a figure repeated thrice:

The initial pickup ranges from *g* to *e♭* (in the key of E♭) before settling on a whole-note *c* ("when whip-poor-wills / CALL"). The next pickups are increasingly lower, leading to *b♭* (in bar 3) and *f* (in bar 5). After a repeat of the *A* (of *A-A-B-A*), Donaldson jumps an octave from low *e♭* to three repeated notes that lead into the bridge ("YOU'LL SEE A smiling face, a fireplace, a cozy room"):

The melody descends gently for a return to those pickup notes to the *A*. The lightheartedly romantic lyric, here, paints a picture that struck a sentimental chord at the time: "Just Molly and me / and baby makes three."

Lyricist George A. Whiting—no relation to composer Richard A. Whiting—was a vaudeville singer who, it is said, was sitting in the room at the Friars Club when Donaldson conjured the tune. The prolific composer was writing more than forty songs a year with myriad lyricists; so, when Whiting offered to add a lyric so he could sing the fresh-off-the-keyboard song in his act—which is to say, an immediate guaranteed performance—Donaldson agreed. "Blue Heaven," as they called it, was published in the winter of 1925. Two years later, the initial recording by singer Gene Austin was an immediate sensation, becoming the best-selling record of the decade with sales topping *five million* copies.

MY FUNNY VALENTINE

music by Richard Rodgers, lyric by Lorenz Hart
from the musical *Babes in Arms* (1937)

Looking for ways to more closely integrate words and music, Rodgers and Hart determined it was time to start writing their own scripts. This worked out successfully on two musicals, after which Rodgers recognized that although his increasingly unreliable partner was able to dash off lyrics on the fly—and on a perpetual bender—Hart was unable to concentrate on dramatic construction. What makes this relevant to our discussion is that when Rodgers handed Hart the haunting music for what became **My Funny Valentine**, and Hart recognized that the word "valentine" fit the music and the mood perfectly, it was a simple matter for them to pick up a stubby pencil and change the name of their hero to: well, Val, thus neatly fitting this perfect romantic ballad into the dramatic narrative. (Musical comedy practice at the time, needless to say, was to insert any song in any show regardless of how or whether it fit.)

Rodgers puts his melody in a minor key (C-minor, in the published music) and constructs the first five bars with only three notes of the scale (*c–d–e♭*). At the same time, he roots the base line on descending chromatic whole notes (*c–b♮–b♭–a♮–a♭*). It isn't until bar 6 that he gives us a different note in the melody, leaping a fifth to *b♭* ("you make me SMILE with my heart"). *A¹* repeats the pattern, starting on *e♭*. In the bridge (of *A-A¹-B-A²*), he briefly moves into the major mode. Here the melody starts on a higher note—*b♭* in bar 1, high *c* in bar 3, *d* in bar 5—that in each case drops down to a consistent *e♭* ("is your FI-GURE less than Greek"), thus steadily increasing the interval by a step. *A²*, which starts with the initial two-bar pattern (low *c*), proceeds to the *e♭* variation (from *A¹*) and builds to a climax with a high *e♭* ("stay little valentine, STAY"). Finally, Rodgers tempers the emotion with a four-bar coda ("each day is Valentine's Day"). As it turns out, they needn't have changed that character name; the song works perfectly well even when sung to or about someone *not* named Valentine.

THE NEARNESS OF YOU

music by Hoagy Carmichael, lyric by Ned Washington
non-production song (1940)

This stand-alone, oh-so-right love song was repurposed by Carmichael from an unused film assignment and transformed for the recording studio. The lyric came from Ned Washington, one of those little-known journeymen who had an even bigger hit simultaneously: the Oscar-winning "When You Wish Upon a Star" [page 190] from *Pinocchio*.

The magic of **The Nearness of You** comes from the nonchalance of the melody, which is craftier than it looks. Bar 1 of the *A* section (in *A-A¹-B-A²*) has a moderate jump of a minor third, from *a* to *c* (in the key of F). It then steps down to a *g*, starting bar 2, and jumps another minor third to *b♭*. In the next bar we have an *f*, going up a major third to *a*, and bar 4 gives us another minor third, *e* to *g*. Thus, it's like a descending staircase, with occasional step-ups. The final *A* holds steady until bar 7: the melody, instead of landing on the expected *f*, jars us with a *c* over a F#-diminished chord. This leads to a four-bar tag that, in Carmichael's typically breezy manner, resolves itself splendidly.

NEVER NEVER LAND

music by Jule Styne, lyric by Betty Comden and Adolph Green
from the musical *Peter Pan* (1954)

A most unusual situation resulted in Styne, Comden, and Green—who at that point had only briefly collaborated, on an undistinguished 1951 revue—being brought together for what would become a string of musicals. Jerome Robbins, on a mission to establish himself as a director, cobbled together a musical version of *Peter Pan* starring Mary Martin. Faced with a lackluster reception during the West Coast tryout, he did *not* fire songwriters Moose Charlap and Carolyn Leigh; they had come up with at least half of a good score, including "I've Gotta Crow," "I'm Flying," and "I Won't Grow Up." Instead, Robbins sent a rescue call to his pals Comden and Green (from *On the Town*) and Styne (from *High Button Shoes*) to supplement the score with juicy material for Martin and costar Cyril Ritchard. The six Comden-Green-Styne efforts included a non-comedic theme song, **Never Never Land,** which—uncharacteristically for Styne, at the time—is straightforward with a hint of melancholy.

The *A* (of *A-A¹-B-A²*) has an anthem-like purity. Styne starts simply, with mostly quarter notes until he fills in the melody starting in bar 5. That is to say, bar 1: "know a place where," compared to bar 5: "not on any chart, you must." The *B* ("you'll have a treasure if you stay there") takes a colorful turn as Styne shifts keys, culminating in a two-bar tag that extends the title phrase for a most lovely ending. Like Peter Pan, the character that J. M. Barrie devised in 1904, "Never Never Land" remains eternal.

NIGHT AND DAY

music and lyric by Cole Porter
from the musical *Gay Divorcee* (1932)

Porter devised one of the earliest of what we might call "Astaire songs," and one of the best, **Night and Day.** He grabs us from the first notes of the verse. "Like the beat, beat, beat of the tom-tom"; "like the tick, tick, tock of the stately clock." Porter makes his point by using repeated notes, and plenty of them: no fewer than thirty-five $b\flat$s (in the key of E♭) over the first eight bars. He then goes up a half step to $b\natural$, nine of them over two bars; up to five cs; and then finishes his sixteen-bar verse by falling back with another fourteen $b\flat$s, ending with the title phrase leading into the refrain. All of this is against a mysterioso set of chromatic octaves in the bass. Is it any wonder we're hooked? Porter halts those incessant repeated notes by holding "day"—in the title phrase, at the start of the refrain—for six beats. Even so, the melody continues to hit us with repeated quarter notes like the beat, beat, beat of a metronomic heartbeat.

The form starts out in straightforward manner, although Porter goes where the melody leads him. We can call it *A-B-A¹-B-C-B¹*, in eight-bar sections. He offers a bit of sleight of hand in bar 6 of the second *A*. What in the initial section had been "only / you beneath the / MOON AND under the / sun" is altered—melodically, as well as lyrically—to "that this / longing for you / FOLLOWS WHERE-E-VER I / go." But that's not all; in the final *B*, he takes what had been "it's no / matter darling / WHERE YOU ARE I / think of you," and changes the rhythm to a climactic "till you / let me spend my / LIFE MAKING LOVE / TO YOU / day and night." This slight-but-determined melodic alteration in otherwise repeated sections, mind you, would become a common device for Porter.

As for the "Astaire song" label, this was pretty much the song that took Astaire from Broadway to Hollywood. Porter corrupts the rhythm for two bars in the *C* section, at "Oh, such a hungry / yearning burning in- / -side of me"—the better to dance with, although Porter-the-lyricist clearly delighted in fashioning wordplay such as "oh such a hungry YEARNING BURNING inside of me."

NOT MINE

music by Victor Schertzinger, lyric by Johnny Mercer
from the motion picture *The Fleet's In* (1942)

Here's a case where the musical magic, I'd guess, was enhanced by the lyricist. Mercer, mind you, was himself a more-than-adequate composer. Following a warmly melodic twelve-bar verse—which, after two somewhat romantically ascending four-bar sections, ends with a downbeat resolution—the refrain begins with the title phrase "It's somebody else's moon above, **Not Mine**." This phrase is built around a set of melancholy triplets:

The triplets are used five times in the refrain (*A-B-A¹-C/A*); unlike in most such lyrics, Mercer uses the words "some-bod-y else's" each time. This ties into the theme of the song in such a manner that one suspects Mercer dictated the melodic phrase—or at least, the rhythmical phrase—to Schertzinger, who at the same time was directing *The Fleet's In* (see "I Remember You" [page 74]).

OL' MAN RIVER

music by Jerome Kern, lyric by Oscar Hammerstein 2nd
from the musical *Show Boat* (1927)

By any manner of definition, **Ol' Man River**※ is one of the important/superlative/monumental creations of the American musical theatre, the *Great American Songbook*, and the great any-old-thing you care to characterize it as. This for the power of Kern's music; the power of Hammerstein's words; the power of what the song says; and the power of how it says it. So, does it matter why, when, and how it was written?

Hammerstein has said that he recognized that his sprawling libretto, based on Edna Ferber's sprawling novel, needed an underlying theme that he could occasionally return to over the forty-year course of the plot. He settled on the image of the mighty Mississippi upon which the Cotton Blossom showboat floated from town to town. When Kern said he was too busy with other parts of the score to address this immediately, Oscar suggested they take the "Cotton Blossom" theme from the opening number, slow it down, and alter it for use. Kern did just that, inverting the banjo-friendly title phrase—which for the purpose of comparison we will transpose to the later song's key of E♭—from the descending figure *e♭* (cot-) *e♭* (-ton) *c* (blos-) *b♭* (-som) to an ascending figure of *b♭* (ol') *b♭* (man) *c* (riv-) *e♭* (-er). And there you have it. Although the "Cotton Blossom"/"Ol' Man River" interdependence has been noted occasionally, these pages seem to be the proper place to examine it. With deep apologies to readers who might find it too musicological for comfort: we promise not to do it again!

"Cotton Blossom" is written in two sections, sung by the "colored chorus" toiling away under the sun, on the one hand, and the "mincing maidens and their beaux" on the other. There are four interweaved themes, all of them up-tempo, in what can be described as *A-B-A-C-D-C-D*. "Ol' Man River" is *A-A¹-B-A²*, in the standard thirty-two bars. The *A* section ("ol' man river, dat ol' man river, he must know sumpin', but don't say nothin'") is clearly derived from the earlier song's *C* section ("Cotton Blossom, Cotton Blossom, Cap'n Andy's floating show"). By converting "Cotton Blossom" from the 2/4 time in which it is printed, we offer a direct comparison.

The banjo-plunk rhythm of the initial "cotton blossom" figure—quarter/ quarter/eighth/dotted quarter, as above—runs throughout the *A* sections of "Ol' Man River," eighteen times over the thirty-two bars. This is not the case in the more varied course of "Cotton Blossom."

Kern has said "the melody of 'Ol' Man River' was conceived immediately after my first hearing Paul Robeson's speaking voice"; this was in the tryout of the play *Black Boy* in September 1926, long before *Show Boat* opened in December 1927. "Robeson's organ-like tones are entitled to no small share of 'that thing called inspiration.'" (This quote, from a 1938 letter, might not reflect how Kern actually felt when the singer was unavailable—or purposely made himself unavailable—to appear in the original production of *Show Boat*. He later played the role, initially in the London production, and was forever identified with the song.)

In any event, it can be said that in converting that short "Cotton Blossom" phrase into all those sustained notes of "Ol' Man River," Kern had Robeson's voice in mind. If the *A* section was specifically contrived to fit the singer, the rest of the song was lifted intact from "Cotton Blossom," literally so. Kern's original manuscript of "Ol' Man River" delineates the three eight-bar A sections; but in place of both verse and bridge, he simply scrawls "copy from opening chorus." That verse—"colored folks work on the Mississippi" in Hammerstein's 1946 revision, although the original lyric included what is nowadays referred to as the "n word"—starts with what we have deemed the *A* section of "Cotton Blossom." As for the bridge, what had been "git yo'self a bran' new gal" is transformed into the immortal "tote dat barge! Lift dat bale!"

All of this is to say, "Ol' Man River" is indeed monumental. Would the song exist without the prior existence of the ornamental "Cotton Blossom"? Would Hammerstein's proposed river song be as powerful if Kern had buckled down and composed one on purpose, rather than taking Oscar's suggestion of digging it out of the opening chorus? In any case, it seems to have worked out. And while we're looking at the original manuscript, let us note Kern's instruction—most likely to arranger Robert Russell Bennett—at the bottom of the page: "N.B. After Joe's 2nd verse, male octette (double 4tette) takes up Refrain with him. Work up big finish." Big finish, indeed!

OLD DEVIL MOON

music by Burton Lane, lyric by E. Y. Harburg
from the musical *Finian's Rainbow* (1947; published 1946)

Here's a romantic ballad—a "moon" song, in fact—
with a difference and something of a glint in the eye—
or, rather, the ear. Lane, a Gershwin protégé whose
lack of ambition resulted in a sporadic if distinctive
output, was well matched with Harburg for the postwar satire, *Finian's Rainbow*.

The eight-bar *A* section begins melodically
enough, with whole notes in the odd-numbered bars
interrupted by mouthfuls of words in the others:

This culminates in a highly rhythmic cadence leading to the title phrase ("It's
that / **Old Devil Moon**") that begins the bridge. After starting bars 1 and 3 of
this section on *c* (in the key of F), Lane slyly—or devilishly?—raises it to a *d♭* in
bar 5. He then shifts into a very different-sounding *C* section, with abrupt chords
punctuating the melody ("You and your glance / [slam] make this romance /
[slam] too hot to handle"). "Glance and (ro-)mance are eighth notes (ending one
bar) tied to quarters (starting the next), adding propulsion to the interior of what
turns out to be a lengthy, forty-eight-bar song. Lane and Harburg take us back
into the *A* with the astonishing interjection "to—your razzle-dazzle":

Then comes a second bridge ("wanna cry, wanna croon") and finally a new
melodic phrase ("just when I think I'm free as a dove") that seems to say oh,
yes, this is supposed to be a real love song. Thus: *A-B-C-A-B-C/A*. It's not your
standard love song; but then one would expect something rather more than a
standard ballad from Lane and Harburg, and they certainly delivered.

ONE FOR MY BABY (AND ONE MORE FOR THE ROAD)

music by Harold Arlen, lyric by Johnny Mercer
from the motion picture *The Sky's the Limit* (1943)

Eighteen months and sixteen or so songs from the start of their collaboration with "Blues in the Night" [page 16], Arlen and Mercer turned out what might well be seen as a follow-up, a barroom plaint with the singer literally wailing that "this torch that I found must be drowned." **One for My Baby**⍟ is just as strong as its predecessor. Given that the earlier song is patterned in the twelve-bar sections of the classic blues (as discussed), it is surprising to find that this second Arlen/Mercer blues is assembled mostly in the standard multiples of eight. That said, it is far from simplistic.

Working as before without a verse, the form is *A*(sixteen)-*A¹*(sixteen)-*B*(eight)-*A²*(eighteen). Arlen sees fit to ratchet up the mood by presenting his second *A* in a different key, modulating (in the printed sheet music) from E♭ to G and remaining there for the rest of the song. The *A* sections amble along over a bluesy rhythm:

The bridge ("you'd never know it, but buddy I'm a kind of poet") turns slashingly if briefly abrupt, with as many as ten syllables to the bar. The final *A* copies the second *A* (i.e., the G major section), with the addition of a two-bar extension that strings out the title phrase. More could be said for "One for My Baby," but Arlen and Mercer speak for themselves, no?

OVER THE RAINBOW

music by Harold Arlen, lyric by E. Y. Harburg
from the motion picture *The Wizard of Oz* (1939)

It is foolhardy to overly rely on songwriter anecdotes, as they can stem from one offhanded innocuous statement (or misstatement) that becomes firmly
rooted through hazy repetition. In this case, Arthur
Freed—a fairly successful lyricist ("Singin' in the
Rain") starting to work his way into the firmament
of MGM as an uncredited string puller behind the
screen of *The Wizard of Oz*—is said to have selected
Arlen and Harburg based on a single song within
their 1937 Broadway musical, *Hooray for What!*: "In
the Shade of the New Apple Tree."

This is a whimsical pastiche of the gently nostalgic Tin Pan Alley songs of
the early century, with Arlen inserting one "wrong" note in the *A* section to add
a welcome twinge of late-Depression neuroticism. Even so, it might seem too
mild a song to merit such fantastical influence. (Hugh Martin—who as a featured
singer in *Hooray for What!* created the vocal arrangement and performed the
song—told me that the number was far more swinging than it appears in the
sheet music version; thus, the Freed story could be accurate.) It is incontest-
able that Arlen and Harburg turned out to be the right men for the *Oz* job.
Although the score is full of wonders, the high spot—and the least typical for
the songwriters—is **Over the Rainbow**.§ Here is a song without a single Arlen-
esque strain, nor any Harburgian whimsy or polemics. Yes, there are several
ungarnished Arlen anthem songs built on pure melody and yearning—"My
Shining Hour," "Out of This World," "A Sleepin' Bee" [page 147]—but "Over
the Rainbow" is the earliest such example among Arlen's work.

The song is marked by an extreme octave jump between the two half notes
("some-where") in the first bar, followed by a slightly smaller interval of a major
sixth in bar 3. Not so simple to sing, but it hasn't harmed the song's popularity.
The bridge (of *A-A-B-A¹*) changes pace with a lulling, running-water-like melody
("someday I'll wish upon a star") as opposed to the hymnlike *A*. Getting back to
our songwriter-anecdote theme, Harburg recalls that while they were searching
for the bridge, he suggested that Arlen use the notes he whistled to call his dog;
Arlen labeled that story nonsense, saying he took his inspiration from the type
of piano exercise you might find in a child's lesson book. One anecdote that *does*

seem accurate—in that both Arlen and Harburg told it, in praise of their mutual friend and sometime collaborator Ira Gershwin—is that when they couldn't come up with a finish, Gershwin pointed out that they already had it: just tack on that running water/dog call/piano exercise phrase from the bridge.

OVERNIGHT

music by Louis Alter, lyric by Billy Rose and Charlotte Kent
from the stage revue *Sweet and Low* (1930)

Louis Alter was one of those relatively unknown but reliable composers of the Depression era who turned out a number of highly interesting songs, including one considerable hit: "Manhattan Serenade," a 1929 instrumental that achieved a second life when a Harold Adamson lyric was added in 1942. More remarkable is **Overnight**,§ written for a Fannie Brice revue produced by her then-husband, Billy Rose. Original title of the Billy (and Fannie) Rose show, during the tryout tour: *Corned Beef and Roses*. Billy, as was his habit, saw fit to muscle in on the songwriter royalties.

"Overnight" is a jigsaw puzzle of minor thirds over shifting chords. The opening phrase starts with two *g*s, in the key of E♭ (on the word ("ov-er") jumping up a minor third to b♭ ("I") and back ("Found"). This is followed by a jump of a minor sixth ("you") in bar 3. This theme is then repeated, one tone lower, in bars 4 through 8 of the sixteen-bar *A* section (of *A-A-B-A*). Alter descends a major fifth into bar 9, where the initial pattern is altered by using a *major* third before reverting to a series of minor thirds. All the while, Alter—who started his career at the piano, accompanying star Nora Bayes in vaudeville—shifts his harmony with a most interesting bass accompaniment, continually inverting the direction of his chords; that is, from *e♭* down to *b♭* in bars 1–2, from *a♮* up to *d* in 3–4, and so on. The eight-bar bridge offers triplets and quarter notes rather than the half and whole notes of the *A*s; what's more, the intervals in this section are major (rather than minor) thirds and sixths. The sixteen-bar verse is highly dramatic if somewhat florid, effectively setting us up for the haunting refrain.

THE PARTY'S OVER

music by Jule Styne, lyric by Betty Comden and Adolph Green
from the musical *Bells Are Ringing* (1956)

The Styne-Comden-Green **The Party's Over**[§] is, by any description, a strongly effective ballad hit. Upon examination, we find that it is built on pickup notes—not only built, but altogether dependent. By my count, there are three-note pickups—that is, initial phrases starting mid-bar that lead directly to the downbeat of the next—fourteen times within thirty-two bars, all, mind you, most effectively:

The *A* sections (of *A-B-A¹-B¹*) have three sets of ascending pickup notes—*b♭* ["the"], *e♭* ["par-"], *f* ["-ty's"], in the key of E♭—leading to bars 1, 3, and 5. Note how Styne completes the phrase by detouring to *a♭* before landing on the expected *g*, starting the refrain with a melancholic twinge that characterizes the song. (Without that *a♭*, we'd have—well, "how dry I am.") The *B*s have repeated-note pickups ("IT'S TIME TO / wind up") leading into bars 1, 3, 5, and 7. (The *A* pickups are always identical, but Styne descends his repeated-note *B* pickups; the first begins on *b♭*, the next *a♭*, then *g*, and finally *f*.)

Although we tend to believe that composers come by these devices sub-consciously, Styne seems to have carefully plotted it out. It is dangerous to put too much credence in his anecdotes, as he was wildly imaginative and seems not to have let facts stand in the way of a good story. But Styne claims that the vocally insecure Judy Holliday believed herself incapable of singing a ballad. He explained that her part of "The Party's Over" was not the melody; it was an ornamental obligato while the leading man sang the actual song. After Judy learned it (and well), Jule says, she realized that she *could* sing a ballad. Whether this tale be real or imagined, it can be seen that these constant pickup notes make the song "easier" to sing: the vocalist is eased into the big notes rather than having to hit them head-on, as contrasted with two ballads Styne soon thereafter wrote for decidedly *non*-insecure leading ladies: "Small World" and "People."

PAST THE AGE OF INNOCENCE

music by Moose Charlap, lyric by Norman Gimbel
from the musical *The Conquering Hero* (1961; published 1956)

Past the Age of Innocence⅗ is another song from a calamitous, blink-and-you'll-miss-it musical comedy. This is the one during the tryout of which the bemused book writer, Larry Gelbart, quipped, "If Hitler's alive, I hope he's out of town with a musical." But what a lovely, if melancholic, song of unrequited love!

The plaintively pure melody combines with intricate harmonics to make this *A-A-B-A¹* song strikingly arresting. The bridge includes three sets of triplets, adding to the tentative nature of the lyric, intended for a young girl trying to convince the boy-next-door that she is—well—"past the age of innocence." In the enigmatic origins category, this song was part of the Moose Charlap/Norman Gimbel score for the 1961 Bob Fosse musical in which it was included. (Director/choreographer/conceiver Fosse was fired in Philadelphia: "now that it's all gone wrong," complained Fosse, "I guess they have to blame *somebody*.") The song fits right into the plot, but it turns out that it was previously recorded and copyrighted in 1956, listing Gimbel as lyricist but one "Bill Sawens" as composer. It was first heard in 1951 in a negligible film called *Rhythm Inn*, with the credited composers being Charlap and Sawens; as best I can decipher, Sawens seems to have been Charlap's pseudonym for several years. In any event, it's a wonderful—if almost thoroughly unknown—song.

PENNIES FROM HEAVEN

music by Arthur Johnston, lyric by Johnny Burke
from the motion picture *Pennies from Heaven* (1936)

Given the prime place of honor held in the big-studio movie musical world by Warren and Dubin on the one hand and Burke and Van Heusen on the other, it seems surprising—at least, I was surprised—to find that **Pennies from Heaven** comes from neither team. Yes, Johnny Burke did the lyric; his first hit, and one that demonstrated his penchant for catchy title phrases (such as "pennies from heaven"). The music was by Arthur Johnston, one of those hidden-in-the-shadows musical assistants to Irving Berlin whose own catalog includes only one other title that stands out, "Cocktails for Two." No matter; "Pennies from Heaven" fits easily on the top shelf with the hits of Warren/Dubin and Burke/Van Heusen.

The main phrase ("ev'ry time it / rains, it rains / pennies from heaven") is instantly memorable, in part due to the quarter notes (starting with three repeated *c*s, in the key of C) and that extended first syllable of "heaven" ending the title phrase (that consists of four *a*s followed by a *g*):

The bridge ("you'll find your fortune falling") consists of mostly quarter notes, climbing in chord-like patterns. The A^1 (of A-B-A^1-B^1) repeats the melody into bar 6, at which point it replaces what had been the title phrase (on repeated *a*s) with repeated *e*s—the highest note in the melody—leading to a *d* ("you must have show-ers"). This takes us into D-minor, Johnston culminating with the title phrase here set to the only triplets used in the song. The results are cheerfully hopeful with a twinge of melancholy, which was just the thing for the mid-Depression nation.

PERSONALITY

music by Jimmy Van Heusen, lyric by Johnny Burke
from the motion picture *Road to Utopia* (1946; published 1945)

A joyfully sly melody meets a raised-eyebrow lyric, built around an altogether innocent-sounding title phrase, in **Personality**. This was written for the fourth of the "Road" pictures—starring Bing Crosby, Bob Hope, and Dorothy Lamour—that came out of Paramount in the 1940s. (*Utopia*, lest you're curious, was a Gold Rush yarn set in Alaska.) The song takes the form of a history lesson, explaining the allure of folk such as Madame DuBarry. What made her the toast of Paree? "She had a well-developed—*personality*," which is to say, clearly, personality had little to do with it.

The melody breezes along in swingy fashion, skipping up and down and over the scale until reaching the title in bar 7 of the *A*. Van Heusen plays some harmonic tricks—including an A-7 chord built upon an unexpected *c#* (in the key of G) in the first bar—and offers a supportively humorous baseline. Burke, meanwhile, manages the feat of constructing each stanza so that the innocuous "personality" pays off each time. The bridge (of *A-A-B-A*) offers a change up, starting each of the first five bars with three syncopated repeated notes ("what did / RO-ME-O see in / JU-LI-ET"). After giving us "Ju-pi-ter" in bar 5, Burke and Van Heusen surprise us with the two-syllable "Ju-no." They then answer the question at hand ("what did," etc.) with a two-word punchline: "*you know*," which lands grandly and is punctuated by a six-bar rest—allowing room for plenty of laughter—before moving on.

PICK YOURSELF UP

music by Jerome Kern, lyric by Dorothy Fields
from the motion picture *Swing Time* (1936)

Swing Time, Kern's one wholly satisfying original motion picture score, offered several charmers including "The Way You Look Tonight" [page 187]. I find myself equally delighted by **Pick Yourself Up**, which is—to borrow a word from Dorothy Fields's lyric—nifty. Designed to fit the talents and screen personalities of Fred Astaire and Ginger Rogers, this is a polka with attitude.

The eight-bar *A* is built on three distinct rhythms: bar 1 has an ascending/descending six-note phrase ("Nothing's impossible") while bars 2, 3, and 4 consist of two quarter notes followed by a dotted quarter and eighth, resulting in an exaggerated third beat ("I have FOUND—that . . ."). What's more, Kern uses a series of thirds that descend as he goes along. In the key of F: *a–a–c* in bar 2, *g–g–b♭* in bar 3, *f–f–a* in the next. After that he gives us two eighths followed by two quarters ("pick my-self up") leading to the section's end. Kern then modulates from the key of F to G, taking the *A¹* a full step up. Continuing in what one supposes was a playful mood, the composer moves into A-minor for the first half of the *B* ("work like a soul inspired"); then moves into C before returning to the original key of F for *A²* (that, for film-staging purposes, is extended to twelve bars). A sixteen-bar interlude ("I'll get some self-assurance") leads back to a full repeat of *A-A¹-B-A²*. The burthen is preceded by an eighteen-bar verse ("please teacher, teach me something"), which is perhaps dispensable. Even so, the latter half of this verse undergoes some eyebrow-raising harmonics, enroute from the key of D to the F of the burthen, suiting the "awkward as a camel" Astaire—that phrase comes from the self-deprecating lyric—quite nicely.

PUT ON A HAPPY FACE

music by Charles Strouse, lyric by Lee Adams
from the musical *Bye Bye Birdie* (1960)

Launching a Broadway musical from a group of untried novices—composer, lyricist, book writer, director, producer, first-timers all—was, and remains, a recipe for instant ignominy. *Bye Bye Birdie* turned out to be a Cinderella story among musical comedies, thanks to a combination of attributes led by the fact that it was funny, brashly refreshing, and mightily tuneful. This is handily represented by Charles Strouse and Lee Adams's irrepressibly breezy—**Put on a Happy Face**. Here is a cheer-up song with melody matching message, promising that "gray skies are gonna clear up" if only you follow the lyricist's lead.

Strouse starts his *A* section with a lightly rhythmic string climbing an octave-plus—from *bb* (in the key of E♭) to *c*, and then descending back to middle *c*. Repeating the phrase for the final half of the *A*, he finishes not on *c* but *db*, literally changing the tone:

The bridge ("take off the gloomy mask of tragedy") starts with a similar lope up from *c* to *c* before heading in a different direction. Note the distinctly descending chromatic line, with Strouse's melody centering—on the first and third beats of each bar—on the next half-step down: "take off that gloom[*c*]-y / mask[*b*] of tra[*bb*]-ge-dy / it's[*a*] not[*ab*] your / style[*g*]." Speaking of which, we are told that Mr. Sondheim was delighted by the way Adams rhymed "tragedy" with "glad-ja-dee-" (as in "glad you decided"). The *C* (of *A-B-A-C*) starts with a more placid progression of whole notes, halves, and quarters. And what happens when you "spread sunshine all over the place"? You get the title once more, only set to a different musical phrase. As evidence of the canny construction of this sprightly song, the composer—who has thus far, through thirty-one bars, carefully avoided resting on the key tone—finally lands on *eb*, effectively spreading that musical sunshine—sunshine that begins, mind you, with Strouse's supremely delightful introductory vamp.

PUTTIN' ON THE RITZ

music and lyric by Irving Berlin
from the motion picture *Puttin' On the Ritz* (1930; published 1929)

As America's most successful and prolific composer of the time, Irving Berlin had a keen sense of what the market wanted. That being the case, he fueled his personal soundtrack of the 1920s with songs gentle and sentimental (such as "Say It with Music," "What'll I Do," and "Always")—even while the younger generation (Gershwin, Kern, DeSylva-Brown-Henderson) were jazzing up the works with fascinating rhythms. That's not to say that Berlin wasn't capable of that, too. This he proved indisputably with the uncanny **Puttin' on the Ritz**, the most startlingly syncopated item he'd turned out since "Alexander's Ragtime Band" (1912) and "I Love a Piano" (1915) [page 71].

Unlike typical songwriters hungry for a hit who rush their newest wares to the market in fear that they may become outdated, Berlin saw fit to hold "Puttin' on the Ritz" until he could prominently place it, as the title song of a major talking picture, perhaps. Except when he wrote the song in the spring of 1927, there *was* no such thing as a talking picture. For whatever reason, Berlin filed it away until he could indeed use it as the title song of a major talking musical. ("Puttin' on the Ritz" was finally published in December of 1929, prior to the release of *Puttin' on the Ritz* in March 1930.) The melody has immediate impact.

Berlin builds the song on an ascending four-note phrase: *f–a♭–c* followed by an octave drop to middle *c* (in the key of A♭). This is repeated four times in succession—but the wily Berlin starts the second hearing of the phrase on the final half beat of bar 1. This throws everything off-kilter, resulting in a most irrepressible rhythm ("IF you're blue and YOU / don't know where to / GO to"). It's so irrepressible that we're jarred, in bar 4, when Berlin reverts to four straight quarter notes. After all of that, he ends the *A* (of *A-A-B-A*) with the title phrase on a half scale of descending eighth notes:

The enervated jumpiness of the song is enhanced by the use of no fewer than twelve octave drops, *c* to *c*, over thirty-two bars. By 1946, the lyric—about Harlem swells up on Lenox Avenue who "spend their last two bits"—did, indeed, become outdated, bordering on the objectionable; so Berlin relocated to Park Avenue, where his denizens "mix with the Rockefellers."

SATIN DOLL

"words and music" by Duke Ellington, Billy Strayhorn, and Johnny Mercer
non-production song, 1960

This sinuous jazz standard evokes an entire world of what you might call stylishly high nightlife. **Satin Doll** is built—in traditional *A-A-B-A* style—on the initial two-bar phrase ("cigarette holder which wigs me"), set on alternating *a*s and *g*s (in the key of C):

The next two bars repeat this up a step; bars 5 and 6 take the rhythmic figure from bar 2 ("which wigs me") and play it over different notes to lead to the title phrase and the end of the *A*. During this we get a colorful array of harmonies. The bridge ("she's nobody's fool so I'm playing it cool as can be") is a syncopated chain, from high *c* down to *g* up to *c* down to *g* up to *c*. ("From *c* down to *g* up to *c* down to *g* up to *c*" would work as a lyric here, in fact.) This is then repeated up a step, after which a spoken tag (spelled "Swich-E-Roo-ney" in the sheet music) serves as a percussive link back to the *A*.

I am as strong a fan of the lyricist as you're likely to find, and it goes without saying—or maybe with saying—that if any *Songbook* writer could fluently speak hepcat slang, it was Johnny "Hang on to Your Lids, Kids" Mercer. So, I'm chagrined to say that the "Satin Doll" lyric sounds like an aging square trying to sound hip. I mean, "Swich-e-Roo-ney?" As for the authorship: the music was written and recorded as an instrumental in 1953. The song version was written in 1958 and published in 1960. Decades later, the estates of Duke

Ellington and his longtime collaborator, Billy Strayhorn, battled it out in court. As best I can interpret it, Ellington's heirs claimed that Strayhorn—whom they described as author of the harmonies but not the melody—wasn't entitled to a share of the composer's copyright renewal. If you have the will/stamina/interest, track down *Tempo Music v. Famous Music 838 F. Supp. 162 (S.D.N.Y. 1993)*. Ellington lost.

SENTIMENTAL JOURNEY

music by Les Brown and Ben Homer, lyric by Bud Green
non-production song 1944

Bandleader Les Brown joined with collaborators Ben Homer and Bud Green to write **Sentimental Journey**, a wartime hit looking forward to better days ("gonna make a sentimental journey, to renew old memories"). The melody provides as good an example of an earworm as you can find. The *A* section is centered around an interval of a third—*e* to *c* (in the key of C)—in teetering rhythm:

Following the first three bars, the *e* slides chromatically down to *d*. The distinctive touch of the song comes in bar 6, where that *e* is briefly altered to *e♭*. The restricted melodic span of the *A* is expanded in the bridge (of *A-A-B-A*), which teeters an octave higher, centered around high *c*. Then it's back to that sinuous earworm. Once you catch it, just try to lose it.

SENTIMENTAL RHAPSODY

music by Alfred Newman, lyric by Harold Adamson
from the motion picture *Street Scene* (1931; published 1942)

Back in the days when you could only watch old movies in old movie houses, I caught the 1931 early talkie version of Elmer Rice's Pulitzer-winning play *Street Scene* and was struck by the atmospheric musical theme that permeated the film. Over the years, I heard this again and again in numerous old movies, used as musical shorthand to instantly evoke the atmosphere of Manhattan between the wars. I long attempted to identify just what this music actually was; I eventually found four bars of **Sentimental Rhapsody** advertised on the back of a random sheet music cover—a 1942 song with, it turns out, "melody based on a theme from the motion picture *Street Scene*"! Go figure.

The song perfectly captures the dreamy, lazy New York milieu, thanks in part to Gershwin-esque blue notes and interval jumps. Alfred Newman was best known as a Hollywood composer, with nine Oscars on his shelf. He knew a thing or two about showtunes, though: in his pre-Hollywood days, he was musical director for multiple Gershwin and Rodgers musicals and thus on the podium when the world first heard such songs as "How Long Has This Been Going On?" [page 58] and "A Ship Without a Sail" [page 145]. As for the conversion from theme to song: the theme itself was published in 1933, used as background music for various films, and frequently recorded. A song version ("Sentimental Rhapsody") was written, with lyric by Harold Adamson, and published in 1942. The music continued to be regularly featured, especially in film noirs of the time, and was prominently placed in the 1947 crime thriller *Kiss of Death*.

SEPTEMBER SONG

music by Kurt Weill, lyric by Maxwell Anderson
from the musical *Knickerbocker Holiday* (1938)

When distinguished stage-and-screen star Walter Huston agreed, at the age of fifty-five, to make his Broadway musical debut as the dictatorial Peter Stuyvesant of old New Amsterdam—in *Knickerbocker Holiday*, Maxwell Anderson's thinly veiled attack on what he saw as the fascism of Franklin Delano Roosevelt—he asked, not surprisingly: what about my love song? And so it was that Weill and Anderson wrote **September Song**; not a love ballad, but a wistful reverie of romance at a time when "the days dwindle down to a precious few." Weill sets it to something of a rocking beat; is that a rocking chair, one wonders?

Three pickup quarter notes—*c-e-b* (in the key of C)—lead to three *a*s in bar 1. On the next hearing, those pickup notes drop to *c-e♭-a♭* leading to *g*. In bar 5 the melody is forced up to high *d*—too high, perhaps, for this overaged character. Weill apparently took his aim directly from Anderson, an acclaimed dramatist here attempting his first musical. This high *d* comes at the top of the phrase "but the days go SHORT." In the second *A*, the high note comes within "one hasn't got TIME." The bridge (of *A-A¹-B-A²*) is more impassioned (*poco expressivo*) and is clearly intended to stress the character with extended notes on high *d* and *eb*. This is followed by the final *A*, dampening the implied ardor with a *calmato* finish. The song includes a purposely non-challenging verse, which wends its way up and down the scale with sets of repeated notes in minor thirds—a verse so intrinsic that you really want (and need) to hear it a second time, with the second lyric provided by Anderson. Let it be added that a hall-mark of the song are the two sets of triplets Weill inserts in the first *A* section ("from May-to-De- / cember" and "when you-reach-Sep- / tember"):

The composer otherwise avoids triplets, even though one would logically expect them in the restated *A* sections. But this, clearly, is precisely what Weill intended.

A SHIP WITHOUT A SAIL

music by Richard Rodgers, lyric by Lorenz Hart
from the musical *Heads Up!* (1929)

Rodgers and Hart's final show of the 1920s was an undistinguished item called, for little reason, *Heads Up!* (During the tryout they called it *Me for You*—more reasonably so, as they likely expected the duet "Me for You" to be the song hit of the show.) The team's fourteenth full musical in four-and-a-half years—yes, their fourteenth full musical in four-and-a-half years!—includes one of the first of Hart's haunting ballads of forlorn unrequited love. **A Ship Without a Sail**, is something of an art song, and unconventionally shaped.

Rodgers gives us the standard thirty-two bars, but he does so in an unconventional *A*(twelve)-*B*(eight)-*A¹*(twelve); in effect, this is an eight-bar *A* with an extended four bars to include the title phrase ("Like a ship without a sail"). Each of the first four bars features interval drops of a major sixth, from *c* to *eb* and then from *g* to *bb* (in the key of E♭). Rodgers adds an unusual but very noticeable vocalized triplet ("when there's no love to *ho-o-old* my love") at the midpoint of his *A*s. A bar later, he inserts an out-of-key *d♭*; significantly, Hart sets the first to "heart" and the second to "love" (as in "love-less"). The bridge seems to be going in a different direction altogether; Rodgers's sheet music arrangement places it atop an accompaniment of staccato quarter notes (a device he returned to occasionally over his career). The refrain is preceded by a tentative and contemplative twenty-four-bar verse that is quite lovely. As for *Heads Up!*, or *Me for You*, the only smash they encountered was the one on Wall Street, having opened their Philadelphia tryout on the Friday after Black Thursday.

SKYLARK

music by Hoagy Carmichael, lyric by Johnny Mercer
non-production song, 1942

Carmichael and Mercer—or Hoagy and Johnny, as they were referred to within the trade—paired infrequently, apparently due to Carmichael's cavalier treatment of Mercer on their first encounter a decade earlier. At that time Mercer, who was ten years younger, was just starting out, and Carmichael had already written "Star Dust." Compounding the problem, it seems, is that while the Indiana-born Carmichael specialized in folksy songs of the South, the Savannah-born Mercer truly did have Georgia on his mind. That is to say that while Hoagy seems to have conscientiously cultivated that homey flavor in his lyrics, he was sensitive to the fact that Johnny just naturally breathed it.

Skylark was completed and published in 1942, but the composer apparently gave the music to his lyricist back before Mercer joined with Arlen to write the instant-classic "Blues in the Night" [page 16]. "Skylark" demonstrates just how well suited these two countrified music men were; their other significant collaborations, neither included in this book, were the folksy 1933 "Lazybones" and the 1951 Oscar-winning "In the Cool, Cool, Cool of the Evening." They also paired for a bloodbath of a musical comedy, the 1940 *Walk with Music*—that brought forth at least six published songs, each of which I find uncharacteristically colorless.

The *A* sections of "Skylark" start with the title in half notes, followed by torrents up and down the scale in thirds and fourths. After wending a melodic path, the sections seem to end in parenthetical asides. The bridge of this *A-A-B-A* song is something else again; perhaps not the most remarkable bridge ever, but certainly among them. Novice piano players beware! It consists of two distinct sections, with three sets of triplets over the first five bars and an altogether remarkable modulation that stunningly, and startlingly, works its way back to the "Skylark" half notes to start the final *A*. The song culminates quietly with yet another parenthetical, but keenly satisfying, afterthought.

A SLEEPIN' BEE

music by Harold Arlen, lyric by Truman Capote and Harold Arlen
from the musical *House of Flowers* (1954)

Twenty years on since "Stormy Weather" [page 163], Arlen reached the peak of his career—or I suppose we should say, one of the many peaks—with **A Sleepin' Bee**.※ This jewel is, perhaps, more of an art song than typically suited for popular consumption, but that hasn't prevented adventurous singers and musicians from succumbing to this particular magic.

The music is distinctively Arlen but at his most pristine. The first four bars of the *A* ("When a bee lies sleepin' in the palm o' your hand") are built on a pure vocal line, with six quarter notes extending from middle *c* (in the key of A♭) to a high *e♭*, after which quarter-note triplets wend back down to *a♭*:

In the reiteration of this phrase in the subsequent bars, Arlen raises the stakes with a high *f*. The bridge ("where you'll see a sun-up sky") is gently syncopated, with a slightly pulsating accompaniment built on Arlen-esquely chromatic descending chords:

The thirty-six-bar song (A-B-A^1-B^1/A^2) culminates as gently as it starts. The introductory verse—written for other characters, who literally set up the premise of the song—is significantly more active, in rhythm and harmonics, than the refrain and serves to accentuate the enchantment that follows. Make that "pure enchantment." The musical in question—derived from a short story by Truman Capote—was beset by problems we needn't go into. Capote, at twenty-one, wrote the book and collaborated on the lyrics with Arlen; the two did a notable job, coming up with a clutch of winning-if-specialized songs (other treasures including "I Never Has Seen Snow," "Two Ladies in de Shade of de Banana Tree" and "House of Flowers").

SMOKE GETS IN YOUR EYES (WHEN YOUR HEART'S ON FIRE)

music by Jerome Kern, lyric by Otto Harbach
from the musical *Roberta* (1933)

"In my country, there's an old proverb that I think all men should study very carefully," says an exotic Russian with a guitar whom the hero—dazzled by a flashy woman who doesn't appreciate him—really *should* love and does by the final curtain (and it's revealed that she's a princess, too). Said proverb: "When your heart's on fire, **Smoke Gets in Your Eyes.**⚹" She then launches into this simple song, strumming on that guitar.

It turns out that the song is anything *but* simple, as can be seen by a drastic leap in bar 2 of a minor seventh, capped by the song's high note. That's an f, in the key of E♭; the lowest note is g, almost two octaves down. The bridge (of A-A-B-A) veers wildly into B-major, with five sharps; try playing *that* on your guitar. (For all this, it appears that the music was written as a vibrant march, as theme music for a 1932 radio program that never aired.)

The lyric comes from Otto Harbach, and it is something of a marvel. The first phrase begins "they asked me how I knew" and goes on for a full eight bars; the song, in fact, consists of a mere four extended sentences strung across its length. This lyric occasionally is cited as containing the most archaic and/or tortured musical comedy rhyme of the century: "so I chaffed them and I / gayly laughed." As for Harbach: back in 1920, he was asked by his producer (Arthur Hammerstein) to teach nephew Oscar everything he knew about writing lyrics and librettos. Otto—who was twenty-two years older than Oscar, and twelve years older than Kern, even—did just that, well enough to lay the foundation for the *Show Boat/Oklahoma!* revolution. Oscar later passed it all on to Sondheim for further development.

Harbach first came to Broadway in 1908 and collaborated with the likes of Friml, Kern, Youmans, Gershwin, and Romberg on such hits as *The Firefly*, *No, No, Nanette*, *Rose-Marie*, *Sunny*, *The Desert Song*, and *The Cat and the Fiddle*. Despite this impressive output, you'll find that "Smoke Gets in Your Eyes" is the one and only Harbach song in this book. In some ways, he deserves credit for setting the stage, as it were, for the American musical theatre; but all of his celebrated collaborators did their finest work, to my taste anyway, without him, as can be seen in connection with his collaborators Kern and Hammerstein. Harbach worked frequently with either or both of them, from 1920 through 1938; but the Kern/Hammerstein songs included herein (including "Can't Help Lovin' Dat Man" [page 22], "Why Was I Born?" [page 193], "The Song Is You" [page 155], "All the Things You Are" [page 5]) came from the musicals Jerry and Oscar wrote *without* Otto in the room.

SO IN LOVE

music and lyric by Cole Porter
from the musical *Kiss Me, Kate* (1948)

Porter is at, or near, his best with this haunting ballad of unrequited love, one with a tinge of the masochistic ("so taunt me, and hurt me, deceive me, desert me"). **So in Love**, ⌘ in some ways, reveals part of the composer's formula for hits. First: devise a more-than-powerful musical theme, which is the hard part. Then: repeat the theme in customary song form, but with subtle alterations that catch the listener unaware and raise the musical temperature.

The sixteen-bar *A* section, in F-minor, is melodically robust: the first bars are rooted on the interval between c and a melancholic $d\flat$ ("strange, DEAR—but true, DEAR—"). The section builds from middle c up to a high $d\flat$ ("the stars FILL the sky") in bar 10. A^1 (of A-A^1-B-A^2) repeats this stunning theme until bar 10, at which point Porter takes that note up a step to $e\flat$ ("you know DAR-ling why"), altering the underlying chord from what had been E♭-7 to D♭. This prepares us for bar 10 of A^2, where he climaxes the melody by peaking at f ("I'm yours 'TIL I die"), with the sheet music marked *passionately*. He then provides an extended ending—repeating the title three more times—as he steps his way down from that high f to the key note of $a♭$. As if to compound this pattern, the bridge section ("in love with the night mysterious") does the very same thing in miniature, substituting a reasonable $e♭$ in bar 2 ("night") with an extreme $f♭$ ("joy") in bar 10. Thus, we have a theme—an exceptionally strong one—with cannily devised alterations.

SOME GIRL IS ON HIS MIND

music by Jerome Kern, lyric by Oscar Hammerstein 2nd
from the musical *Sweet Adeline* (1929)

It might be considered problematic to include the Kern-Hammerstein **Some Girl Is on His Mind** within our collection, in that it is somewhat inaccessible. The song has been commercially recorded; and come 2025, the music will enter the public domain. However, it has never been published in standard sheet music form, and it's not immediately apparent whether the lyric—which has been printed independent of the music and can be located, free of charge though not necessarily legally, online—was ever properly registered for copyright. All of this is beside the point, for me at any rate; the song is stunningly beautiful, ranking high among both the Kern and the Kern/Hammerstein catalogs.

It was written for the nostalgically fin de siècle musical *Sweet Adeline* ("Why Was I Born?" [page 193]), devised by the authors as a direct follow-up to their *Show Boat*. "Some Girl Is on His Mind" is a tavern-scene chorale for the male ensemble drinking to "girls they left behind," devised to have a similar effect to sentimental ballads of the then not-so-distant era like—well, the 1903 barbershop favorite "Sweet Adeline."

The form is most unusual for Kern, or for Broadway at the time: A-A-B-A^1, yes, but with the A sections constructed of not the usual eight bars but twelve. In the manner, though not the flavor, of the American blues as described by W. C. Handy (see "Blues in the Night" [page 16]), Kern starts with a four-bar phrase, beginning and ending with whole notes but filled with eighths in between:

This is then repeated, down a minor third; all through, Kern uses a chromatically descending bass line of quarter notes. The section concludes with the title phrase, twice. After an exact repeat of the twelve-bar *A*, Kern moves to an eight-bar *B* built on a more fluid two-bar figure:

In the first bar, Kern jumps from *e♭* (in the key of E♭) to *b♭*, leading to that quarter note within the phrase. In bar 3, he goes from *e♭* to *c*; in bar 5, he makes this jump a full octave. The song resolves with an eight-bar reduction of the original *A* section (that in the stage version is intended to be sung by a full-throated male chorus). The forty-bar song is unlike anything from Kern thus far in his career (which began in 1904), or any of the then-reigning Broadway boys. It is simply the right song for the right spot and it's inspired, a musical treat.

SOME OTHER TIME

music by Leonard Bernstein, lyric by Betty Comden and Adolph Green
from the musical *On the Town* (1944; published 1945)

Leonard Bernstein, assistant conductor at the New York Philharmonic, was not looking to write a Broadway musical comedy when the opportunity irresistibly presented itself. His 1944 ballet *Fancy Free*, choreographed by Jerome Robbins, was so immediately successful that the pair were urged to devise a theatrical version using the skeletal concept—three soldiers on a twenty-four-hour leave in New York, New York—though none of the musical material or choreography. The score for *On the Town* included five bona fide ballets; a considerable number of satirical songs, already the specialty of the composer's lyricist pals, Betty Comden and Adolph Green; a couple of standard ballads; and **Some Other Time**.※ This is a lovely, contemplative, and—for Bernstein, especially—simple song, though not quite as simple as it seems.

It is in standard, thirty-two-bar *A-A-B-A* form (after a rubato, eight-bar verse); but Bernstein wrote it, within the context of the musical, as a contrapuntal quartet. The first half of the *A* is set against a simple chord progression, although Bernstein—perhaps intentionally—throws in a Gershwin-esque blue note (a *b♭* in the key of C) in bar 3. Bar 5, meanwhile, builds to a high *e* and drops an octave; so much for simplicity. The harmony in the bridge moves into A♭, before returning to C with another octave drop; in the penultimate measure, on *d* this time. Then back to a restatement of the *A*.

"Some Other Time" was written to give *On the Town* a moment of repose before the final, frenetic ballet. The song developed into a full-blown quartet, but the verse and initial refrain were written for and sung as a solo by Comden (who, along with Green, was featured in the original production).

SOMEONE TO WATCH OVER ME

music by George Gershwin, lyric by Ira Gershwin
from the musical *Oh, Kay!* (1926)

With *Lady, Be Good!* at the tail end of 1924, George and Ira Gershwin started turning out jazz-age musical comedies distinguished by a parade of peppy dance tunes. Ten months before, mind you, George's hagiographers started proclaiming his appointment with greatness by virtue of "Rhapsody in Blue." In the fall of 1926, **Someone to Watch over Me** was devised as yet another peppy dance tune to be used in their latest upcoming musical. George, who had a tendency to sit at the piano and improvise for hours, at some point started to play this as-yet-unlyricized tune at a slow tempo. The brothers simultaneously scratched their respective chins, puffing on their ever-present cigars, and a melancholy ballad hit was born. Not just a hit, but the first such warmly romantic ballad from the brothers. ("The Man I Love" [page 117] was cut during the tryout of *Lady, Be Good!* and did not find a substantial audience until 1928.)

The melody of "Someone to Watch over Me" suggests the initial inspiration: following a rhythmic first bar consisting of six notes skipping up an octave ("there's a somebody I'm longing to see"), George uses a four-note pattern ("I hope that he" on *f-f-e♭-d*, in the key of E♭) in bar 2; repeats it a step lower in bar 3; and another step lower in bar 4. Bar 5 starts with an auspicious rest, followed by three quarter notes (yet another step lower) that lead to a high $e\flat$ half note—over an unexpected $a\natural$ in the accompaniment—followed by a severe octave drop:

♪♩♩♩♩♩♩♩♩♩♩♩♩♩♩♩♩♩♩♩

Play "Someone to Watch over Me" at a frisky pace and it sounds, indeed, like a happy cousin of "Fascinating Rhythm" [page 40]. Catchy for a dance specialty, yes; but this "slowed-up ex-jazz tune," to quote Ira, turned out to have an intrinsically sentimental throb in its throat.

SOMETHING TO REMEMBER YOU BY

music by Arthur Schwartz, lyric by Howard Dietz
from the stage revue *Three's a Crowd* (1930)

This early Schwartz/Dietz hit is a wistfully resigned song of lost love. "Oh, give me **Something to Remember You By**" is set to a string of quarter notes with subtly shifting harmonies. The first and fifth bars of the anthem-like *A* sections (in *A-A¹-B-A*) start with three repeated notes, then proceed in descending intervals. Schwartz uses all quarter notes in the *A* sections, except for the cadences:

♩♩♩♩♩♩♩♩♩♩♩♩o ♩♩♩♩♩♩♩♩o o

This is pointed up by a bit of mild syncopation at the start of the bridge and compounded by an even trickier figure before the composer returns to the final *A*.

As fitting as the words are, the music was first written with another lyricist altogether. While Schwartz was just getting a foothold on Broadway—thanks in great part to the acclaim afforded the risqué "I Guess I'll Have to Change My Plan" [page 68]—he started 1930 with two West End musicals. "I Have No Words (to Say How Much I Love You)"—with lyrics by Desmond Carter, an Englishman who also wrote London musicals with George Gershwin, Vernon Duke, and Kurt Weill—was introduced in *Little Tommy Tucker*. This is an up-tempo comedic insult duet ("I've fallen arches and a birthmark or two, so why the deuce have I no words?"), perhaps patterned on Rodgers and Hart songs such as "I Feel at Home with You" from *A Connecticut Yankee* (1927). Dietz urged Schwartz to slow it down and add color to the harmonies while maintaining the precise melody. "Something to Remember You By" immediately displaced the earlier song and remains a standard.

The true hit of *Three's a Crowd*, though, was an interpolation that also arrived via London: Johnny Green's "Body and Soul" [page 17].

SOMETHING'S GOTTA GIVE

music and lyric by Johnny Mercer
from the motion picture *Daddy Long Legs* (1955; published 1954)

Johnny Mercer skirted the conundrum of how to justify a screen romance between a middle-aged star and his thirty-two-year younger leading lady by conjuring up this song hit. "When an irresistible force such as you" (think Leslie Caron) "meets an old immovable object like me" (think Fred Astaire). Thanks to the propulsive drive of **Something's Gotta Give** and that ol' Astaire charm, it worked.

The rhythmic beat seems specifically contrived to give Fred something to dance to:

Witness the series of highly combustible, multisyllabically syncopated words ("irresistible," "immovable," "irrepressible," "implacable") woven into the *A* sections (of *A-A¹-B-A²*, sixteen bars each). Further, Mercer caps his *A* with the percussive title phrase repeated thrice, over three bars, in tortured tempo:

The first eleven of those repeated notes are *d* (in the key of C) before he steps down to the expected, and gratifying, *c*—as if to say that the singer is trying to convince himself that after all, and after all those unresolved tones, something indeed *will* give. Add in a contrasting *B* that calms the rhythm with six bars of strongly declarative whole notes (starting "so en / GARDE"), and the results are indeed irresistibly irrepressible. As for Astaire, while he continued to work into his 80s in the'80s—having started as a six-year-old vaudevillian, in a kid act with sister Adele in 1905—this was to be the final hit "Astaire song."

THE SONG IS YOU

music by Jerome Kern, lyric by Oscar Hammerstein 2nd
from the musical *Music in the Air* (1932)

Kern and Hammerstein's toweringly romantic **The Song Is You** positively soars with grandeur.

The main melodic statement is purposely note heavy; the first bar alone contains eight eighth notes (to the lyric "I hear music when I look at / you") that circle the key note of C: *b–c–c–b–b–c–c–b/f*. A set of triplets takes us to bar 3 and the same eight-note pattern, now starting on *g*. The accompaniment also includes numerous triplets, further restraining the pace. The bridge (of *A-A¹-B-A²*) is somewhat calmer but no less grand, starting with a leap of a seventh ("I alone"), from *e* to *d#*. Six repeated *d#*s, that is, after which Kern cascades through a succession of keys before slyly finding his way back home to C for *A²*.

The loquaciously flowery lyric—which frequently requires seven or eight notes to the bar—demands that the music be performed at a stately pace; one is surprised to find that this emotionally buoyant ballad is a mere thirty-two bars long. It is perhaps surprising to relate that the song—in the context of the musical for which it was created—is considerably less than romantic: it is sung by the preening, overly conceited lothario of the piece who "gazes complacently at his reflection in mirror of dressing table, takes up framed photograph of himself, blows a bit of dust off and finally polishes the frame lightly with his handkerchief. Curtain." The song is you? Or, the song is *me*?

SOON IT'S GONNA RAIN

music by Harvey Schmidt, lyric by Tom Jones
from the musical *The Fantasticks* (1960)

Composer Harvey Schmidt and lyricist Tom Jones brought a new and unconventional sound to musical theatre with *The Fantasticks* and subsequent work. "Hear how the wind begins to whisper" starts the verse of **Soon It's Gonna Rain**, lulling us into the intended mood. This leads into a gently soothing vamp—featuring four repeated eighth notes, followed by two quarters—that will serve as undercurrent through the refrain:

The title phrase, at the start of the *A* (of *A-A-B-A¹*), is built on that same pattern of repeated eighth notes; the vamp, in fact, serves as the final two bars of the A sections. The bridge changes the pattern, rising from a *d* dotted half note (in the key of C) up to *b* and back ("we'll find four limbs of a tree"). Schmidt then repeats this two-bar phrase starting on *e* (ascending to *c*) and then *f* going to *d*. He returns to those repeated *g*s for the final A, which in the end resolves with a gentle tag and fades out with that shimmering vamp. Jones, meanwhile, weaves an evocative spell of velvet rain falling out where the fields are warm and dry, importuning the listener to run inside and stay—or, at least, to luxuriate in the fantastical sense imagery of it all.

SOPHISTICATED LADY

music by Duke Ellington, lyric by Irving Mills and Mitchell Parish
non-production song (1933)

Duke Ellington's **Sophisticated Lady**⸎ emerged in the spring of 1933 as an instrumental recorded by the Ellington orchestra. Five months later, Mitchell Parish added an evocative and altogether fitting lyric incorporating the already existing title, as he had similarly done in 1929 for the immortal "Star Dust" [page 162]. Publisher Irving Mills added his name to the copyright (as was his tendency); it also has been claimed that the music was composed by a pair of Ellington soloists, with Duke deeming it his creation (as was his tendency). A couple of lifetimes later, it doesn't really matter, does it? "Sophisticated Lady" is silkily smooth and then some, and certainly demonstrates what we know of as the Ellington touch.

The initial phrase ("they / say into your / early life ro-mance / came") starts with a *g♭* pickup (in the key of A♭) leading to *f*, which over bar 1 builds to a high *g♭*, then works its half-step way back down to *g*. The melody then steps up from *f* to *e♭*, with a second distinctive chromatic slide. The creamy smooth harmonies are pure Ellington, whatever "pure Ellington" connotates. The bridge ("smoking, drinking, never thinking") is equally phenomenal. Having moved temporarily into G-major, we start on *d♮*; drop a minor third to *b♮*, up a fourth to *e♮*, then back to *b* and up a minor sixth to *g* and onward. The second half of the bridge (of *A-A¹-B-A²*) starts with the very same initial two bars before culminating in an exceptional cadence with "some man in a restaurant."

Parish—née Michael Hyman Pashelinsky, from Lithuania—was a proficient staff lyricist at Mills Music, regularly assigned to add words to tunes from distinctive musician-composers including Carmichael and Ellington. His work was typically sturdy if rarely flashy, allowing the music—and the composers—to remain solely in the spotlight. That said, Parish munificently out-earned many of the better-known songwriters of his time thanks to fully equal shares of "Sophisticated Lady" and "Star Dust" as well as "Sleigh Ride," "Deep Purple," "Moonlight Serenade," and "Stars Fell on Alabama."

SPEAK LOW

music by Kurt Weill, lyric by Ogden Nash
from the musical *One Touch of Venus* (1943)

Kurt Weill, midway through his fourteen (final) years in America, came up with this intriguingly moody ballad. Set against a gently throbbing pulse that you might describe as a syncopated heartbeat, he and lyricist Ogden Nash leisurely introduce their title phrase—"**Speak Low**⸬ when you speak, love"—over the course of four bars, with "low" and "love" both held for six beats (in 4/4 time):

The song might be described as A-A^1-B-A^2, but for our purposes let's divide the sixteen-bar As in half, which gives us seven eight-bar sections: Ax/Ay-Ax/Ay^1-B-Ax/Az. Those extended six-beat notes appear at the start of six of the seven sections of the song, missing only from the B (the lyric of which starts "time is so old and love so brief"). The bridge replaces the pulsing rhythm—briefly—with a rhapsodic accompaniment. After that it's back to the heartbeat for the rest of the song. Countering those extended notes, mind you, are twenty sets of quarter-note triplets over the fifty-six bars.

All the while, the unsettled romance of the song remains (as reflected in the lyric "love is a spark, lost in the dark, too soon"). Weill accentuates this by scrupulously refusing to rest on the key note except as he prepares to move into the rhapsodic bridge, thirty-one bars in ("and always too SOON"). That is to say, those extended notes—except within the brief bridge—conspicuously avoid the f (in the key of F) Weill propels us to expect, landing instead on a, d, and c. He even ends the song on a high d, leaving us with a provocatively romantic, if uneasy, ballad. But this description is too technical. Just listen to the music.

SPRING CAN REALLY HANG YOU UP THE MOST

music by Tommy Wolf, lyric by Fran Landesman
from the musical *The Nervous Set* (1955; published 1961)

"Spring is here, why doesn't my heart go dancing?" asked Hart and Rodgers [page 160] back in 1938. Fran Landesman and Tommy Wolf expressed more or less the same sentiment a generation later—or rather a *beat* generation later—with **Spring Can Really Hang You Up the Most.**

They start in a friendly manner ("spring is here, there's no mistaking"), the melody skipping along from *e* up to *c* (in the key of C). The *A* continues, in chordal patterns, until concluding with the sardonic title phrase. This descends not to the expected middle *c* but down to a low *g*—that is repeated, emphatically, five times. Yes, "spring is here" . . . "but not for me," to quote a similarly unrequited Gershwin ballad. The bridge is built on a four-note figure that seesaws against altered harmonies, resulting in a detour from C major to G minor. Rather than creating a typical modulation for the start of A^2 (of A-A^1-B-A^2-C), Wolf diverts to G major for one bar only before abruptly jumping to the original key.

A second arresting deviation comes four bars later, when what had been *g* (over an E-minor chord) in bar 6 of the prior A sections becomes *a♭* (over E♭-minor). Once again, Wolf simply shrugs it off, hoping—one supposes—that the vocalist can follow. Then comes an eight-bar tag, culminating with the title phrase presented in a nine-note chromatic scale descending to that low, low *g*. As listeners in the jazz club at the time might have said, "Crazy, man."

The song has a clouded history. *The Nervous Set* was a 1959 musical that lasted only three weeks on Broadway (and included "The Ballad of the Sad Young Men" [page 12]). It was developed, though, at the Crystal Palace nightclub in St. Louis. "Spring" was written for the original *Nervous Set* in 1955, at which point it was recorded and gradually grew to become a jazz favorite despite not being published. When a revised version of the musical made its way to Broadway, "Spring"—for reasons unknown—was not used. Ella Fitzgerald got around to recording it in 1961, at which point the song was finally published: accurately labeled as "from the original production of *The Nervous Set*," although it was not from the original *Broadway* production. But no matter: what a song!

SPRING IS HERE

music by Richard Rodgers, lyric by Lorenz Hart
from the musical *I Married an Angel* (1938)

It is impossible to call **Spring Is Here** the very most unrequited of Rodgers and Hart's many unrequited love songs, but this stunningly poignant ballad certainly qualifies for consideration. The glories of the song begin with the three-note title phrase. Rodgers starts on g (in the key of A♭), raises a half step to $a♭$, then lands on f. Thus, there's tension (on "spring") and partial release (on "here"). Those three notes, over the first two bars, are countered by five repeated gs in bar 3. The rest of the A repeats this figure two steps lower:

In the bridge (of A-B-A-B^1), Rodgers gives us two ascending scales of quarter notes, the second with a slight tonal alteration—raising the second and third notes a half step—this makes all the difference. The final section resolves with an amended title phrase: "spring is here—I hear." Although the answer to the initial query comes somewhat earlier. "Why doesn't my heart go dancing?" the lyric asks. "Maybe it's because nobody loves me," answers the perhaps autobiographical Hart, heart on sleeve, wiping tear aside.

It might be noted that Rodgers and Hart wrote one of their greatest songs for the 1929 musical *Spring Is Here*. This was *not* "Spring Is Here," but "With a Song in My Heart" [page 196]. There was, indeed, a title song, an altogether different "Spring Is Here" of little distinction (unpublished, understandably so). In 1933, the boys—with writer Moss Hart—worked up an MGM film project called *I Married an Angel*, which went unproduced. Following their unhappy sojourn in Hollywood, they returned to Broadway with a string of six consecutive hit musicals, songs from which are scattered among these pages. Included in these was the stage version of *I Married an Angel*, written without Moss, which included mostly new material including the sparkling, second "Spring Is Here." The show was such a success that MGM produced a 1942 screen adaptation of the stage adaptation. A bemused

Rodgers noted, "Larry and I ended up in the curious but happy position of being paid for the same material three times: as a movie that was never filmed, as a stage musical, and as a movie that was filmed but—from what I've heard about it—never should have been."

ST. LOUIS BLUES

music and lyric by W. C. Handy
non-production song (1914)

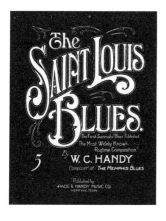

W. C. Handy called himself the Father of the Blues. Although he didn't invent the form, he popularized it thanks in great part to the instantaneous success of the genre-defining **St. Louis Blues.**⸸ Having naively sold off the rights to his 1912 "Memphis Blues," he realized the wisdom of setting up his own publishing company in time to profit from his 1914 opus.

The song is composed in three distinct sections. First comes a twelve-bar blues, consisting of a four-bar phrase ("I hate to see de ev'nin' sun go down"), which is then repeated and followed by a final four bars. This entire section is then repeated, with a different lyric. The middle section—set to a tangoish rhythm—consists of an eight-bar phrase ("St. Louis woman, wid her diamon' rings") that is then repeated. After the music grinds down to a dramatic pause, we continue to what is marked Chorus ("got de St. Louis Blues, jes as blue as Ah can be"). This, like the initial part, is twelve bars. Thus, sixty-four bars all told. Despite its age, "St. Louis Blues" more than retains its strength.

For those musically interested: Handy's original printing—published in Memphis, rather than New York—is in 2/4 time, unlike the later printings that have been converted to common time (4/4). The chorus is labeled with the legend: Melody from "The Jogo Blues," which was an instrumental "rag"—also known as "The Memphis Itch"—published by Handy in 1913. It will be noted that the original cover bears the name "The Saint Louis Blues," which is also the spelling on the copyright registration. The title page, though—and all mentions within the lyric—use "St. Louis."

STAR DUST

music by Hoagy Carmichael, lyric by Mitchell Parish
non-production song (1929)

It has been seen that several of our 201 favorites have had outsized influence over the world of popular song. By any measure, Hoagy Carmichael's **Star Dust**※ ranks high among them. For forty or fifty years, this was claimed to be the most recorded song ever; sitting here in a different world in another century, that distinction is probably outdated and—given the new media universe—likely nontrackable. I would imagine that at least some readers of these pages, who surely know and love a fair number of these *Great American Songbook* standards, are unfamiliar with this immortal favorite. Even so, examining or reexamining this almost-hundred-year-old song is likely to firmly establish it in your inner musical memory.

Carmichael was one of the first—and one of the most notable—of a new breed of child-of-the-century Americans who lived to make music; he was a practicing lawyer, in fact, but that didn't last long. Sitting around waiting in rehearsal halls, recording studios, and driving from town to town to meet the next gig, insistently melodic strains would pop out of the ether. Carmichael's first major piece to make it into the recording studio, "Washboard Blues" (1925), was so unconventional that it became an instant cause of wonderment in musical circles. Then came "Star Dust," which Carmichael first recorded as an instrumental in 1927. The song's revolutionary nature can be gleaned from the start: one can't help feeling that the words are following, and practically struggling, to keep up with the music. That ethereal melody—filled with arpeggiated octave jumps and spurts of improvisatory stretches—had to have been conceived with cornet or sax in mind, which goes a long way toward explaining the song's instant allure for musicians and bandleaders.

As was the case with several of these band-grown instrumentals, Carmichael's canny publisher soon assigned a staff lyricist (Mitchell Parish) to add words and turn the instant jazz classic into an ultra-lucrative pop song standard. Parish's lyric in 1929 did precisely that, although the title and the notion of a "stardust melody" came from Carmichael's initial, not fully realized lyric for the song. As for the question of rule breaking, a famous contemporary songwriter noted that it "rambles and roams like a truant schoolboy in a meadow. Its structure is loose, its pattern complex. Yet it has attained the kind of long-lived popularity that few songs can claim. What has it got? I'm not certain. I know only that it is beautiful and I like to hear it." So said Oscar Hammerstein, in his invaluable 1949 book *Lyrics*. "It is something very special, all by itself. Anyone who tried to imitate it would be a fool."

STORMY WEATHER (KEEPS RAININ' ALL THE TIME)

music by Harold Arlen, lyric by Ted Koehler
from the stage revue *Cotton Club Parade*, 22nd edition (1933)

Stormy Weather❧ begins with a wail, almost literally so ("Don't know why"). This was the starting point not only for the song but for the song slot; the Cotton Club folks had lined up singing bandleader Cab Calloway to star in the next edition, so Arlen searched for and found what he thought of as a "front shout" similar to the "Hi-de-ho" chant in Cab's self-written 1931 song hit, "Minnie the Moocher." (By the time this edition of the *Parade* was ready for production, Calloway was unavailable and replaced—most fortuitously for "Stormy Weather"—by Ethel Waters.)

The pickup notes of the front shout (*b♮* and *c* leading to *e♭*, in the key of A♭) are heard again leading into bar 2 and bar 3; the third time, Arlen takes the *e♭* on a startling octave drop ("stormy WEA-THER"). There are other surprises along the way, like the *c♭* leading to *c♮* ("keeps raining ALL the TI-IME") in bars 6–7; and the repetition of the final two bars of the *A* section in *A¹*, resulting in an unconventional *A*(eight)-*A¹*(ten)-*B*(eight)-*A¹*(ten). This is matched by one of the great torch song lyrics from Ted Koehler. Let us note that Arlen and Koehler also wrote a somewhat busy twelve-bar interlude, which is rarely used and was eventually published in a 1985 edition of the sheet music (issued in the key of G).

As best I can tell—although the evidence is inconclusive—this was added for a vaudeville tour Arlen undertook, starting May 1933 at Radio City Music Hall, while Waters was still singing the song at the Cotton Club. This act included not only the composer/singer but a chorus, wind machines, and rain effects, which might explain the desire for the "rain pourin' down" interlude. Waters included the interlude in her May recording of the song, but it was not used in Arlen's own chart-topping recording (from February, five weeks before the opening of this edition of *Cotton Club Parade*.) Although I typically welcome intrinsically connected if infrequently heard "extra" song material from the workbench of the authors, I find the "Stormy Weather" interlude an overly busy attempt to add drama—or you could say, *sturm und drang*—to a song that is already perfectly "sturmy" in itself.

SUMMERTIME

music by George Gershwin, lyric by DuBose Heyward
from the "folk opera" *Porgy and Bess* (1935)

Following the creation of numerous musical comedies, an instantly world-famous rhapsody, a full-fledged piano concerto, and other musical miscellanea, George Gershwin cleared his typically frenetic schedule to embark on the creation of nothing less than a real, genuine, and thoroughly grand opera—or at least a Gershwin opera, which meant that it inevitably contained a couple of handfuls of prime Broadway material. Gershwin determined that *Porgy and Bess* would be different, and it was from the start.

Summertime⁎ serves as the opening number following a brief instrumental prologue, although it was not so intended; a fully staged 150-bar opening sequence was cut during the final rehearsals prior to the Boston premiere. It seems untoward to attempt to describe the sixteen altogether perfect bars of "Summertime" in song-shop terms; but it might be instructive to break it down into four, four-bar mini sections that—for lack of better nomenclature—we'll label A-A^x-A-A^y. First comes that classic opening statement ("Summertime, an' the livin' is easy"). This is set to spare chords, alternating from A minor to E7 (in the key of C) for the full four bars until Gershwin moves to D minor for A^x. This section ("fish are jumpin'") is a little more intricate, featuring a countermelody in the accompaniment and Gershwin-esque harmonics. The A is then repeated verbatim ("Oh, yo' daddy's rich"), with Gershwin making small melodic adjustments to accommodate his collaborator; novelist DuBose Heyward was something of a poet but nothing of a lyricist, although *Porgy and Bess* worked out just fine. (Ira Gershwin stepped into the project along the way, concentrating on the more urbane and less folksy songs including "It Ain't

Necessarily So" and "There's a Boat Dat's Leavin' Soon for New York.") Then comes the A^y ("so hush, little baby"), which ends with the sole rhyme using the final words of bars 8 and 16 (high/cry, and later sky/by).

"Summertime" was written with two refrains, and it is unthinkable to perform it with only the first. Gershwin saw to it that the song was published using a piano-reduction of the full stage arrangement—including the seven-bar instrumental lead-in from the brief overture/prelude; the extra two-bar break between the two refrains; the chromatic fills and countermelodies in the second refrain; and the seven-bar orchestral ending following the last word. All of that makes for thirty-nine glorious bars of what George's score labels "lullaby, with much expression."

SWANEE

music by George Gershwin, lyric by I. (Irving) Caesar
from the stage revue *Capitol Revue* (1919)

The twenty-year-old George Gershwin seemed to come out of nowhere with **Swanee**,⁂ his first and—in terms of sheet music and record sales—likely the most lucrative hit during his lifetime. It's one that, as it turns out, sounds very little like anything he was to write.

The verse ("I've been away from you a long time") is so very driving that one has to wonder where this young man came up with such a thing. It turns out that he more or less pulled it off the piano rack: someone else's piano rack. "Hindustan," by Oliver G. Wallace and Harold Weeks, was a "one-step" suitable for energetic ballroom dancing. George and his lyricist at the time, Irving Caesar, looked at the big novelty hit of the fall of 1918 and decided to write their own—not copying the music or lyric, mind you; but featuring a similarly driving minor-key verse and a similar modulation to the geographical title that starts the major-key refrain. "Hindustan" writer Wallace was British, hence the not-so-authentic song of India; Gershwin and Caesar wrote an American-themed rouser with the flavor of, and incorporation of a quote from, Stephen Foster's "Old Folks at Home."

That "Swanee" turned out to be an even bigger hit than "Hindustan" was something of a fluke. The song was introduced as part of the stage show accompanying the October 1919 opening of New York's 5,200-seat Capitol Theatre, self-described as the "world's largest and foremost motion picture palace." It was performed, we are told, by chorus girls with electric lights on their slipper, and quickly forgotten. Several months later, though, Gershwin's occasional lyricist B. G. DeSylva took George to a party with Al Jolson. (DeSylva had already written several Jolson hits, including "I'll Say She Does.") George, an electrifying pianist, characteristically found himself sitting at the piano. Jolson heard "Swanee," immediately inserted it into his then-running musical, and recorded it. And in case you're wondering, Caesar's lyric—which tells of mammy waiting for me down by the Swanee shore—was written and performed prior to Jolson's involvement. The very fact that the song had been published in conjunction with the *Capitol Revue* made it impossible for Jolson to demand authorship credit (as he frequently did with songwriters, including DeSylva) and seize a cut of the substantial royalties generated.

SWEET GEORGIA BROWN

music and lyric by Ben Bernie, Maceo Pinkard, and Kenneth Casey
non-production song (1925)

Jazz, with a capital "J," means different things to different people. In 1924 it was even more indistinct, along the lines of "don't know how to describe it, but I know it when I hear it." The big musical event of the year—at least within the intersection of New York sophisticates and music makers—was a concert officially titled "An Experiment in Modern Music" assembled by Paul Whiteman, known to one and all at the time as the "King of Jazz" (so much so that Universal Pictures built a 1930 movie musical around him: *King of Jazz.*)

Written to order for the concert—dashed off in about three weeks—was George Gershwin's *Rhapsody in Blue*, which indeed defined the jazz age. But were Gershwin, Whiteman, Berlin, and brethren true jazzmen? That's not for us to determine. At that point in time, such songs as W. C. Handy's 1914 "St. Louis Blues" [page 161] and the 1923 Cecil Mack-Jimmy Johnson "Charleston" [page 25] had broken through the barriers, professional and racial, to Tin Pan Alley success.

In 1925 along came a new and significant American pop/standard/classic, **Sweet Georgia Brown**. The authors, or their publishers, labeled it a "Charleston-Swing Song," which I suppose is an accurate description. Maceo Pinkard, a black songwriter from West Virginia who had already served as composer-lyricist for a Broadway musical (*Liza*, in 1922), seems to have been mostly responsible for the music. His official coauthors were bandleader Ben Bernie (born Bernard Anzelevitz), whose band introduced the song and who received first billing; and Kenneth Casey (see below). In any case, "Sweet Georgia Brown" epitomizes American jazz, or Charleston Swing, or whatever you want to call it.

The song is built on a wonderfully swinging four-bar figure, which is repeated twice in the *A* (of *A-B-A-C*); makes up half of the eight-bar bridge; and after a four-bar stretch is immediately heard twice more:

The *C* brings a different musical phrase ("fellers—she can't get, are fellers—she ain't met"). but not so new, as it is derived from a two-bar phrase heard four times within the twenty-bar verse.

Standing out among little-known songwriters represented in this book is Casey, who appears to have written the lyric. Born in 1899, he might reasonably be deemed the movies' first child star. "The Vitagraph Boy," they called him; his angelic, waiflike face appeared in more than fifty films from the powerful Vitagraph Studio between 1909 and 1913, after which he smashed into the wall of obsolescence. A 1915 vaudeville reviewer noted that the washed-up sixteen-year-old's stage act included one of his films—in which he was about three years younger ("and looks it")—but that "he plays the piano, cornet and violin, sings and dances, and does every one of them well." Casey thereafter drifted from career to career, including a stint as a dance band leader that put him in proximity of Bernie and Pinkard. Casey and Bernie—writing without Pinkard—in 1939 turned out something called "The Daughter of Sweet Georgia Brown." If you've never heard it, no wonder.

SWINGING ON A STAR

music by Jimmy Van Heusen, lyric by Johnny Burke
from the motion picture *Going My Way* (1944)

Talk about **Swinging on a Star**. Burke and Van Heusen had been writing songs for Bing Crosby films since 1941 and had already brought forth a substantial 1942 hit in "Moonlight Becomes You." Burke had, with prior collaborators, been writing for Bing since the 1936 "Pennies from Heaven" [page 137]. The team faced an unconventional situation with *Going My Way* in that the star was playing a young New York City priest; no crooning love songs here, needless to say. They came up with a story song so charming, and in its own way swinging, that they won an Oscar; at the same time, Crosby won himself an Oscar as did the producers/ directors/writers. (Given eligibility rules that obviously needed a tad of fine-tuning, costar Barry Fitzgerald was nominated for both Best Actor and Best Featured Actor. He won the latter, probably a good idea as it would have been unwise for him to defeat Bing.)

The song is an unconventional thirty bars and quite unlike anything you might hear. It consists of two distinct parts, both of which follow the title by swinging along as they go. The title section ("would you like to swing on a star"), for example:

$$ \text{♩. ♪ | ♩ ♩ ♩ ♫ | ♩} \quad \text{♩. ♪ | ♩ ♩ ♩ ♫ | ♩} $$

Van Heusen features intervals that dip a fifth and jump back in bars 1 (*d* to *g*, in the key of B♭), 3 (*c* to *f*), and 5 (*d* to *g*). The "story" section—this is, mind you, a priest singing to the kids—describes various recalcitrant animals ("a mule is an animal with long funny ears"; in subsequent refrains we get a pig and a fish). This section is subdivided into three four-bar sections, the last a variation of the first. The middle section—which displays characteristics of said critters ("his back is brawny but his brain is weak")—is built on intervals of thirds (starting each of the four bars) followed by repeated notes. Van Heusen constructs it so that each bar starts one step up; the first includes a drop of a fifth, the second a major sixth, the third a minor seventh. It might sound complicated, but it *sounds* perfectly simple. If we must label the form, I'd call it *A-B-C-B¹-A¹*. The results are a kid-friendly song that can't help but delight listeners of any age. Let us add that Van Heusen—working with his later collaborator, Sammy Cahn—came up with a worthy and not-dissimilar successor: "High Hopes," written for Frank Sinatra in the 1959 film *A Hole in the Head*. That also won the Best Song Oscar. Me, I much prefer to keep swinging on a star.

'S WONDERFUL

music by George Gershwin, lyric by Ira Gershwin
from the musical *Funny Face* (1927)

The playfully bright and breezy roaring twenties style of the brothers Gershwin is typified by **'S Wonderful**—which, among other things, demonstrates the growing contribution of Ira's words to George's music. Ira's title phrase contraction propels the song. One can imagine how relatively weak the melody would be if they had added a fourth syllable, "it's," as a pickup note; using what is pronounced "swon-" instead of "it's won-" makes all the difference. (This doesn't stop some performers from nevertheless adding the pickup note, which is enough to drive a songwriter nuts. And while we're at it, the accurate punctuation of the song title is not Swonderful or S'Wonderful but 'S Wonderful.)

George sets that golden phrase in three notes: a dotted quarter ($b\flat$), an eighth ($b\flat$), and a half note g tied to a whole note in the next bar (in the key of E$\flat$):

That two-bar figure is used seven times over the course of thirty-two bars, plus two additional times—on different pitches—in the B (of A-A¹-B-A²). The A and A¹ sections, in fact, consist entirely of those two tones, $b\flat$ and g, with a final $e\flat$ (or c, in A¹) for the cadence. As for the bridge ("you've made my life so glamorous"), George gives us fourteen repeated ds within eighteen notes, driving the song delightfully. Let us add that at a time when competitors such as Youmans and Rodgers were lavishing attention on musically colorful verses, the less-than-distinguished twenty-four-bar verse to "'S Wonderful" is an example of how repeated notes—even from Gershwin—can sound pedestrian.

TAKING A CHANCE ON LOVE

music by Vernon Duke, lyric by John Latouche and Ted Fetter
from the musical *Cabin in the Sky* (1940)

Vernon Duke, whose music was usually—and almost literally, in the words of Shakespeare, "caviar to the general"—found his one truly successful Broadway musical with this Deep South folk fable about the Lord and the Devil fighting over the soul of Little Joe, husband of the devout Petunia (in the person of Ethel Waters).

How Duke and fellow Russian emigree George Balanchine found themselves on *Cabin in the Sky* is another tale in itself. The composer's publisher, Jack Robbins, who also had Ellington on his roster, kept complaining that they got "the wrong Duke." But Vernon's score turned out to be altogether right for the material, led by the exuberant **Taking a Chance on Love.**§

The leisurely melody of the first two bars ("here I go again"), with two notes and three notes respectively, is upended by a syncopated figure in bar 3 with a leap up a sixth and back down ("I hear THOSE-TRUMP-ETS blow again"). The *A* (of *A-A¹-B-A²*) ends with the less-starkly syncopated title phrase, so delectably set that we grow to look forward to it every time it reappears.

It's almost as if those triplets set our heart a-leaping, which is perfectly fitting for this song about gambling on romance. The composer enhances our joy by providing striking harmonics throughout, especially so in the latter half of the bridge. After that he moves jauntily back to the *A*, where—here we go again—"taking a chance on love."

How do songwriters find a hit? The underfinanced *Cabin in the Sky*, unable to afford a pre-Broadway tryout, scheduled four New York previews. Discovering that the first act closing—something of an offbeat lullaby—was uncompelling, Waters demanded that the songwriters give her some "meat and potatoes." On the morning of day two, Duke rummaged through his trunk to find "Fooling Around with Love," a song he had written for an abandoned George Abbott musical with Ted Fetter (who, as it happens, was cousin to Cole Porter). Duke and Fetter had in 1936 written a fine song called "Now," which we couldn't quite find space for in this book. Latouche tweaked Fetter's existing lyric, with the latter's acquiescence, and wrote the four encores that were needed to placate enthralled audiences. Problem solved, show saved, and a song standard pulled out of the fire.

TEA FOR TWO

music by Vincent Youmans, lyric by Irving Caesar
from the musical *No, No, Nanette* (1925; published 1924)

Vincent Youmans led jazz-age Broadway away from reigning operetta hits (including his own 1923 *Wildflower*) to the modern era of musical comedy with *No, No, Nanette*, complete with one of the biggest song hits of the time: **Tea for Two**. (Introduced in the spring of 1924 during the extended Chicago tryout, the song was an instant hit long before the show reached Broadway in 1925.) Although Youmans was soon to develop a stunning musical complexity ("More Than You Know" [page 123]), his early hits were marked by musical phrases so catchy as to be irrepressible. "Tea for Two," a soft-shoe to end all soft-shoes, offers a simple pattern of dotted quarter and eighth notes in slightly varying intervals: "picture you up- / -on my knee just / tea for two and / two for tea" is set in the key of Ab-major, with *ab–f–g–f* / *ab–f–g–eb* / *g–eb–d–eb* / *g–eb–f–eb*. That is to say, it pivots with a drop of a minor third interval in bars 1 and 2, a major third in 3 and 4. In *A¹* (of *A-A¹-A²-B/A*), Youmans moved the initial pattern into C-major (*c -a♮ -b♮ -a♮* / etc.). At the same time, he alters the melody by adding sixteenth notes, to vary the rhythm or perhaps just to help out lyricist Irving Caesar. Thus, what had been "pic-ture you u- / -pon my knee" becomes "no-*bo-dy* near-us to / see-*us or* hear-us." The section ends with an abrupt cadence of two whole notes, an *e♮* moving to *eb* (over an Eb-7 chord), which takes us back to where we started. The *A²* again offers a surprise final cadence, jumping an octave on *eb* ("all the boys TO / SEE"). Youmans resolves it all by moving stepwise— retaining his dotted-quarter-and-eighth-note pattern—from high *f* down to *ab*; thus *f–f–eb–eb* / *d–d–c–c* / etc.) As for the notion of hit songs comprised of catchy musical phrases presented over and over again, "Tea for Two" was one of three top Youmans hits from 1924–1925 built upon similarly canny construction, the others being "I Want to Be Happy" (also from *Nanette*) and "Sometimes I'm Happy" (from *Hit the Deck*).

THANKS FOR THE MEMORY

music and lyric by Leo Robin and Ralph Rainger
from the motion picture *The Big Broadcast of 1938* (published 1937)

This Oscar-winning song about a failed relationship and "all those little dreams that never did come true" was more or less hijacked over the years by Bob Hope, who in younger days introduced it in a non-descript Paramount extravaganza. **Thanks for the Memory** is a bittersweet song of wistful regrets and whimsical recollections that still holds up for anyone who ever mused about what could have/would have/should have been. (The clip from the film can easily be found on the internet. Song cue: "You know, I kind of miss you singing in the bathtub.")

The song is simply but sturdily constructed. The *A* (of *A-A-B-A¹*) starts with the title phrase in a descending scale over two bars. We then get three specific "memories" (two in single bars, the third over two bars) built upon gently repeated notes:

These eventually climb to a high *d* (in the key of F); and the section ends with an octave drop on the tag line "how/ LOVE-LY it / was." The subsequent *A* and *A¹* follow suit, with lists of three additional memories and ending with "thank you so much." The bridge ("many's the time that we feasted") has a more casual rhythm, with triplets.

Leo Robin—a prolific lyricist whose collaborators included Youmans, Arlen, Schwartz, Kern, and Styne (with whom he wrote "Diamonds Are a Girl's Best Friend")—provided numerous refrains; the initial printing of the sheet music contained two plus a page including three "extra choruses." Some of the Depression-era "memories" are dated ("motor trips and burning lips and burning toast and prunes"); others were so suggestive as to be censorable ("that weekend at Niagara when we hardly saw the falls"). Even so, "Thanks for the

Memory" retains its charm. It all adds up to a sad, funny, rueful recounting of romantic heartbreak.

THAT OLD BLACK MAGIC

music by Harold Arlen, lyric by Johnny Mercer
from the motion picture *Star Spangled Rhythm* (1942)

The first three years of what was to be the occasional collaboration of Harold Arlen and Johnny Mercer included three remarkable tapeworms, as Arlen termed them: songs that eschewed formula and went on to whatever lengths the composer heard in his inner ear. Midway between "Blues in the Night" [page 16] and "One for My Baby" [page 132], buried within another long-forgotten film, came **That Old Black Magic.**✳

Arlen starts with a persistent sustained figure in the bass lasting eighteen bars, with one interior alteration. ("Rhythmically but sustained" is the tempo marking.) Against this comes the initial phrase "that old black magic has me in its spell," on a string of mostly *g*s (in the key of E♭):

In bar 2 of *A¹* (of what you could call *A-A¹-B-A²-C*) he steps up from those insistent *g*s to an unearthly *d♭*, on "I" within the phrase "the same old tingle that I feel so well." This announces that, to borrow an image from Mercer's lyric, we are off on that elevator ride: bar 13 starts on high *c*; moves through the aforementioned *d♭* up to *e♭*; and then presses the "down" button to land, ultimately, on the low *e♭* that ends the section. At this point, that steadily rolling eight-notes-to-the-bar bass is abruptly halted, after thirty-one bars—which is to say, 248 consecutive eighth notes. But who's counting? Then comes the bridge ("I should stay away but what can I do"), which starts up on that high *e♭* and gradually descends. Leading to the cadence, Arlen throws in yet another unearthly tone, his lowest of the song: *c♭*—four of them, a quarter note followed by triplets—within the phrase "only your kiss CAN PUT-OUT-THE fire." Then it's back to *A²*, which starts like its predecessors with repeated *g*s but fills in the harmony; interrupts itself to add a sequence of repeated high *d♭*s ("the mate that fate had me created for); and climaxes with a string of high e♭s before moving back to the "down and down I go" section. Finally, we have an extended ending ("in a spin, loving the spin I'm in") after seventy-five bars of Arlen/Mercer magic.

THERE BUT FOR YOU GO I

music by Frederick Loewe, lyric by Alan Jay Lerner
from the musical *Brigadoon* (1947)

Brigadoon, a tale of a mystically enchanted land that addressed issues of mortality and life-after-death very much on the mind of postwar audiences, contained the stunning **There But for You Go I**. Too complex for a popular song, surely; but its steady pace and contemplative tone provide enduring strength. This was, I suppose, the precise aim of composer Loewe and lyricist Lerner. The song is in the form of an anecdote told by the character—a disillusioned chap fleeing upper-class Manhattan—explaining how he was just one of all those lonely men "trying not to cry" until he found the girl in question, who, in dramaturgical terms, lives in a world that comes to life only one day for every hundred years, thus complicating the courtship. That time-traveling plot accounts for the somewhat formalized construction of the song.

The *A* section is built on a string of quarter notes interrupted—on the second beat, in five of the eight bars—by pairs of eighth notes with which composer and lyricist effectively force an introspective tempo:

Loewe builds his melody on intervals, namely a drop of a minor sixth at the start of bar 1; a major sixth at bar 3; and, after two bars working their way up from middle *c*, an octave drop ("THERE—BUT for you go I") leading to the title phrase. The bridge (of *A-A-B-A¹*) more or less takes us, musically speaking, from the past to the present as Lerner speaks of those "lonely men around me." The music grows impassioned, the key moving to E-minor from C, as Loewe now restricts his melody to nothing shorter than quarter notes. All through the song thus far, including the verse, Loewe has clinically avoided any and all accidentals in his melody (although his accompaniment is full of chromaticism throughout). In bar 5 of that moody *B*, he gives us his first foreign tone: a *b♭* ("till the DAY you / found me") that almost jars us with its mellow tonality. He ends the section with an *e♭* ("there a- / -MONG them") during a quick detour from D through E♭-major to G, on his way back to C. The closing section becomes even more impassioned as Loewe, and Lerner, build to a heightened final appearance of the title phrase. It's supremely effective, emotionally, if decidedly too serious for commercial popularity.

Loewe would turn out well more than a dozen significant song hits—*My Fair Lady* and *Gigi*, combined, have a couple of handfuls of imperishable standards—but he hardly fit in with any of his peers. "I am not a songwriter," Loewe said (as quoted by his mistress from 1947, when she was a twenty-one-year-old in *Brigadoon*, through the premiere of *Gigi* in 1958). "I am a dramatic composer. Give me a story, and I can translate the locale into music."

THERE'S NO HOLDING ME

music by Arthur Schwartz, lyric by Ira Gershwin
from the musical *Park Avenue* (1946)

The Arthur Schwartz-Ira Gershwin-George S. Kaufman musical *Park Avenue* sought to present divorce among Manhattan's upper set as a source of amusement, with bittersweet—or, more accurately— simply bitter results. "Good-bye to All That" [page 45] was a regretful ballad of lost love near the end of the second act; **There's No Holding Me**⁑ was a romantic ballad in the midst of the first, slotted just after a valse-Viennese paean to divorce called "Sweet Nevada." You can't quite have divorce without marriage, can you? At least, not on Park Avenue.

Schwartz presents an attractive, lightly rhythmic melody with subtle tricks that not only keep it interesting but make it engaging. The refrain begins with four rhythmic pickup notes leading to a half note ("name your heart's de- /-sire"). That's in bar 1, leading to four descending notes. The same pickup notes take us into bar 2; but this time, we get a two-syllable word ("starlight") set to an eighth and dotted quarter. This slight interruption brings jaunty charm to the song, after which Schwartz ends the final bars steadily on the beat:

♪♫♪|♩ ♪♪ ♪♪|♩ ♪♫♫|♪♪. ♪♪ ♪♪|♩ ♫♫|♩. ♪♪ ♩ |♩ ♩ ♩ ♩ |𝅝

The bridge (of *A-A¹-B-A²*) changes the rhythm, starting with dotted half notes in the first bars before Schwartz livens it up. There's a drop of a major sixth going from bar 1 to 2; when we next hear it, going into bar 6, the melody remains the same, but the underlying chord is radically altered. As with the jaunty alterations in the *A* sections, this catches our ear; propels us forward, and marks the song as one to be remembered. Although I personally favor "Goodbye to All That," "There's No Holding Me" also deserves its place—not in the least because it was an especial favorite of S. Sondheim.

THEY CAN'T TAKE THAT AWAY FROM ME

music by George Gershwin, lyric by Ira Gershwin
from the motion picture *Shall We Dance* (1937)

Gershwin's penchant for repeated notes—and the potential power of both repeated and pickup notes—can be seen in **They Can't Take That Away from Me.**⁑ He uses a figure of five repeated pickup notes ("the way you wear your—") nine times within thirty-six bars:

♪ ♫♫♩ ♩ ♫♩|𝅝 |♪ ♫♫♩ ♫♩|𝅝

The *A* sections (of *A-A¹-B-A²*) are built with a list stating: the way you do THIS; the way you do THAT; the way you do THIS. The effect of those repeated *eb* pickups (in the key of Eb) is to accentuate the final words of each phrase: hat, tea, dreams, and more, which are thus accentuated, courtesy of all those repeated notes. Gershwin goes up a major third from the *eb* to *g* in the first case; down a fourth to *bb* in the second; and up a fifth to a high *bb* in the third. The title phrase is similarly accentuated, starting with three *c* pickup notes ("oh, no, they") leading to—and highlighting—the title phrase. The bridge ("we may never never meet again") is less note dense and less syncopated, resting our ears—until, that is, those pickups return to take us to *A²* and build to a climactic and extended ending. The verse is something of a curiosity, starting with two five-bar sections, followed by a seven-bar ending, which might appear intriguing but aren't, alas.

THEY DIDN'T BELIEVE ME

music by Jerome Kern, lyric by Herbert Reynolds
from the musical *The Girl from Utah* (1914)

By any description, Jerome Kern's **They Didn't Believe Me** is a groundbreaking landmark among the annals of American popular song. That said, I hesitated to include it in this book on the grounds that although it opened a magic musical door for the composer and those budding teenagers—Gershwin, Rodgers, Youmans, Schwartz—he directly inspired, they were to find considerably richer territory on the other side. The fruits of that, mind you, are scattered among these pages. I tentatively settled on this exclusion despite the fact that when I first broached the idea of this book to Mr. Sondheim, he collegially rejected a theory I floated by barking: take a look at "They Didn't Believe Me." While selecting my final treasures for our candy box, though, I stumbled on a 1926 article by Mr. Gershwin saying just about the same thing. With GG and SS—nearly a century apart—calling out to me, what's a person to do? (I might say that I couldn't help but feel the *burthen*, if you know what I mean; if not and you care to, see "All the Things You Are" [page 5].) Kern, who had been writing typically charming, often slightly raggy numbers for the first decade of his career, starts with a verse that—given what follows—turns out to be most interesting.

This consists of a charming, slightly raggy four-bar figure of alternating notes in intervals of one or two steps:

This figure is used four times within the sixteen-bar verse. Then come three quarter-note pickups leading to two half notes and a relatively straightforward *A* section—until Kern, in baseball parlance, throws a few curves. The first comes at the cadence in bar 8, which he underpins with that dotted eighth and sixteenth figure from the verse. This leads to the bridge, which starts with no fewer than fifteen consecutive quarter notes ("your lips your / eyes your cheeks your / hair") in a staggered stepwise pattern that take us back to what promises to be a restatement of the *A*. But it's not. The revolution Kern jump-started—which, according to multiple reports, caused the "boys" over on Tin Pan Alley to choke on their cigars—came from the rhythmic disruption wreaked by one little set of eighth-note triplets (in bar 18, if you're following the public domain sheet music, which can easily be accessed on the internet):

If those eighth-note triplets are revolutionary, the lyric here is notably awkward: "and when I / tell them / and I cert-n'ly-am goin' to / tell them." Although I imagine vocalists since 1914 have sung "and I'm cert-'n-ly goin' to tell them" to few complaints. The composer shakes us up similarly, if not so startlingly, with some severe interval drops (minor sevenths and sixths) and—at the end of the bridge—an unexpected diversion into C-minor (the song is in the key of A♭). Thus, I bow to Messrs. Kern, Gershwin, and Sondheim and this song that can be said—with some exaggeration, but not too much—to have singlehandedly launched both the American musical theatre and the Great American Songbook.

THIS IS MY BELOVED

music by Harry Revel, lyric by Arnold B. Horwitt
from the musical *Are You with It?* (1945)

Among the Hollywood refugees from an unwelcoming Broadway was Harry Revel, who was indeed a refugee; his parents fled Russia for London, where Harry Glaser was born in 1905, ten days prior to and just across town from that other child of Russian refugees, Julius Stein (AKA Jule Styne). Revel had a fairly active career partnering with Mack Gordon on dozens of films (with songs including "Did You Ever See a Dream Walking?" and—for Shirley Temple—"When I'm with You," "Oh, My Goodness," and the immortal "You've Gotta Eat Your Spinach, Baby"). His only Broadway success was the postwar, carnival midway musical *Are You with It?*, which played a season. The score, with lyrics by Arnold B. Horwitt (a revue sketch writer and lyricist of the 1955 musical *Plain and Fancy*), includes the arrestingly interesting **This Is My Beloved**.§ It is not, in any way, to be confused with the Borodin-derived "And This Is My Beloved" from the 1953 operetta *Kismet*.

The verse sets up what's to come, with its flowery poesy interrupted midway by a lively contemporary vamp. The twelve-bar *A* section starts with two broadly melodic bars, followed by two harmonically colored bars suitable to a big band crooner (ending in an octave drop), followed by four swinging bars, and ending (with a leap of a seventh) in another four broadly melodic bars:

That final whole note is accompanied by an uncannily harmonic cadence of descending thirds. Then it's back to a restatement of the full *A*, identical until we move to the bridge (of *A-A¹-B-A²*). This turns mellow for half of the eight bars, after which Revel changes pace before moving back to that broad, croony, swingy *A*. The effect of this forty-four-bar ballad is one of lulling us with melody—and catching us, every time, when they break into swing.

THIS TIME THE DREAM'S ON ME

music by Harold Arlen, lyric by Johnny Mercer
from the motion picture *Blues in the Night* (1941)

The pairing of blues-happy Arlen and folksy colloquial Mercer brought forth a clutch of great songs, often with a melancholic twinge—colored, perhaps, by the less than happy home lives of the thirty-something songwriters. Both married exotic-to-them chorus girls (interfaith) from one of their early shows and neither lived happily ever after. This deep-veined malaise can be seen in what might be their most remarkable songs, "Blues in the Night" [page 16] and "One for My Baby" [page 132]. A similar lost-love message—albeit more resigned and less bitter—came in what appears to have been their first effort, **This Time the Dream's on Me**. (They wrote five songs for the 1941 film *Blues in the Night*; the title number was the final one they tackled.)

Arlen provides a straightforward, almost anthem-like melody. Gently wistful, he restricts himself to only one significantly rhythmic figure, the second complete bar of the *A* (of *A-A¹-B-A²*):

Arlen's melodic progress seems intrinsically tied to Mercer's lyric. The three pickup notes ("somewhere some-"/) are repeated *d*s (in the key of G). This jumps—in hopes of a positive romance?—an octave to the whole note in the first full bar ("day"). In bar three there's a drop of a—disheartening?—minor seventh. The repeated *d*s in bar four also jump, but only a sixth this time ("oh by the / WAY"). Then comes the title phrase, a six-note descent from high *c* down to *e*. That is to say, both music and lyric can be seen as starting on a hopeful high—that octave leap—but conclude with a deflating descent. Harmonically, Arlen keeps his melody on key with only a few touches of pessimistic color; that is, the G#-diminished chord in bar 2 ("we'll be CLOSE together") and a neatly chromatic harmonic progression into the bridge. Here, the writers turn more optimistically hopeful: "it would be fun to be certain that I'm the one"; while Mercer crafts a sly triple rhyme ("to know that *I* at least supp*ly* the shoulder you *cry* upon"). But it's only a pipe dream, alas. The final *A* takes the singer—and the lyricist, and us—back down to the realistic realization that this time, indeed, the dream's on me. "So set 'em up, Joe," as Mercer memorably wrote soon thereafter.

THOU SWELL

music by Richard Rodgers, lyric by Lorenz Hart
from the musical *A Connecticut Yankee* (1927)

Rodgers and Hart, who arrived on Broadway in 1925, were initially considered "collegiate" songwriters—not only by virtue of the brash freshness of their early songs ("Manhattan," "Mountain Greenery"), but because they were pure Ivy League, right out of Columbia University on upper Broadway. This compared to their immediate predecessors, Kern, Berlin, Gershwin, and Youmans, all of whom spent their formative years struggling on the bare-knuckled campus of Tin Pan Alley. (Cole Porter was, famously, a creature of Yale; although eleven years older than Rodgers, he did not start his Broadway career until 1928.) The first eight Rodgers and Hart scores (over just two years) were relatively manicured and polite. But with *A Connecticut Yankee* in the fall of 1927, they demonstrated that they were as versatile, "adult," and jazz age as any of their peers. This can be seen—or, rather, heard—in the splendid **Thou Swell**.

Rodgers builds the song on a persistent pickup note, which usually leads to monosyllable ("THOU / swell") and occasionally to two syllables ("THOU / witty"):

♩ | ♩. ♩ | ♫♩ ♩♩ | ♩. ♩ | ♩. ♩ | ♩. ♩ | ♫♩ ♩♩ | ♩. ♩ | ♩

This pickup note leads into all eight bars of the *A* (of *A-B-A-B/A*), a total of nineteen times over thirty-two bars. The bridge is remarkable, too, with Rodgers tricking up the rhythm:

♩ ♩| ♫ ♬♩ ♪| ♫ ♬♩ ♪| o___ ♩.

This provides Hart the opportunity to make one of the most remarkable of the many remarkable rhymes he dashed off during his twenty-year career: "hear me / holler I choose a sweet / lollapaloosa in thee." The song title, itself, was indicative of the nature of the piece: Mark Twain's tale had a modern-day fellow (1889 in the novel, 1927 in the musical) time travel to King Arthur's Camelot, circa 543. How to court a demure demoiselle if not by mixing "thou" with then current-day slang? (This raffish Rodgers and Hart Camelot is rather more to my taste than the other one, but that's just me.) The verse, which—given the way it dovetails into the pickup note pattern of the refrain—seems to be intrinsic—is even more explosive, featuring a severely accented rhythm ("BABE we are well MET / AS in a spell MET / I lift my hel-MET") plus off-the-beat interval leaps of fifths and sixths. The romantic ballad "My Heart Stood Still"—first heard in a London musical earlier that year—was the song hit of *Connecticut Yankee*, but "Thou Swell" is pure exuberance.

TIME ON MY HANDS (YOU IN MY ARMS)

music by Vincent Youmans, lyric by Harold Adamson and Mack Gordon
from the musical *Smiles* (1930)

Youmans, at his self-assured best, makes it seem simple with the penthouse reverie **Time on My Hands**.※ The title phrase is set to a triplet figure, repeated no fewer than ten times over shifting harmonies:

A close look reveals that Youmans interrupts the song's leisurely pace with just one snatch of syncopation, in the bridge of this *A-A-B-A²* ballad. An introspective, leisurely verse—the composer is known to have slaved over his verses—is filled with notes: fifty-five over twelve bars, compared to sixty-two over the lazy thirty-two-bar refrain.

Despite the storm clouds hanging over Broadway, the nation, and Youmans's career, "Time on My Hands" was and is yet another Youmans gem. *Smiles*—which predated *Guys and Dolls* by having its heroine in Salvation Army garb—was not. With the stock market wolf at the door, producer Florenz Ziegfeld went all out to assemble a can't-miss hit featuring not one but three of Broadway's biggest stars at the time: Marilyn Miller (from Kern's *Sally* and *Sunny*) plus the sibling team Fred and Adele Astaire (from the Gershwins' *Lady, Be Good!* and *Funny Face*) and a story from golden boy Noël Coward, no less. *Smiles* proved mirthless, alas, further plunging the showman into the insolvency that would bury him even before his death in 1932.

TOO LATE NOW

music by Burton Lane, lyric by Alan Jay Lerner
from the motion picture *Royal Wedding* (1951)

Following the success of the third Lerner and Loewe musical, *Brigadoon* (1947), composer Frederick Loewe chose to withdraw from the stressful collaboration. This left lyricist Lerner searching for a new partner. What appeared to be a fruitful collaboration with Kurt Weill ended with the latter's death in 1950. Next up was Burton Lane, who himself had withdrawn from an acrimonious collaboration with Yip Harburg on the hit 1947 musical *Finian's Rainbow*. Lerner and Lane joined for the latest Fred Astaire MGM vehicle, *Royal Wedding*. The collaboration brought forth several treats including the exceedingly fine **Too Late Now**,※ a ballad of bittersweet-love-at-last-because-it's-too-late-to-consider-us-apart as related by Lerner. (The lovelorn lyricist was just then starting his third of eight marriages.)

The *A-A¹-B-A²* song sounds quite simple in its melancholy way, but it is carefully and keenly constructed. Working in the key of C, Lane starts every two bars of his eight-bar *A* sections with ascending quarter notes of *e* ("too"), *g* ("late"), and *b* ("now"). This descends to *a* the first time, rises to *c* the second, and finally builds to *e*. All told, Lane gives us that *e–g–b* figure nine times over the thirty-four bars. The bridge starts on the high *e* and features a gently swung rhythm that fully suggests romantic yearning.

In 1951, Lerner returned to Broadway to rejoin Loewe for several more projects beginning with *Paint Your Wagon*. After Loewe officially retired in 1960, Lerner and Lane would uneasily team again on the troubled Broadway musicals *On a Clear Day You Can See Forever* (1965) and *Carmelina* (1979).

TOO MARVELOUS FOR WORDS

music by Richard A. Whiting, lyric by Johnny Mercer
from the motion picture *Ready, Willing and Able* (1937)

"You're just **Too Marvelous for Words**"⸓ the song goes, but Johnny Mercer—still in the earlier stages of his career—has a bushelful, and then some. "There aren't any magic adjectives to tell you all you are," goes the verse, after which Mercer shoots the works with magic adjectives. The lyric is made possible by Richard A. Whiting's delightful and functional melody. The *A* section starts with four casual bars, to a rocking melody, stringing out that opening statement; then the composer provides lyricist sufficient melodic space for all those marvelous words—"like glorious, glamourous, and that old standby amorous":

♩ | ♩. ♩ | ♩. ♫ ♩ ♩ | ♩ ♩ ♩ ♩ | ♩. ♩ | ♩ ♩ ♫ ♩ | ♩ ♫ ♩. ♪ | ♩ ♩ ♩ ♩ | ♫ ♩

The bridge (of *A-A¹-B-A²*) follows this pattern, starting casually but giving way to the wordsmith who here coins that imperishable phrase, "you're much too much / and just too very very / to ever be in / Webster's Dictionary." The published song is a breezy thirty-two bars, preceded by that eight-bar "magic adjective" verse. For the seven-minute version in the original film, though, Mercer embarks on a veritable Websterian field day bursting with multiple refrains and patter. To quote from midway through, "you're simply too spectacular / to be in my vernacular."

TRY TO REMEMBER

music by Harvey Schmidt, lyric by Tom Jones
from the musical *The Fantasticks* (1960)

When Harvey Schmidt was first working as a graphic artist for NBC television, he told me, he would sometimes rent a piano in the Steinway Hall rehearsal studio on West 57th Street: "One night I had been working on some aggressively hostile, dissonant, jazzy concoction and just abruptly stopped, overcome by big-city heat and no air-conditioning. I was drifting ever deeper into a semi-comatose state when I suddenly realized 'Hey, I'm paying a lot of money to play this piano so I'd better keep playing!' I removed my soaked shirt and tie and set forth to establish a complete change of pace. In the quiet of the moment out came this simple pure melody, totally intact, with no conscious effort on my part. 'Well, that's kinda pretty,' I thought, but because of its instant accessibility, I decided it was probably just some well-known folk song, possibly even 'Streets of Laredo'!" But it wasn't; it was Harvey's own **Try to Remember**. "When Jerry Orbach was cast as El Gallo, I asked him whether or not he might need the key to be raised or lowered, but he said it was just fine as written. So, amazingly, the music for this song is note-for-note exactly as I first encountered it."

THE VARSITY DRAG

music by Ray Henderson, lyric by B. G. DeSylva and Lew Brown
from the musical *Good News!* (1927)

Cecil Mack and Jimmy Johnson's 1923 "Charleston" [page 25] popularized the dance of that name, near and far, across the nation—so much so that the craze, "made in Carolina," as the lyric establishes, soon swept into all corners of the nation, embraced by sheiks and swains, coeds and flappers. One of the numerous hot-band follow-ups came from Broadway's DeSylva, Brown, and Henderson, who in the revue *George White's Scandals of 1926* had melodically investigated "The Birth of the Blues" [page 14] and explicated the "Black Bottom" before Ma Rainey got to it. With those two song hits under their collective belts, they formed their own publishing firm and wrote the smashingly successful musical *Good News!* "The Best Things in Life Are Free" was the ballad hit, but just as or even more popular was their **The Varsity Drag**.⸋ Cannily, DB&H not only provided a dance-happy melody; they instructed everyone just what to do: "here is the drag, see how it goes, down on the heels, up on the toes." The rhythm is beyond catchy:

♪♩ ♪♩ ⸹ | ♪♩ ♪♩ ⸹ | ♪♩ ♪♩ ⸹ | ♪♩ ♪♩ ⸹ | ♩ ♩ ♩ ♩ | ♩ ♫ ♫♩ | 𝅝 __ 𝅝

Henderson uses repeated notes in the *A* (of *A-A¹-B-A¹*) to jump from middle *c* to high *c*; in bars 1–2 via *e* and *g* (in the key of C), in 3–4 via *f* and *a♭*). The bridge ("you can pass many a class") also varies the harmony, traversing from E-major to C, F-minor, F-major, and G before returning home. The verse is not to be overlooked in that it promises an explosive refrain by giving us a propulsive rhythm—punctuated by those insistent quarter notes—over chromatically shifting chords:

♪♩ ♪♩ ♫♩♫♩ ♪♩ ♪♩ ♩ ⸹ ⸹ ♩ | - ♩ ⸹

"Why should a sheik learn how / to speak Latin and / Greek—bad- / -ly" when he or she can just say it with feet? Gladly.

THE WAY YOU LOOK TONIGHT

music by Jerome Kern, lyric by Dorothy Fields
from the motion picture *Swing Time* (1936)

It is outside the parameters of our mission to consider how economic conditions and related matters caused Broadway's most accomplished composers to gather on the far coast in the mid-1930s and turn out a stream of songs demonstrating that they were not only at the top of their creative powers but still expanding their craft and forging a new foundation for what we now blithely call the *Great American Songbook*. Berlin, Gershwin, Porter, and even the great Kern made the trip with golden—and gold-bearing—results. Kern, who had upended Broadway operetta land in 1915 and reforged the field in 1927 with *Show Boat*, now was happily ensconced a continent away from his Bronxville manse. But rather than sitting around collecting plaudits and royalties, **The Way You Look Tonight** demonstrates that he was as astonishing as ever.

The song starts with a warmly romantic strain ("some / day/ when I'm awf'ly / low") featuring three whole notes over four bars. But this is not to be one of those standard thirty-two-bar songs: the *A* extends sixteen bars, featuring an octave drop midway ("a- / glow just thinking / OF / YOU") with the title phrase ranging across four bars near the end of the section. Kern and Dorothy Fields—and yes, the young lyricist seems to have altogether rejuvenated the composer after all those years with Wodehouse and Harbach and Hammerstein—move into the restatement of the *A* (of *A-A-B-A¹*) with three pickup notes ("OH, BUT YOU'RE / lovely") that we couldn't possibly do without. Those pickup notes reappear at the end of the second *A*, not sung but in the accompaniment as Kern confounds us with new harmonies in the bridge (starting with four repeated half notes: "WITH EACH / WORD YOUR / tenderness grows"). He takes us from the original key of E♭ into G♭, cycling his way through chords of B♭-minor, A♭-minor, and D♭, and back again, until retreating to E♭ for an exact repetition of *A* with a four-bar tag of the title phrase. So much for the simple thirty-two-bar ballad. For his efforts, Kern became the first "Broadway" composer to win an Oscar.

WHAT IS THERE TO SAY?

music by Vernon Duke, lyric by E. Y. Harburg
from the stage revue *Ziegfeld Follies of 1934* (1933)

The acrimonious collaboration of Vernon Duke and E. Y. Harburg—a partnership originally brokered by Duke's mentor Gershwin (George) and Harburg's college pal Gershwin (Ira)—ran aground during the tryout of this Shubert-produced edition of the *Follies*. (The rights were bought from Billie Burke Ziegfeld; her husband, the "Great Ziegfeld," had died in 1932.) The breakup was centered, as it happens, around the delightfully light-as-air **What Is There to Say?**※ During the tryout—which was so troubled that what had been called the *Ziegfeld Follies of 1933* didn't reach town until the first week of 1934—Duke discovered Harburg at work with a new composer, secretly setting the lyric for "What Is There to Say?" to an alternate melody. Duke intervened, and his version remained in the show; but it was the end of the collaboration.

Harburg moved on to a new Shubert revue with Arlen and Ira Gershwin, *Life Begins at 8:40*, while Duke moved on to a second Shubert-produced *Follies*—also with Ira ("I Can't Get Started" [page 59]). Duke starts his *A* (of *A-A-B-A¹*) with the title phrase of ascending quarter notes leading to a dotted half, a pattern that then repeats. There follow two bars of the most felicitous cascading quarter-note triplets:

The bridge features a recurring three-note phrase of pickup notes as well as another bar of six triplets. Harburg, meanwhile, is at his whimsical best; who else was likely to take advantage of those delicious triplets with something like "my / heart's-in-a dead-lock-I'd / e-ven-face wed-lock-with / you"?

WHEN DID I FALL IN LOVE?

music by Jerry Bock, lyric by Sheldon Harnick
from the musical *Fiorello!* (1959)

The theatrically dramatic work of Jerry Bock and Sheldon Harnick is outside the range of our concentration, generally speaking, but **When Did I Fall in Love?** certainly belongs in our group of favorites. This "slow and tender" ballad is simplicity itself; not a song of love unrequited but of love unrecognized, until it is—recognized—in the final eight bars.

The title phrase starts gently, on the second beat, with ascending quarter notes (*c–c–d/e–g–g*, in the key of C). In the next bar, though, Bock jars us on the second beat with *f#–g*:

In A^1 (of a most unusual A-A^1-A^2-A^3), he starts the pattern on *a* (over an A-minor chord), making the discordant tone a *d#*. The third section returns to the original tones of the title phrase repeats. In the triumphant A^3—where the unanticipated love is suddenly proclaimed—Bock starts the pattern on *f* (over a F chord) as he builds to a triumphant end. All the while, the composer—in the original arrangement—augments the lyric with exquisite harmonics. The gentleness of the A and A^2 sections is belied by the discord on the second beat of practically every bar—a discordant *f#–eb–d* or *f#–eb–db*, as desired. A^1, meanwhile, is distinguished by a rhapsodic accompaniment; and A^3 becomes even more lush. The standard published version excludes the original forty-bar verse ("there he goes, my congressman"), understandably so as it is heavily plot-related. But it also excludes the shimmeringly romantic sixteen-bar interlude ("when did respect first become affection"), which is intrinsic to the song and not to be overlooked.

WHEN THE SUN COMES OUT

music by Harold Arlen, lyric by Ted Koehler
non-production song (1941)

Following the success of the Arlen-Harburg score for the 1939 motion picture *The Wizard of Oz*, Yip jumped the train back to Broadway. Harold chose to remain in Hollywood, where he temporarily reunited with his *Cotton Club* lyricist, Koehler, while awaiting further developments—specifically, the pairing with another partner on a level with (or, in my opinion, somewhat above) Harburg: Johnny Mercer. It was a collaboration inaugurated with the 1941 instant classic "Blues in the Night" [page 16].

In the meantime, Arlen and Koehler reunited for several songs, one of which fits on the shelf with the pair's earlier efforts ("Stormy Weather" [page 162], "I Gotta Right to Sing the Blues" [page 67], "Ill Wind" [page 81], and more).

When the Sun Comes Out—a verseless song of thirty-eight bars—starts with a wailing plaint of a title phrase. The *B* section—in what is roughly *A-A-B-A¹*—provides a casual counterpoint to the nearly overwrought *A*; the final *A* breaks out into a slightly extended coda. The lyric is straightforward compared to what the infinitely more skillful Harburg or Mercer might have wrought; but I suppose we could make the same claim about most of the other Arlen-Koehler songs. Musically, though, you can see that Harold's sure got the blues.

WHEN YOU WISH UPON A STAR

music by Leigh Harline, lyric by Ned Washington
from the motion picture *Pinocchio* (1940)

Much has been said—at least in places where people discuss such things—of the unconventional octave jump that starts the refrain of that folklike children's anthem "Over the Rainbow" [page 133]. **When You Wish Upon a Star** begins with another octave jump! Although the songs were officially introduced upon the release of their respective films—*The Wizard of Oz* in 1939, *Pinocchio* in 1940—both were registered as unpublished manuscripts at the Copyright

Office in the summer of 1938. Something must have been in the Culver City songwriters' water that spring.

The *Pinocchio* song proceeds most interestingly: that octave jump from low *g* (the lowest note in the melody) then descends before working its way up to an *a* (on "star," in the key of C). Bar 3 has another octave jump, from *b*, and works its way up to high *c*. Bar 5, on the other hand moves up a tone to *d* but then descends in a scale pattern to the cadence. The *A* (of *A-A¹-B-A¹*) is as sweet and calming as a lullaby, despite a pair of colorful accidentals (*c#* in bar 2, *f#* in bar 4). Those descending scales are contrasted by rising patterns in the bridge ("fate is kind"), which include even more chromaticism with soothing effect.

Composer Harline was a Disney staffer who went on to score numerous mainstream films after leaving animation land. If he wrote songs in addition to his five *Pinocchio* titles (including "Give a Little Whistle," "Hi-Diddle-Dee-Dee," and "I've Got No Strings"), I can't find them. But "When You Wish Upon a Star" and the overall *Pinocchio* score earned him and lyricist Ned Washington ("The Nearness of You" [page 126]) two Oscars, for Best Score and Best Song, the first such awards won by an animated feature.

WHERE OR WHEN

music by Richard Rodgers, lyric by Lorenz Hart
from the musical *Babes in Arms* (1937)

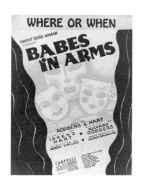

Rodgers and Hart had written numerous song hits (and numerous Songbook standards) since 1925, but *Babes in Arms*—their twentieth full musical over a twelve-year period—contained three at once: **Where or When**, "My Funny Valentine" [page 125], and "The Lady Is a Tramp," along with the equally worthy "Johnny One Note" and "I Wish I Was in Love Again."

"Where or When" practically defines the notion of déjà vu. Rodgers conjures a most haunting melody with just enough mystery to carry Hart's existential question: "It seems we stood and talked like this before . . . but who knows where or when?"

The composer's tools, here, are repeated notes and the ascending scale. Bar 1 has three *b♭*s (in the key of A♭); bar 2 has four *c*s. After landing on *d* in the next two bars, he gives us seven $e\flat$s in bar 5, and goes on from there. Note the unusual layout: two *A* sections, of ten bars each, followed by a straightforward bridge consisting of two four-bar sections. Then comes a twelve-bar final section. Rodgers starts with the first two bars of the original *A*, the first on a low $b\flat$ and the second on *c*. He then builds his way up the scale—step by step, bar by bar, two repeated notes per bar—until he ends the song on a high, and somewhat triumphant, $e\flat$. Mind you, this clinical discourse on strong construction is merely illustrative. Clearly cognizant of what made effective music, Rodgers likely was oblivious to any such structures or strictures. He just wrote what sounded instinctively right to him, and that was the key to his astonishing output over forty years.

WHY DID I CHOOSE YOU?

music by Michael Leonard, lyric by Herbert Martin
from the musical *The Yearling* (1965)

Howard Taubman, briefly the first-string drama critic of the *New York Times*, suggested that "the po' white folks in *The Yearling* could use an antipoverty program, and so could the musical." That was Saturday morning after a Friday opening, with the scenery hauled to the dump on Sunday. But composer Michael Leonard—as related in our discussion of "I'm All Smiles" [page 82]—was able to get one of his former students to record some of the songs. Streisand made **Why Did I Choose You?**❋ an instant near-classic.

This stunning *A-B-A-C* ballad culminates with the *C* extended to twelve bars instead of eight, which makes for a strong but gentle climax (as Barbra and other interpreters discovered). How many similarly worthy songs have disappeared beneath the wreckage of other instant flops, one wonders? Although we do, in fact, find more than a handful—for instance, "Here's That Rainy Day" [page 53]—among our *201 Favorites*.

Let's Go
Milton Schafer-Ira Levin
(page 105)

Lorna's Here
Charles Strouse-Lee Adams
(page 107)

Lullaby of Broadway
Harry Warren-Al Dubin
(page 111)

Mack the Knife
Kurt Weill-Bert Brecht-Marc Blitzstein
(page 112)

Makin' Whoopee!
Walter Donaldson-Gus Kahn
(page 116)

The Man I Love
George Gershwin-Ira Gershwin
(page 117)

The Man That Got Away
Harold Arlen-Ira Gershwin
(page 118)

Moonglow
Will Hudson-Eddie De Lange-Irving Mills
(page 122)

Never Never Land
Jule Styne-Betty Comden-Adolph Green
(page 126)

Night and Day
Cole Porter
(page 127)

Ol' Man River
Jerome Kern-Oscar Hammerstein 2nd
(page 129)

One for My Baby
(And One More for the Road)
Harold Arlen-Johnny Mercer
(page 132)

Over the Rainbow
Harold Arlen-E. Y. Harburg
(page 133)

Overnight
Louis Alter-Billy Rose-Charlotte Kent
(page 134)

The Party's Over
Jule Styne-Betty Comden-Adolph Green
(page 135)

Past the Age of Innocence
Moose Charlap-Norman Gimbel
(page 136)

Pennies from Heaven
Arthur Johnston-Johnny Burke
(page 137)

Satin Doll
Duke Ellington-Billy Strayhorn-Johnny Mercer
(page 142)

A Sleepin' Bee
Harold Arlen-Truman Capote
(page 147)

Smoke Gets in Your Eyes
Jerome Kern-Otto Harbach
(page 148)

So in Love
Cole Porter
(page 149)

Some Other Time
Leonard Bernstein-Betty Comden-
Adolph Green
(page 151)

Sophisticated Lady
Duke Ellington-Irving Mills-Mitchell Parish
(page 157)

Speak Low
Kurt Weill-Ogden Nash
(page 158)

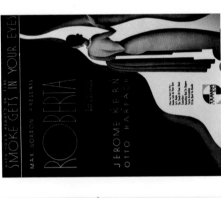

St. Louis Blues
W. C. Handy
(page 161)

Star Dust
Hoagy Carmichael-Mitchell Parish
(page 162)

Stormy Weather
Harold Arlen-Ted Koehler
(page 163)

Summertime
George Gershwin-DuBose Heyward
(page 164)

Swanee
George Gershwin-Irving Caesar
(page 165)

'S Wonderful
George Gershwin-Ira Gershwin
(page 169)

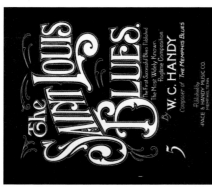

Taking a Chance on Love
Vernon Duke-John Latouche
(page 170)

That Old Black Magic
Harold Arlen-Johnny Mercer
(page 173)

There's No Holding Me
Arthur Schwartz-Ira Gershwin
(page 175)

They Can't Take That Away from Me
George Gershwin-Ira Gershwin
(page 176)

They Didn't Believe Me
Jerome Kern-Herbert Reynolds
(page 177)

This Is My Beloved
Harry Revel-Arnold B. Horwitt
(page 178)

Time on My Hands (You in My Arms)
Vincent Youmans-Harold Adamson-
Mack Gordon
(page 182)

Too Late Now
Burton Lane-Alan Jay Lerner
(page 183)

Too Marvelous for Words
Richard A. Whiting-Johnny Mercer
(page 184)

The Varsity Drag
B. G. DeSylva-Lew Brown-Ray Henderson
(page 186)

The Way You Look Tonight
Jerome Kern-Dorothy Fields
(page 187)

What Is There to Say?
Vernon Duke-E. Y. Harburg
(page 188)

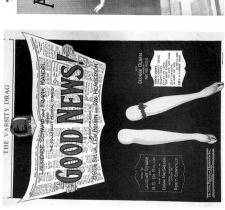

Where or When
Richard Rodgers-Lorenz Hart
(page 191)

Why Did I Choose You?
Michael Leonard-Herbert Martin
(page 192)

Why Was I Born?
Jerome Kern-Oscar Hammerstein 2nd
(page 193)

Witchcraft
Cy Coleman-Carolyn Leigh
(page 195)

Without a Song
Vincent Youmans-William Rose-
Edward Eliscu
(page 197)

Zing! Went the Strings of My Heart
James F. Hanley
(page 203)

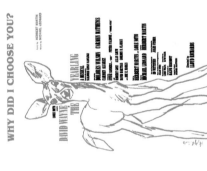

WHY WAS I BORN?

music by Jerome Kern, lyric by Oscar Hammerstein 2nd
from the musical *Sweet Adeline* (1929)

Kern and Hammerstein followed their landmark *Show Boat* (1927) with *Sweet Adeline*, a mild slice of turn-of-the-century nostalgia with a score worthy of their talents. Standing out was **Why Was I Born?**⁑ a supremely effective torch song.

The construction is practically mathematical; why that should work so well, we can't quite say. Every other bar of the *A* (of *A-B-A-B/A*) consists of a rest (or hold) followed by three repeated quarter notes:

In bars 2 and 6 we get a fourth repeated (whole) note. In 4 and 8, there are two notes, the repeated tone from the prior bar plus a dotted half note up a tone. The *B* is built on a simple ascending chord-like figure of mostly quarter notes. The second *A* is an exact copy; the final section starts with the ascending quarter notes that build to a high *g*—held for nine beats—after which we get those repeated high *e♭*s dropping an octave for the finish.

The songwriters most certainly didn't sit there calculating how effective these repeated notes would be; it was instinctual on their part. But they likely did realize that this pattern would provide Helen Morgan—who sang "Can't Help Lovin' Dat Man" [page 22] and "Bill" in *Show Boat*, and for whom they wrote *Sweet Adeline*—a series of most effective whole notes that she could "torch" to great effect.

WILLOW WEEP FOR ME

music and lyric by Ann Ronell
non-production song (1932)

When a twenty-one-year-old Radcliffe student arrived to interview the great George Gershwin, he divined that she possessed distinctive musical talent. Gershwin convinced Ann Rosenblatt of Omaha to change her name to Ronell and placed her as rehearsal pianist for his 1928 musical *Rosalie*. Her career proceeded slowly, faced as she was with resistance to both her gender and her musical complexity. Ronell's most familiar song is unquestionably "Who's Afraid of the Big Bad Wolf," written with Frank Churchill for Walt Disney's 1933 short *Three Little Pigs*, but her masterwork is unquestionably **Willow Weep for Me**.

This is an astonishing song, in league with Johnny Green's "Body and Soul" [page 17]. The music is distinctive, certainly; Ronell works within the confines of the thirty-two-bar *A-A-B-A* form, but that's just about the only pattern she follows. The title phrase, in the first bar, consists of a dotted eighth and sixteenth—which drops an octave—followed by eighth-note triplets, the final note tied to a half note. This figure is repeated in bar 2, whereas bar 3 completes the phrase with a second set of triplets that run on to even more triplets in bar 4. Then comes the extraordinary bar 5, in which Ronell breaks into double time with a stride-piano accompaniment, immediately returning to her dotted eighth and sixteenth/triplet rhythm:

All of those initial notes—except the tied tone in bar 4 and the final whole note—are incessant and insistent high *d*s (in the key of G). The *A* section is heard three times; in each case, that double-time bar startles before quickly vanishing. Who's counting, but Ronell gives us the octave drop *twelve* times; and I count twenty-three sets of eighth-note triplets, *plus* another eight in the sixteen-bar verse. Atop the sheet music—which was published by Irving Berlin's firm—appears "Dedicated to George Gershwin." No wonder.

WITCHCRAFT

music by Cy Coleman, lyric by Carolyn Leigh
non-production song (1957)

A child prodigy at the keyboard, Cy Coleman moved from the concert hall to cabaret with his Cy Coleman Trio. His songwriting—which would eventually lead to an impressive Broadway career—started in earnest when he was paired with the similarly ambitious Carolyn Leigh, who had already written a Sinatra hit ("Young at Heart," music by Johnny Richards) and half a Broadway score (for Mary Martin's *Peter Pan*, music by Moose Charlap). While waiting for Broadway to call, Coleman and Leigh turned out a string of contemporary pop songs. At a time when Rodgers and Hammerstein were still creating hits in competition with Lerner and Loewe and while Loesser and Styne and Bernstein were creating classic musicals of their own, the considerably younger Coleman pointed forward from the start—that is to say, with the jazzy vamp to **Witchcraft**✲:

After a chromatically syncopated verse comes the refrain, with the tempo direction in the sheet music labeled "with a swingin' feeling." The initial section is built on a snappy two-bar phrase ("those fingers in my hair") that is repeated three times, against differing chords. *A¹* takes the phrase up two steps, from what had been *d* (in the key of F) to *f*; Coleman adds a couple of extra notes, either to goose the rhythm or to accommodate Leigh, or both. The bridge (of *A-A¹-B-C-A²*) is built around the title phrase ("cause it's *witchcraft*, wicked *witchcraft*") and ends with a striking chord sequence that makes it impossible to return to a restatement of the *A*. Instead, Coleman gives us a new section, which is something of an inverse version of the *A*. After a jazzy cadence accompanied by jazzy chord play, he takes us back where he started for a most satisfactory ending. And let's not overlook the critical contribution of Leigh, with an equally swingin' lyric that catches our immediate notice when she starts off with "shades of old Lucretia Borgia"—shades, methinks, of old Cole Porter.

WITH A SONG IN MY HEART

music by Richard Rodgers, lyric by Lorenz Hart
from the musical *Spring Is Here* (1929)

Rodgers seems to have been in a somewhat more noble—or perhaps more Kern-like—frame of mind than usual when he wrote **With a Song in My Heart**. Hart's words came after the music was written, as usual, but the melody seems to have put him in a similarly lofty mood. The refrain starts with the anthem-like title phrase and develops in stately manner with the tempo marking "rather slow but with rhythm."

Actually, it starts with three preliminary pickup notes with which Rodgers temporarily jolts us from the key of E♭ (which ends the verse and starts the refrain), namely e♮ ("I") f ("greet") b♮ ("you"):

The main melodic figure, which is repeated throughout the song, is notable for the way it more or less circles the b♭ Rodgers wants to concentrate on: b♭–a♮–c–b♭–a♮–b♭. The bridge (of *A-B-A-B¹/A¹*) is relatively spare, starting with a leap of a sixth ("when the music SWELLS"), featuring nothing briefer than a quarter note and concluding with a canny cadence of two whole notes leading back to the *A* ("standing NEAR—AND—"). Rodgers was known to consider "With a Song in My Heart" one of his very favorite songs. I think it's grand, too.

WITHOUT A SONG

music by Vincent Youmans, lyric by William (Billy) Rose and Edward Eliscu
from the musical *Great Day!* (1929)

Youmans entered what you might call his mature period—beginning when he turned thirty-one and lasting just four years, as he became incapacitated by tuberculosis—with *Great Day!*, an epic self-described "Musical Play of the Southland." Composed, conceived, and produced by Youmans himself, who seems to have consciously determined to outdo *Show Boat*. Instead, he all but sabotaged what remained of his career. **Without a Song** is a strong, spare, and noble song, which most clearly seems intended to rival "Ol' Man River." It doesn't, quite—although it might have if *Great Day!* hadn't opened a week before the stock market crash and closed within the month. (The lyric includes one impossibly ethnic word that can no longer be sung; but then, "Ol' Man River" had several.)

Youmans builds "Without a Song" on the title phrase, setting it to three pickup eighth notes leading to a half note:

This is repeated, in a descending pattern, four times within each of the *A* sections (of *A-A-B-A*); that's twelve times over thirty-two bars. In each case, Youmans starts the pattern a third lower; on *d* (in the key of E♭) in bar 1, *b♭* in bar 3, then *g*, and finally *e♭*. The bridge is more straightforward, in anthem-like manner, consisting of stepwise patterns rather than chain of intervals jumps in the *A*. Despite the musical's quick failure, *Great Day!* also included a second standard: "More Than You Know" [page 123].

YOU ARE FOR LOVING

music and lyrics by Hugh Martin (credited to Hugh Martin and Ralph Blane)
from the stage musical *Meet Me in St. Louis* (1960)

A 1960 summer stock attempt to convert MGM's 1944 *Meet Me in St. Louis* into a stage musical proved ill advised. Nevertheless, it brought forth a gem: **You Are for Loving**. This jewellike song is as exquisite as "The Boy Next Door" [page 19], although without Judy Garland to introduce it, it has remained all but unknown.

A series of intervals adds a certain tentativeness to the melody: an upward fifth in bar 2, a major sixth in bar 4, another fifth in bar 6; then a series of downward fourths in the bridge. The *C* (of *A-B-A-C*), unlike the eight-bar sections preceding it, is extended with an extra four bars that serve to cap the lyric with a deceptively poignant twist.

The seven songs written for the stock production disappeared, but "You Are for Loving" was rescued in the 1963 off-Broadway revival of *Best Foot Forward*. (It was sung—shades of Judy Garland—by a seventeen-year-old newcomer named Liza Minnelli). The song was also included, naturally enough, in the 1989 Broadway revival of *Meet Me in St. Louis*, which just as naturally failed. But what a song! Although the song is credited to Martin and Blane, it was written by Martin. (See authorship note on page 39.)

YOU BETTER GO NOW

music by Robert Graham, lyric by Bickley Reichner
from the stage revue *New Faces of 1936* (1936)

Producer Leonard Sillman started his *New Faces* series in 1934, the first of seven that managed to reach Broadway. The purported purpose was to discover new stars; that first edition brought forth a young actor named Henry Fonda, who within seven months was playing a leading role on Broadway and within seventeen months was a Hollywood movie star. (Ultimately, about twenty of Sillman's "new faces" went on to substantial careers, including Van Johnson, Eartha Kitt, Maggie Smith, and Madeline Kahn.)

The producer's song-choosing skill, though, was less than notable. With the exception of the 1952 edition, which included "Guess Who I Saw Today" [page 46] and several other entertaining numbers, the first and only other standout among the varied editions was **You Better Go Now** from *New Faces of 1936*. (Composer Robert Graham is not quite so unknown as it appears; after a thorough search, I discovered that he soon thereafter changed his name to Irvin Graham, with the 1953 inspirational standard "I Believe" among his credits.)

"You Better Go Now" starts with a verse somewhat along the lines of the jaded "party" songs of Messrs. Porter and Coward ("I understand he married her for money, well after all a gentleman must dine"). It veers, abruptly, into something more moving, a contemplative, wearily wise admission that "you better go, because I like you much too much." The effect is not dissimilar to that of Kurt Weill's "September Song" [page 144], which came along two years later. But "You Better Go Now" strikes a rather more ruminative, if gently world-weary, chord.

YOU HAVE CAST YOUR SHADOW ON THE SEA

music by Richard Rodgers, lyric by Lorenz Hart
from the musical *The Boys from Syracuse* (1938)

Rodgers and Hart's second 1938 musical, *The Boys from Syracuse*, had no fewer than five marvelous songs—the others being "Falling in Love with Love," "The Shortest Day of the Year," "Sing for Your Supper," and "This Can't Be Love." (Their first show of the year, *I Married an Angel*, contained merely one instant classic, "Spring Is Here" [page 160].) I have no qualms in selecting **You Have Cast Your Shadow on the Sea** for our favorites list, although ask me last year or next, and I might switch to one or three of the others.

The *A* section (of *A-A¹-B-A²*) is built around the descending chromatic passage in the first two bars, redolent of a boat—or a "bark," as in the lyric—floating downstream. "Slowly, with expression," it says; somewhat lazy, and thoroughly lovely. The bridge, too, is fine, marked by the three insistent repeated notes leading from the prior cadence (on the words "SINCE YOU HAVE made"). There is a smoothly placid twenty-bar verse, with the nautical nature of the piece reflected by the "watery" accompaniment figure. Hart, for his part, slips in a line about "the edge of this flat old world," the action taking place in ancient Greece.

YOU TOOK ADVANTAGE OF ME

music by Richard Rodgers, lyric by Lorenz Hart
from the musical *Present Arms!* (1928)

As related in our discussion of "Thou Swell" [page 180], the formerly "collegiate" Rodgers and Hart came of age as 1927 turned to 1928 with items such as the aforementioned slang-slinging swingfest and the wryly droll-but-wise **You Took Advantage of Me**. Not only were both melodic, tuneful, and effective; they show Rodgers writing music that, in itself, is as humorous as Hart's lyrics.

The latter is a deftly cobbled soft-shoe, with a casually syncopated *A* section ("I'm a sentimental / sap that's all") marked by playful intervals—dropping a fifth, jumping a seventh—within the very first bar. In the latter half of the *A*, Rodgers steps down from high *f* to low *e♭* (in the key of E♭). The bridge (of *A-A-B-A*) resembles nothing so much as tipsily stumbling on a flight of irregular musical stairs for three bars ("I'm so hot and bothered that I don't know my elbow from my ear"), pulling oneself together in unsteady balance, and then doing it once more. You'll perhaps need to look at or listen to the music to see what I mean, but that just about describes it. Rodgers being Rodgers, he is careful to stoke that fall with a couple of wildly errant notes: *d♭* here ("I DON'T know"), *c♭* there ("el-BOW from"). "So what's the use," asks Hart, "you've cooked my goose, 'cause you took advantage of me." All told, it's a sprightly chromatic romp that'll set you beaming.

YOU'RE ALL THE WORLD TO ME

music by Burton Lane, lyric by Alan Jay Lerner
from the motion picture *Royal Wedding* (1951)

What sort of song do you write when you need your fifty-year-old leading man to doff his top hat, snuff out his cigarette, and explode into happiness so unrestrainable that he dances with the chair, leaps on the couch, walks up the wall, and terps across the ceiling for five minutes? Have I got a song for you! That's precisely what's demanded of **You're All the World to Me**, which serves its purpose spectacularly well, although, admittedly, the sight of Fred Astaire hopping over the ceiling sconce would likely entertain picture audiences no matter what music the MGM orchestra blasts out. This song is so very joyous one can understand his tripping the light fantastic, even above that light fixture.

The music is built around an off-the-beat four-bar figure ("you're like Paris in April and May"):

The form is *A-B-A-B²*; this figure recurs every four bars throughout, albeit on different pitches. Lane propels the melody with a bright, scale-like fill of nine notes in bars 4 and 8 of the *A* sections. Lerner, for his part, offers verbal acrobatics; has anyone else, even Yip Harburg, ever thought to slip in a rhyme for "Aurora Borealis"? (Further song scoping reveals, we sheepishly admit, that Johnny Mercer—to music by Sonny Burke and Lionel Hampton—offered a *triple* chalice-palace-borealis rhyme in the 1947 "Midnight Sun.")

The song is such a perfect fit for the occasion that we must confess it did not pop out of a Lerner-Lane work session with stern Fred impatiently tapping his toe. Lane wrote it while Alan was still at boarding school, to a perfectly serviceable Harold Adamson lyric that by 1950 was too insensitive for use. "I Want to Be a Minstrel Man" was sung, danced, and scatted by thirteen-year-old Harold Nicholas surrounded by an extremely white bevy of Goldwyn Girls in the 1934 Eddie Cantor film *Kid Millions*. The refrains are identical except for a slightly extended climax of the final section. Lerner and Lane did, however, write an entirely new verse that serves to get Fred out of his reverie, out of his chair, up on his feet, and high off the floor.

ZING! WENT THE STRINGS OF MY HEART

music and lyric by James F. Hanley
from the stage revue *Thumbs Up!* (1934)

Why is this song so joyous? Songwriter James F. Hanley uses an arpeggiated chord of three eighth notes leading into just about every phrase of the sixteen-bar *A* sections—six times within the *A*, to be precise, leading to different chords. This thrusts us forward eighteen times over the course of the song:

Add to this the title phrase at the end of each *A*, starting with an exuberant "Zing!"—that's Hanley's exclamation mark, there—interrupted by a one-beat pause from the rest of the phrase:

The composer repeatedly builds us up, never lets us down. The bridge (of *A-A-B-A*) literally builds, starting on a low *eb* (in the key of Eb) and gradually wending its way to high *f*.

The song is long—fifty-six bars, plus an eight-bar verse—but it is a breezy, self-propelling delight. Hanley, who is otherwise best known for two early Fannie Brice hits ("Second Hand Rose" and "Rose of Washington Square"), wrote five songs for this undistinguished revue. (In fashioning his downbeat notice in the *New York Times*, Brooks Atkinson ended with "P.S.—According to the sailor in the adjoining seat, the girls are O.K.") The enduring song hit of the show was an interpolation from Vernon Duke: "Autumn in New York" [page 11]. But **Zing! Went the Strings of My Heart**⌘ flies along on wings—or, rather, *zings* along.

SONGWRITERS!

Certain fabled songwriters appear frequently throughout this book. That being the case, we present a chronological list of their songs contained herein (along with the usual biographical data), after which we do the same for songwriters who are less visible on these pages. This is not a reflection of their songs or their careers; in some cases, they are supremely accomplished, but the bulk of their work falls outside our area of concentration. But I say, everybody who had a hand in even one song among our favorites deserves their place.

words and music mostly by . . .

Harold Arlen | composer
born: February 15, 1905, Buffalo, New York
died: April 23, 1986, New York, New York
1930 **Get Happy** [page 44]
1932 **I Gotta Right to Sing the Blues** [page 67]
1932 **I've Got the World on a String** [page 95]
1932 **It's Only a Paper Moon** [page 92]
1933 **Stormy Weather** [page 163]
1934 **As Long as I Live** [page 10]
1934 **Ill Wind (You're Blowin' Me No Good)** [page 81]
1939 **Over the Rainbow** [page 133]
1941 **Blues in the Night (My Mama Done Tol' Me)** [page 16]
1941 **This Time the Dream's on Me** [page 179]
1941 **When the Sun Comes Out** [page 190]

1942 **That Old Black Magic** [page 173]
1943 **One for My Baby (And One More for the Road)** [page 132]
1944 **Ac-cent-tchu-ate the Positive** [page 1]
1946 **Come Rain or Come Shine** [page 28]
1946 **I Wonder What Became of Me** [page 79]
1954 **The Man That Got Away** [page 118]
1954 **A Sleepin' Bee** [page 147]
1973 **I Had a Love Once** [page 69]

Irving Berlin | composer/lyricist
born: May 11, 1888, Mohilev, Russia
died: September 22, 1989, New York, New York
1915 **I Love a Piano** [page 71]
1929 **Puttin' on the Ritz** [page 141]
1935 **Cheek to Cheek** [page 26]
1936 **Let Yourself Go** [page 101]
1936 **Let's Face the Music and Dance** [page 104]
1942 **I Left My Heart at the Stage Door Canteen** [page 70]

Johnny Burke | lyricist
born: October 3, 1908, Antioch, California
died: February 25, 1964, New York, New York
1936 **Pennies from Heaven** [page 137]
1944 **Swinging on a Star** [page 168]
1946 **Personality** [page 138]
1953 **Here's That Rainy Day** [page 53]
1955 **Misty** [page 121]

Hoagy Carmichael | composer/lyricist
born: November 22, 1899, Bloomington, Indiana
died: December 27, 1981, Rancho Mirage, California
1928 **Star Dust** [page 162]
1930 **Georgia on My Mind** [page 43]
1931 **Lazy River** [page 100]
1939 **I Get Along Without You Very Well (Except Sometimes)** [page 65]
1940 **The Nearness of You** [page 126]
1942 **Skylark** [page 146]
1945 **Memphis in June** [page 120]

Betty Comden | lyricist
born: May 3, 1917, Brooklyn, New York
died: November 23, 2006, New York, New York
1944 **Some Other Time** [page 151]
1954 **Never Never Land** [page 126]
1956 **Just in Time** [page 97]
1956 **The Party's Over** [page 135]
1960 **Make Someone Happy** [page 115]

Howard Dietz | lyricist
born: September 8, 1896, New York, New York
died: July 30, 1983, New York, New York
1929 **I Guess I'll Have to Change My Plan (The Blue Pajama Song)**
    [page 68]
1930 **Something to Remember You By** [page 153]
1931 **Dancing in the Dark** [page 31]
1932 **Alone Together** [page 7]
1937 **I See Your Face Before Me** [page 75]
1961 **Magic Moment** [page 114]

Vernon Duke | composer
born: October 10, 1903, Parafianovo, Russia
died: January 17, 1969, Santa Monica, California
1932 **April in Paris** [page 9]
1933 **What Is There to Say?** [page 188]
1934 **Autumn in New York** [page 11]
1936 **I Can't Get Started** [page 59]
1940 **Love Turned the Light Out** [page 108]
1940 **Taking a Chance on Love** [page 170]
1956 **Born Too Late** [page 18]

Duke Ellington | composer
born: April 29, 1899, Washington, DC
died: May 24, 1974, New York, New York
1933 **Sophisticated Lady** [page 157]
1942 **Don't Get Around Much Anymore** [page 35]
1944 **I'm Beginning to See the Light** [page 84]
1960 **Satin Doll** [page 142]

Dorothy Fields | lyricist
born: July 15, 1905, Allenhurst, New Jersey
died: March 28, 1974, New York, New York
1928 **I Can't Give You Anything but Love** [page 60]
1935 **I'm in the Mood for Love** [page 85]
1936 **Pick Yourself Up** [page 139]
1936 **The Way You Look Tonight** [page 187]

George Gershwin | composer
born: September 26, 1898, Brooklyn, New York
died: July 11, 1937, Beverly Hills, California
1919 **Swanee** [page 165]
1924 **Fascinating Rhythm** [page 40]
1924 **The Man I Love** [page 117]
1926 **Someone to Watch over Me** [page 152]
1927 **How Long Has This Been Going On?** [page 58]
1927 **'S Wonderful** [page 169]
1930 **I Got Rhythm** [page 66]
1933 **Isn't It a Pity?** [page 87]
1935 **Summertime** [page 164]
1937 **They Can't Take That Away from Me** [page 176]

Ira Gershwin | lyricist
born: December 6, 1896, New York, New York
died: August 17, 1983, Beverly Hills, California
1924 **Fascinating Rhythm** [page 40]
1924 **The Man I Love** [page 117]
1926 **Someone to Watch over Me** [page 152]
1927 **How Long Has This Been Going On?** [page 58]
1927 **'S Wonderful** [page 169]
1930 **I Got Rhythm** [page 66]
1933 **Isn't It a Pity?** [page 87]
1936 **I Can't Get Started** [page 59]
1937 **They Can't Take That Away from Me** [page 176]
1946 **Good-bye to All That** [page 45]
1946 **There's No Holding Me** [page 175]
1954 **The Man That Got Away** [page 118]

Adolph Green | lyricist
born: December 2, 1914, Bronx, New York
died: October 23, 2002, New York, New York
1944 **Some Other Time** [page 151]
1954 **Never Never Land** [page 126]
1956 **Just in Time** [page 97]
1956 **The Party's Over** [page 135]
1960 **Make Someone Happy** [page 115]

Oscar Hammerstein 2nd | lyricist
born: July 12, 1895, New York, New York
died: August 23, 1960, Doylestown, Pennsylvania
1927 **Can't Help Lovin' Dat Man** [page 22]
1927 **Ol' Man River** [page 129]
1928 **Lover, Come Back to Me!** [page 110]
1929 **Some Girl Is on His Mind** [page 150]
1929 **Why Was I Born?** [page 193]
1932 **The Song Is You** [page 155]
1934 **Hand in Hand** [page 47]
1937 **The Folks Who Live on the Hill** [page 42]
1939 **All the Things You Are** [page 5]

E. Y. "Yip" Harburg | lyricist
born: April 8, 1898, New York, New York
died: March 5, 1981, Los Angeles, California
1932 **April in Paris** [page 9]
1932 **It's Only a Paper Moon** [page 92]
1932 **Brother, Can You Spare a Dime?** [page 20]
1933 **What Is There to Say?** [page 188]
1939 **Over the Rainbow** [page 133]
1947 **How Are Things in Glocca Morra?** [page 56]
1947 **Old Devil Moon** [page 131]

Lorenz Hart | lyricist
born: May 2, 1895, New York, New York
died: November 22, 1943, New York, New York
1927 **Thou Swell** [page 180]
1928 **You Took Advantage of Me** [page 201]

1929 **A Ship Without a Sail** [page 145]

1929 **With a Song in My Heart** [page 196]

1932 **Isn't It Romantic?** [page 88]

1932 **Lover** [page 109]

1936 **Little Girl Blue** [page 106]

1937 **Have You Met Miss Jones?** [page 49]

1937 **My Funny Valentine** [page 125]

1937 **Where or When** [page 191]

1938 **Spring Is Here** [page 160]

1938 **You Have Cast Your Shadow on the Sea** [page 200]

1940 **It Never Entered My Mind** [page 90]

Gus Kahn | lyricist

born: November 6, 1886, Koblenz, Germany

died: October 8, 1941, Beverly Hills, California

1922 **Carolina in the Morning** [page 24]

1924 **It Had to Be You** [page 89]

1928 **Love Me or Leave Me** [page 107]

1928 **Makin' Whoopee!** [page 116]

Jerome Kern | composer

born: January 27, 1885, New York, New York

died: November 11, 1945, New York, New York

1914 **They Didn't Believe Me** [page 177]

1927 **Can't Help Lovin' Dat Man** [page 22]

1927 **Ol' Man River** [page 129]

1929 **Some Girl Is on His Mind** [page 150]

1929 **Why Was I Born?** [page 193]

1932 **The Song Is You** [page 195]

1933 **Smoke Gets in Your Eyes** [page 148]

1934 **Hand in Hand** [page 47]

1936 **Pick Yourself Up** [page 139]

1936 **The Way You Look Tonight** [page 187]

1937 **The Folks Who Live on the Hill** [page 42]

1939 **All the Things You Are** [page 5]

1942 **I'm Old Fashioned** [page 86]

Ted Koehler | lyricist
born: July 14, 1894, Washington, D.C.
died: January 17, 1973, Santa Monica, California
1930 **Get Happy** [page 44]
1932 **I Gotta Right to Sing the Blues** [page 67]
1932 **I've Got the World on a String** [page 95]
1933 **Stormy Weather** [page 163]
1934 **As Long as I Live** [page 10]
1934 **Ill Wind (You're Blowin' Me No Good)** [page 81]
1941 **When the Sun Comes Out** [page 190]

Burton Lane | composer
born: February 2, 1912, New York, New York
died: January 5, 1997, New York, New York
1933 **Everything I Have Is Yours** [page 38]
1941 **How About You?** [page 55]
1947 **How Are Things in Glocca Morra?** [page 56]
1947 **Old Devil Moon** [page 131]
1950 **Too Late Now** [page 183]
1951 **You're All the World to Me** [page 202]

John Latouche | lyricist
born: November 13, 1914, Baltimore, Maryland
died: August 7, 1956, Calais, Vermont
1940 **Love Turned the Light Out** [page 108]
1940 **Taking a Chance on Love** [page 170]
1954 **It's the Going Home Together** [page 93]
1954 **Lazy Afternoon** [page 100]
1955 **I've Always Loved You** [page 94]

Alan Jay Lerner | lyricist
born: August 31, 1918, New York, New York
died: June 14, 1986, New York, New York
1947 **The Heather on the Hill** [page 51]
1947 **There But for You Go I** [page 174]
1948 **Here I'll Stay** [page 52]
1950 **Too Late Now** [page 183]
1951 **Another Autumn** [page 8]
1951 **You're All the World to Me** [page 202]

Hugh Martin | composer/lyricist
born: August 11, 1914, Birmingham, Alabama
died: March 11, 2001, Encinitas, California
1941 **Ev'ry Time** [page 39]
1944 **The Boy Next Door** [page 19]
1944 **Have Yourself a Merry Little Christmas** [page 50]
1960 **You Are for Loving** [page 198]

Johnny Mercer | lyricist
born: November 18, 1909, Savannah, Georgia
died: June 25, 1976, Hollywood, California
1936 **I'm an Old Cowhand (From the Rio Grande)** [page 83]
1937 **Too Marvelous for Words** [page 184]
1938 **Jeepers Creepers** [page 96]
1939 **Day In—Day Out** [page 34]
1939 **I Thought About You** [page 76]
1941 **Blues in the Night (My Mama Done Tol' Me)** [page 16]
1941 **This Time the Dream's on Me** [page 179]
1942 **I Remember You** [page 74]
1942 **I'm Old Fashioned** [page 86]
1942 **Not Mine** [page 128]
1942 **Skylark** [page 146]
1942 **That Old Black Magic** [page 176]
1943 **One for My Baby (And One More for the Road)** [page 132]
1944 **Ac-cent-tchu-ate the Positive** [page 1]
1945 **Laura** [page 99]
1946 **Come Rain or Come Shine** [page 28]
1946 **I Wonder What Became of Me** [page 79]
1952 **Early Autumn** [page 36]
1955 **Something's Gotta Give** [page 154]
1960 **Satin Doll** [page 142]

Cole Porter | composer/lyricist
born: June 9, 1891, Peru, Indiana
died: October 15, 1964, Santa Monica, California
1928 **Let's Do It (Let's Fall in Love)** [page 103]
1932 **Night and Day** [page 127]
1934 **I Get a Kick Out of You** [page 64]
1948 **So in Love** [page 149]

Richard Rodgers | composer
born: June 28, 1902, New York, New York
died: December 30, 1979, New York, New York
1927 **Thou Swell** [page 180]
1928 **You Took Advantage of Me** [page 201]
1929 **A Ship Without a Sail** [page 145]
1929 **With a Song in My Heart** [page 196]
1932 **Isn't It Romantic?** [page 88]
1932 **Lover** [page 109]
1936 **Little Girl Blue** [page 106]
1937 **Have You Met Miss Jones?** [page 49]
1937 **My Funny Valentine** [page 125]
1937 **Where or When** [page 191]
1938 **Spring Is Here** [page 160]
1938 **You Have Cast Your Shadow on the Sea** [page 200]
1940 **It Never Entered My Mind** [page 90]

Billy Rose | lyricist
born: September 6, 1899, New York, New York
died: February 10, 1966, New York, New York
1929 **More Than You Know** [page 193]
1929 **Without a Song** [page 197]
1930 **Overnight** [page 134]
1931 **I Found a Million Dollar Baby (in a Five and Ten Cent Store)** [page 63]
1932 **It's Only a Paper Moon** [page 92]

Arthur Schwartz | composer
born: November 25, 1900, Brooklyn, New York
died: September 3, 1984, Kintnersville, Pennsylvania
1929 **I Guess I'll Have to Change My Plan (The Blue Pajama Song)** [page 68]
1930 **Something to Remember You By** [page 153]
1931 **Dancing in the Dark** [page 31]
1932 **Alone Together** [page 7]
1937 **I See Your Face Before Me** [page 75]
1946 **Good-bye to All That** [page 45]
1946 **There's No Holding Me** [page 175]
1961 **Magic Moment** [page 114]

Jule Styne | composer
born: December 31, 1905, London, England
died: September 20, 1994, New York, New York
1942 **I Don't Want to Walk Without You** [page 62]
1954 **Never Never Land** [page 126]
1956 **Just in Time** [page 97]
1956 **The Party's Over** [page 135]
1960 **Make Someone Happy** [page 115]

Jimmy Van Heusen | composer
born: January 26, 1913, Syracuse, New York
died: February 6, 1990, Rancho Mirage, California
1939 **Darn That Dream** [page 32]
1939 **I Thought About You** [page 76]
1944 **Swinging on a Star** [page 168]
1946 **Personality** [page 138]
1953 **Here's That Rainy Day** [page 53]

Harry Warren | composer
born: December 24, 1893, Brooklyn, New York
died: September 22, 1981, Los Angeles, California
1931 **I Found a Million Dollar Baby (in a Five and Ten Cent Store)**
[page 63]
1934 **I Only Have Eyes for You** [page 73]
1935 **Lullaby of Broadway** [page 111]
1938 **Jeepers Creepers** [page 96]

Kurt Weill | composer
born: March 2, 1900, Dessau, Germany
died: April 3, 1950, New York, New York
1938 **September Song** [page 144]
1943 **Speak Low** [page 158]
1948 **Here I'll Stay** [page 52]
1955 **Mack the Knife** [page 112]

Vincent Youmans | composer
born: September 27, 1898, New York, New York
died: April 5, 1946, Denver, Colorado

1924 **Tea for Two** [page 171]
1929 **Keepin' Myself for You** [page 98]
1929 **More Than You Know** [page 193]
1929 **Without a Song** [page 197]
1930 **Time on My Hands (You in My Arms)** [page 182]
1932 **I Want to Be with You** [page 77]

and also featuring . . .

Lee Adams | lyricist
born: August 14, 1924, Mansfield, Ohio
1960 **Put on a Happy Face** [page 140]
1964 **Lorna's Here** [page 107]

Harold Adamson | lyricist
born: December 10, 1906, Greenville, New Jersey
died: August 17, 1980, Beverly Hills, California
1930 **Time on My Hands (You in My Arms)** [page 182]
1931 **Sentimental Rhapsody** [page 143]
1933 **Everything I Have Is Yours** [page 38]
1948 **It's a Most Unusual Day** [page 91]

Milton Ager | composer
born: October 6, 1893, Chicago, Illinois
died: May 6, 1979, Los Angeles, California
1929 **Happy Days Are Here Again** [page 48]

Louis Alter | composer
born: June 18, 1902, Haverhill, Massachusetts
died: November 5, 1980, New York, New York
1930 **Overnight** [page 134]

Maxwell Anderson | lyricist
born: December 15, 1888, Atlantic, Pennsylvania
died: February 28, 1959, Stamford, Connecticut
1938 **September Song** [page 144]

Sidney Arodin | composer
born: March 29, 1901, Westwego, Louisiana
died: February 6, 1948, New Orleans, Louisiana
1931 **Lazy River** [page 100]

Ben Bernie | composer
born: May 30, 1891, Bayonne, New Jersey
died: October 20, 1943, Beverly Hills, California
1925 **Sweet Georgia Brown** [page 166]

Leonard Bernstein | composer
born: August 25, 1918, Lawrence, Massachusetts
died: October 14, 1990, New York, New York
1944 **Some Other Time** [page 151]

Ralph Blane | composer/lyricist
born: July 26, 1914, Broken Arrow, Oklahoma
died: November 13, 1995, Broken Arrow, Oklahoma
1941 **Ev'ry Time** [page 39]
1944 **The Boy Next Door** [page 19]
1944 **Have Yourself a Merry Little Christmas** [page 50]
1960 **You Are for Loving** [page 198]

Marc Blitzstein | lyricist
born: March 2, 1905, Philadelphia, Pennsylvania
died: January 22, 1964, Martinique, West Indies
1955 **Mack the Knife** [page 112]

Rube Bloom | composer
born: April 24, 1902, New York, New York
died: March 30, 1976, New York, New York
1939 **Day In—Day Out** [page 34]

Jerry Bock | composer
born: November 23, 1928, New Haven, Connecticut
died: November 3, 2010, Mount Kisco, New York
1959 **When Did I Fall in Love** [page 189]

Brooks Bowman | composer/lyricist
born: October 21, 1913, Cleveland, Ohio
died: October 17, 1937, Garrison, New York
1934 **East of the Sun (West of the Moon)** [page 37]

Elisse Boyd | lyricist
born: 1910
died: March 10, 1979, New York, New York
1952 **Guess Who I Saw Today** [page 46]

Bert Brecht | lyricist
born: February 19, 1898, Augsburg, Bavaria
died: August 14, 1956, East Berlin, East Germany
1955 **Mack the Knife** [page 112]

Harry Brooks | composer
born: September 29, 1895, Homestead, Pennsylvania
died: June 22, 1970, Teaneck, New Jersey
1929 **Ain't Misbehavin'** [page 3]

Les Brown | composer
born: March 14, 1912, Reinerton, Pennsylvania
died: January 4, 2001, Pacific Palisades, California
1944 **Sentimental Journey** [page 143]

Lew Brown | lyricist
born: December 10, 1893, Odessa, Ukraine
died: February 5, 1958, New York, New York
1926 **The Birth of the Blues** [page 14]
1927 **The Varsity Drag** [page 186]
1933 **Let's Call It a Day** [page 102]

Walter Bullock | lyricist
born: May 6, 1907, Shelburn, Indiana
died: August 19, 1953, Los Angeles, California
1950 **Blue Day** [page 15]

Ralph Burns | composer
born: June 29, 1922, Newton, Massachusetts
died: November 21, 2001, Los Angeles, California
1952 **Early Autumn** [page 36]

Irving Caesar | lyricist
born: July 4, 1895, New York, New York
died: December 18, 1996, New York, New York
1919 **Swanee** [page 165]
1924 **Tea for Two** [page 172]
1928 **Crazy Rhythm** [page 30]

Truman Capote | lyricist
born: September 30, 1924, New Orleans, Louisiana
died: August 25, 1984, Los Angeles, California
1954 **A Sleepin' Bee** [page 147]

Kenneth Casey | lyricist
born: January 10, 1899, New York, New York
died: August 10, 1965, Cornwall, Connecticut
1925 **Sweet Georgia Brown** [page 166]

Morris "Moose" Charlap | composer
born: December 19, 1928, Philadelphia, Pennsylvania
died: July 8, 1974, New York, New York
1960 **Past the Age of Innocence** [page 136]

Sidney Clare | lyricist
born: August 15, 1892, New York, New York
died: August 29, 1972, Los Angeles, California
1929 **Keepin' Myself for You** [page 98]

Cy Coleman | composer
born: June 14, 1929, Bronx, New York
died: November 4, 2004, New York, New York
1957 **Witchcraft** [page 195]
1959 **The Best Is Yet to Come** [page 13]

Con Conrad | composer
born: June 18, 1891, New York, New York
died: September 18, 1938, Van Nuys, California
1934 **The Continental** [page 29]

Henry Creamer | lyricist
born: June 21, 1879, Richmond, Virginia
died: October 13, 1930, New York, New York
1918 **After You've Gone** [page 2]

Eddie de Lange | lyricist
born: January 15, 1904, Long Island City, New York
died: July 15, 1949, Los Angeles, California
1934 **Moonglow** [page 122]
1939 **Darn That Dream** [page 32]

B. G. "Buddy" DeSylva | lyricist
born: January 27, 1895, New York, New York
died: July 11, 1950, Los Angeles, California
1926 **The Birth of the Blues** [page 14]
1927 **The Varsity Drag** [page 186]
1932 **I Want to Be with You** [page 77]

Mort Dixon | lyricist
born: March 20, 1892, New York, New York
died: March 23, 1956, Bronxville, New York
1931 **I Found a Million Dollar Baby (in a Five and Ten Cent Store)**
[page 63]

Walter Donaldson | composer
born: February 15, 1893, Brooklyn, New York
died: July 15, 1947, Santa Monica, California
1922 **Carolina in the Morning** [page 24]
1927 **My Blue Heaven** [page 124]
1928 **Love Me or Leave Me** [page 107]
1928 **Makin' Whoopee!** [page 116]

THE GREAT AMERICAN SONGBOOK

Al Dubin | lyricist
born: June 10, 1891, Zurich, Switzerland
died: February 11, 1945, New York, New York
1934 **I Only Have Eyes for You** [page 73]
1935 **Lullaby of Broadway** [page 111]

Edward Eliscu | lyricist
born: April 2, 1902, New York, New York
died: June 18, 1998, Newtown, Connecticut
1929 **More Than You Know** [page 123]
1929 **Without a Song** [page 197]

Abraham Ellstein | composer
born: July 7, 1907, New York, New York
died: March 22, 1963, New York, New York
1950 **Blue Day** [page 15]

Frank Eyton | lyricist
born: August 30, 1894, London, England
died: November 11, 1962, London, England
1930 **Body and Soul** [page 17]

Ted Fetter | lyricist
born: June 10, 1910, Ithaca, New York
died: March 13, 1996, New York, New York
1940 **Taking a Chance on Love** [page 170]

Fred Fisher | composer/lyricist
born: September 30, 1875, Cologne, Germany
died: January 14, 1942, New York, New York
1922 **Chicago (That Toddling Town)** [page 27]

Ralph Freed | lyricist
born: May 1, 1907, Vancouver, British Columbia, Canada
died: February 13, 1973, Los Angeles, California
1941 **How About You?** [page 55]

Errol Garner | composer
born: June 15, 1921, Pittsburgh, Pennsylvania
died: January 2, 1977, Los Angeles, California
1955 **Misty** [page 121]

Don George | lyricist
born: August 27, 1909, New York, New York
died: June 27, 1987, New York, New York
1944 **I'm Beginning to See the Light** [page 84]

Norman Gimbel | lyricist
born: November 16, 1927, Brooklyn, New York
died: December 19, 2018, Montecito, California
1960 **Past the Age of Innocence** [page 136]

Mack Gordon | lyricist
born: June 21, 1904, Warsaw, Poland
died: February 28, 1959, New York, New York
1930 **Time on My Hands (You in My Arms)** [page 182]

Jay Gorney | composer
born: December 12, 1896, Bialystok, Russia
died: June 14, 1990, New York, New York
1932 **Brother, Can You Spare a Dime?** [page 20]

Stuart Gorrell | lyricist
born: September 17, 1901, Knox, Indiana
died: August 10, 1963, Ridgewood, New Jersey
1930 **Georgia on My Mind** [page 43]

(Irvin) Robert Graham | composer
born: September 18, 1909, Philadelphia, Pennsylvania
died: December 1, 2001, Englewood, New Jersey
1936 **You Better Go Now** [page 199]

Murray Grand | composer
born: August 27, 1919, Philadelphia, Pennsylvania
died: March 7, 2007, Santa Monica, California
1952 **Guess Who I Saw Today** [page 46]

Bud Green | lyricist
born: November 19, 1897, Austria
died: January 2, 1981, Yonkers, New York
1944 **Sentimental Journey** [page 143]

John W. "Johnny" Green | composer
born: October 10, 1908, New York, New York
died: May 15, 1989, Beverly Hills, California
1930 **Body and Soul** [page 17]
1933 **I Cover the Waterfront** [page 61]

Nancy Hamilton | lyricist
born: July 27, 1908, Sewickley, Pennsylvania
died: February 18, 1985, New York, New York
1940 **How High the Moon** [page 57]

W. C. Handy | composer/lyricist
born: November 16, 1873, Florence, Alabama
died: March 28, 1958, New York, New York
1914 **St. Louis Blues** [page 161]

James F. Hanley | composer/lyricist
born: February 17, 1892, Rensselaer, Indiana
died: February 8, 1942, Douglaston, New York
1934 **Zing! Went the Strings of My Heart** [page 203]

Otto Harbach | lyricist
born: August 18, 1873, Salt Lake City, Utah
died: January 24, 1963, New York, New York
1933 **Smoke Gets in Your Eyes** [page 148]

Leigh Harline | composer
born: March 26, 1907, Salt Lake City, Utah
died: December 10, 1969, Long Beach, California
1940 **When You Wish Upon a Star** [page 190]

Sheldon Harnick | lyricist
born: April 30, 1924, Chicago, Illinois
1959 **When Did I Fall in Love?** [page 189]

Ray Henderson | composer
born: December 1, 1896, Buffalo, New York
died: December 31, 1970, Greenwich, Connecticut
1926 **The Birth of the Blues** [page 14]
1927 **The Varsity Drag** [page 186]
1933 **Let's Call It a Day** [page 102]

Woody Herman | composer
born: May 16, 1913, Milwaukee, Wisconsin
died: October 29, 1987, West Hollywood, California
1952 **Early Autumn** [page 36]

Edward Heyman | lyricist
born: March 14, 1907, New York, New York
died: October 16, 1981, Jalisco, Mexico
1930 **Body and Soul** [page 17]
1933 **I Cover the Waterfront** [page 61]

DuBose Heywood | lyricist
born: August 31, 1885, Charleston, South Carolina
died: June 16, 1940, Tryon, North Carolina
1935 **Summertime** [page 164]

Johnny Hodges | composer
born: July 25, 1907, Cambridge, Massachusetts
died: May 11, 1970, New York, New York
1944 **I'm Beginning to See the Light** [page 84]

Ben Homer | composer
born: June 27, 1917, Meriden, Connecticut
died: February 12, 1975, Los Angeles, California
1944 **Sentimental Journey** [page 143]

Arnold B. Horwitt | lyricist
born: July 20, 1918, New York, New York
died: October 19, 1977, Santa Monica, California
1945 **This Is My Beloved** [page 178]

Bart Howard | composer/lyricist
born: June 1, 1915, Burlington, Iowa
died: February 21, 2004, Carmel, New York
1954 **Fly Me to the Moon (In Other Words)** [page 41]

Will Hudson | composer
born: March 8, 1908, Grimsby, Ontario, Canada
died: July 16, 1981, Isle of Palms, South Carolina
1934 **Moonglow** [page 122]

Harry James | composer
born: March 15, 1916, Albany, Georgia
died: July 5, 1983, Las Vegas, Nevada
1944 **I'm Beginning to See the Light** [page 84]

Paul James (James P. Warburg) | lyricist
born: August 18, 1896, Hamburg, Germany
died: June 3, 1969, Greenwich, Connecticut
1929 **Can't We Be Friends?** [page 23]
1930 **Can This Be Love?** [page 21]

James P. (Jimmy) Johnson | composer
born: February 1, 1894, New Brunswick, New Jersey
died: November 17, 1955, Jamaica, New York
1923 **Charleston** [page 25]

Arthur Johnston | composer
born: January 10, 1898, New York, New York
died: May 1, 1954, Corona del Mar, California
1936 **Pennies from Heaven** [page 137]

Isham Jones | composer
born: January 31, 1894, Coalton, Ohio
died: October 19, 1956, Hollywood, California
1924 **It Had to Be You** [page 89]

Tom Jones | lyricist
born: February 17, 1928, Littlefield, Texas
1960 **Soon It's Gonna Rain** [page 156]
1960 **Try to Remember** [page 185]

Roger Wolfe Kahn | composer
born: October 19, 1907, Morristown, New Jersey
died: July 12, 1962, New York, New York
1928 **Crazy Rhythm** [page 30]

Charlotte Kent | lyricist
born: February 7, 1907, New York, New York
died: (after 1957)
1930 **Overnight** [page 134]

Fran Landesman | lyricist
born: October 21, 1927, New York, New York
died: July 23, 2011, London, England
1955 **Spring Can Really Hang You Up the Most** [page 159]
1959 **The Ballad of the Sad Young Men** [page 12]

J. Turner Layton | composer
born: July 2, 1894, Washington, D.C.
died: February 6, 1978, London, England
1918 **After You've Gone** [page 2]

Carolyn Leigh | lyricist
born: August 21, 1926, Bronx, New York
died: November 19, 1983, New York, New York
1957 **Witchcraft** [page 195]
1959 **The Best Is Yet to Come** [page 13]

Michael Leonard | composer
born: August 16, 1931, Rockville Centre, New York
died: October 31, 2015, New York, New York
1965 **I'm All Smiles** [page 82]
1965 **Why Did I Choose You?** [page 192]

Ira Levin | lyricist
born: August 27, 1929, New York, New York
died: November 12, 2007, New York, New York
1965 **Let's Go** [page 105]

Morgan Lewis | composer
born: December 26, 1906, Rockville, Connecticut
died: December 8, 1968, New York, New York
1940 **How High the Moon** [page 57]

James Lipton | lyricist
born: September 19, 1926, Detroit, Michigan
died: March 2, 2020, New York, New York
1967 **Maybe It's Time for Me** [page 119]

Frank Loesser | lyricist/composer
born: June 29, 1910, New York, New York
died: July 28, 1969, New York, New York
1942 **I Don't Want to Walk Without You** [page 62]
1947 **I Wish I Didn't Love You So** [page 78]

Frederick Loewe | composer
born: June 10, 1901, Berlin, Germany
died: February 14, 1988, Palm Springs, California
1947 **The Heather on the Hill** [page 51]
1947 **There But for You Go I** [page 174]
1951 **Another Autumn** [page 8]

Cecil Mack | lyricist
born: November 6, 1873, Portsmouth, Virginia
died: August 1, 1944, New York, New York
1923 **Charleston** [page 25]

Herb Magidson | lyricist
born: January 7, 1906, Braddock, Pennsylvania
died: January 2, 1986, Beverly Hills, California
1934 **The Continental** [page 29]

Gerald Marks | composer/lyricist
born: October 13, 1900, Saginaw, Michigan
died: January 27, 1997, New York, New York
1931 **All of Me** [page 4]

Herbert Martin | lyricist
born: July 28, 1926, Stamford, Connecticut
died: September 27, 2019, Englewood, New Jersey
1965 **I'm All Smiles** [page 82]
1965 **Why Did I Choose You?** [page 192]

James "Jimmy" McHugh | composer
born: July 10, 1894, Boston, Massachusetts
died: May 23, 1969, Beverly Hills, California
1928 **I Can't Give You Anything but Love** [page 60]
1935 **I'm in the Mood for Love** [page 85]
1948 **It's a Most Unusual Day** [page 91]

Joseph Meyer | composer
born: March 12, 1894, Modesto, California
died: June 22, 1987, New York, New York
1928 **Crazy Rhythm** [page 30]

Irving Mills | lyricist
born: January 16, 1894, New York, New York
died: April 21, 1985, Palm Springs, California
1933 **Sophisticated Lady** [page 157]
1934 **Moonglow** [page 122]

Jerome Moross | composer
born: August 1, 1913, Brooklyn, New York
died: July 25, 1983, Miami, Florida
1954 **It's the Going Home Together** [page 93]
1954 **Lazy Afternoon** [page 100]

James Mundy | composer
born: June 28, 1907, Cincinnati, Ohio
died: April 24, 1938, New York, New York
1955 **I've Always Loved You** [page 94]

J. P. (John) Murray | lyricist
born: October 11, 1906, New York, New York
died: June 17, 1984, Connecticut
1933 **If I Love Again** [page 80]

Ogden Nash | lyricist
born: August 19, 1902, Rye, New York
died: May 19, 1971, Baltimore, Maryland
1943 **Speak Low** [page 158]
1957 **Born Too Late** [page 18]

Alfred Newman | composer
born: March 17, 1900, New Haven, Connecticut
died: February 17, 1970, Hollywood, California
1931 **Sentimental Rhapsody** [page 143]

Ben Oakland | composer
born: September 24, 1907, Brooklyn, New York
died: August 26, 1979, Hollywood, California
1933 **If I Love Again** [page 80]

Mitchell Parish | lyricist
born: July 19, 1900, Lithuania, Russia
died: March 31, 1993, New York, New York
1929 **Star Dust** [page 162]
1933 **Sophisticated Lady** [page 157]

Maceo Pinkard | composer
born: June 27, 1897, Bluefield, West Virginia
died: July 21, 1962, New York, New York
1925 **Sweet Georgia Brown** [page 166]

Ralph Rainger | composer
born: October 7, 1901, New York, New York
died: October 23, 1942, Palm Springs, California
1937 **Thanks for the Memory** [page 172]

David Raksin | composer
born: August 4, 1912, Philadelphia, Pennsylvania
died: August 9, 2004, Los Angeles, California
1945 **Laura** [page 99]

Andy Razaf | lyricist
born: December 16, 1895, Washington, D.C.
died: February 3, 1973, North Hollywood, California
1929 **Ain't Misbehavin'** [page 3]
1929 **Honeysuckle Rose** [page 54]

Bickley Reichner | lyricist
born: June 4, 1905, Philadelphia, Pennsylvania
died: April 9, 1989, Philadelphia, Pennsylvania
1936 **You Better Go Now** [page 199]

Harry Revel | composer
born: December 21, 1905, London, England
died: November 3, 1958, New York, New York
1945 **This Is My Beloved** [page 178]

Herbert Reynolds (M. E. Rourke) | lyricist
born: August 14, 1867, Manchester, England
died: August 26, 1933, New York
1914 **They Didn't Believe Me** [page 177]

Leo Robin | lyricist
born: April 6, 1900, Pittsburgh, Pennsylvania
died: December 29, 1984, Los Angeles, California
1937 **Thanks for the Memory** [page 172]

Ann Ronell | composer/lyricist
born: December 25, 1905, Omaha, Nebraska
died: December 25, 1993, New York, New York
1932 **Willow Weep for Me** [page 194]

Laurence Rosenthal | composer
born: November 4, 1926, Detroit, Michigan
1967 **Maybe It's Time for Me** [page 119]

Harry Ruskin | lyricist
born: November 30, 1894, Cincinnati, Ohio
died: November 16, 1969, Burbank, California
1929 **I May Be Wrong But I Think You're Wonderful!** [page 72]

Bob Russell | lyricist
born: April 25, 1914, Passaic, New Jersey
died: February 18, 1970, Beverly Hills, California
1942 **Don't Get Around Much Anymore** [page 35]

Milton Schafer | composer
born: September 24, 1920
died: April 12, 2020
1965 **Let's Go** [page 105]

Victor Schertzinger | composer
born: April 8, 1888, Mahanoy City, Pennsylvania
died: October 26, 1941, Hollywood, California
1942 **I Remember You** [page 74]
1942 **Not Mine** [page 128]

Harvey Schmidt | composer
born: September 12, 1929, Dallas, Texas
died: February 28, 2018, Tomball, Texas
1960 **Soon It's Gonna Rain** [page 156]
1960 **Try to Remember** [page 185]

Seymour Simons | composer/lyricist
born: January 14, 1896, Detroit, Michigan
died: February 12, 1949, Detroit, Michigan
1931 **All of Me** [page 4]

Robert Sour | lyricist
born: October 31, 1905, New York, New York
died: March 6, 1985, New York, New York
1930 **Body and Soul** [page 17]

Billy Strayhorn | composer/lyricist
born: November 29, 1915, Dayton, Ohio
died: May 31, 1967, New York, New York
1960 **Satin Doll** [page 142]

Charles Strouse | composer
born: June 7, 1928, New York, New York
1960 **Put on a Happy Face** [page 140]
1964 **Lorna's Here** [page 107]

Henry Sullivan | composer
born: December 7, 1895, Worcester, Massachusetts
died: December 1, 1975, New York, New York
1929 **I May Be Wrong But I Think You're Wonderful!** [page 72]

Kay Swift | composer
born: April 19, 1897, New York, New York
died: January 28, 1993, Southington, Connecticut
1929 **Can't We Be Friends?** [page 23]
1930 **Can This Be Love?** [page 21]

Thomas "Fats" Waller | composer
born May 21, 1904, New York, New York
died December 15, 1943, Kansas City, Kansas
1929 **Ain't Misbehavin'** [page 3]
1929 **Honeysuckle Rose** [page 54]

Ned Washington | lyricist
born: August 15, 1901, Scranton, Pennsylvania
died: December 20, 1974, Beverly Hills, California
1940 **The Nearness of You** [page 126]
1940 **When You Wish Upon a Star** [page 190]

George Whiting | lyricist
born: August 16, 1884, Chicago, Illinois
died: December 13, 1943, New York, New York
1927 **My Blue Heaven** [page 124]

Richard A. Whiting | composer
born: November 12, 1891, Peoria, Illinois
died: February 19, 1938, Beverly Hills, California
1937 **Too Marvelous for Words** [page 184]

Tommy Wolf | composer
born: 1925, St. Louis, Missouri
died: January 9, 1979
1955 **Spring Can Really Hang You Up the Most** [page 159]
1959 **The Ballad of the Sad Young Men** [page 12]

Jack Yellen | lyricist
born: July 6, 1892, Raczki, Poland
died: April 17, 1991 Concord, New York
1929 **Happy Days Are Here Again** [page 48]

ACKNOWLEDGMENTS

It is most obvious and most proper to say, first and foremost, that this book could not and would not exist without the songwriters. The iconic ones are renowned, deservedly so. Others are, at this point in time, all but forgotten or in some cases virtually untraceable. But if music be the food of love, the song's the thing—which Shakespeare didn't quite say but *I* did. I give thanks to the songwriters: my aim, in an attempt to recompense them for the years of enjoyment their labors have provided, is to help spread their songs around. Composers and lyricists—and at this writing all but a sparse handful of those included are no longer with us—need only listeners to remain alive: today, tomorrow, and always. That sounds like it should be a song title, or maybe it already is.

Being more of a writer with a keen interest in music than a keen musician with a facility for writing, I recognized the advisability of having someone with a strong and practical music background peering over my shoulder. I wound up with three. The perfect person for the job was Bruce Pomahac, the recently retired longtime director of music at the Rodgers & Hammerstein Organization and one of those unsung people who keep the music of Broadway sounding like Broadway music. Bruce enthusiastically embraced the challenge, devouring my initial song discussions and offering insight, observations, and even a few corrections. We had barely begun when he called from Michigan to inform me that I mustn't rely on him to complete the project; he had suddenly been diagnosed with terminal pancreatic cancer. Typically for Bruce, the call was not to commiserate on his condition but, rather, to *apologize* for his inability to continue offering guidance. We did manage to get through a portion of the unfinished manuscript before he quickly, and peacefully, succumbed.

By that point I had already begun—at Bruce's urging—to work with Michael H. Lavine, a music director/vocal coach/sheet music archivist with as protean a knowledge of popular and theatre music as just about anyone. Michael combed through my song descriptions, refining hazy analysis, questioning certain statements, and pointing out his own observations from coaching countless professional singers through many of these songs. He also urged me not to overlook certain titles that, in retrospect, immediately claimed their place. His contributions have been of enormous value and are most sincerely appreciated.

Another musical Michael—conductor/pianist Michael Gildin—also joined us, illustrating and enhancing the discussions of rhythmic patterns within the songs by devising what we believe is a clear and easily comprehensible form of rhythmic notation. At the same time, he offered valuable insights. Between Michael, Michael, and Bruce, the discussions in this book are far clearer than they would otherwise have been. I am exceedingly grateful, and I expect readers will appreciate the resulting clarity.

Following many years of random music gathering, I was able to pull copies of most of the songs in this book from my own shelves. My concentration has always been on playing copies, many of which are inevitably worn, tattered, and occasionally marred by the scribbling of prior owners. Most fortunately, Michael Lavine possesses a monumental collection of sheet music. After collating all the "clean" cover images Michael and I could find, he referred me to Harold Jacobs, a West Coast collector with a similarly extensive collection. Michael (with whom I was already working) and Harold (whom I had never met) both generously and patiently dug through shelves and files and cartons, eagerly supplying just about all I sought. I offer special gratitude to both of them for these many images, which I trust have enhanced your enjoyment.

Information, advice, and varied support came from Larry Blank, Ted Chapin, Jack Viertel, William Rosenfield, Norm Hirschy, Ken Bloom, Michael Feinstein, and others. In our specialized field of endeavor, it seems, everyone is eager to share information and seek out the next discovery. Mark Eden Horowitz, whose official title at the Music Division of the Library of Congress is senior music specialist, is a valuable resource to anyone researching just about anything in the field and a good friend to many of us as well. No lost score is hidden too deep, no enigmatic mystery is too convoluted for Mark to find the solution or at least propose where to search next.

I have also learned, over the course of time, that a book manuscript is merely a stack of pages (or e-pages) without a publisher to transform it into a book (or e-book). I express my appreciation to and Chris Chappell and John Cerullo at Backbeat Books/Rowman & Littlefield, along with Barbara Claire, Laurel Myers, Ashleigh Cooke, and the rest of their excellent and accommodating staff.

Special thanks go to the estimable John Pizzarelli, not just for his breezily bright foreword but for his astounding facility for songs from the *Great American Songbook*. Every rendition is bright and alive, sounding as if he just played a session with Johnny or Cole or Dick and Larry last week. If you haven't seen him perform or heard any of his dozens of recordings, do! Prepare yourself for pure musical enchantment.

My children, Johanna and Charlie, furloughed back home during that pandemic from medical school on the one hand and university on the other, condescended to allow me to continually play these songs within the not-overly-spacious confines of city living. And if I had to struggle through "Body and Soul" many dozens of times before I could manage to tolerably plunk my way from verse to second ending, my devoted wife, Helen, had to *hear* those chords and discords—well, let's just say, too many times with nary a word of complaint or a roll of the eyes. So, I thank her indeed for gracious tolerance of music in the air, night and day.

BIBLIOGRAPHY

Special acknowledgments are in order for two books written almost simultaneously more than fifty years ago. In 1970, no one seems to have considered the notion of a great, or even not-so-great, American songbook—not even the songwriters, many of whom were still very much around (if more or less relegated to the musical sidelines by the incursions of The Beatles and what followed).

Alec Wilder, an esoteric American composer whose work straddled the classical and art song world, thought otherwise and proved his point with what he called *American Popular Song: The Great Innovators 1900–1950*. Wilder covered a broader field than we have settled on, discussing more than seven hundred songs. His discussions are understandably briefer; and his viewpoint is somewhat different than ours can be, in that he was writing about songs created and popularized during his lifetime. (He was also writing about songs far more popular than his own, resulting in an occasional scent of competitiveness.) That said, Wilder's *American Popular Song* more or less created the notion of "The Great American Songbook" and remains indispensable.

Around this same time, a well-connected writer named Max Wilk thought to sit down with some of those old-time songwriters—who were left languishing in their living rooms, collecting royalties but all but invisible to the marketplace— to ask about the creation of their hits from the horse's mouths, as it were. These songwriters, many of whom were already on the far side of sixty, had a lot to say; not always accurately recalled, but just about always colorfully so. Being a show biz insider—Wilk's father, Jacob, had been head of the story department at Warner Bros.—Max had personal access to many of the writers. Once word got out that he had spoken to the likes of Arlen and Ira Gershwin, everyone wanted to sit with him. *They're Playing Our Song: From Jerome Kern to Stephen Sondheim—The Stories Behind the Words and Music of Two Generations* gives us first-person accounts from Rodgers, Berlin, Mercer, Styne, Loesser, and more. Much of what has come along in subsequent biographies and studies is mined from Wilk's endlessly fascinating conversations, which are well worth seeking out.

The prime source for this book, needless to say, is the published sheet music for the 201 songs included (and, for that matter, the thousands that are not included). The days are past when research was done principally from books, magazines, and printed materials. Much information—accurate or not—can be found on the internet. Databases, clippings, and more offer facts (which, for our purposes, we endeavor to double- and triple-check), as do theatre programs and other memorabilia.

Among the most frequently consulted sources for this book are the annual (and, in some cases, semiannual) *Catalog of Copyright Entries* published by the Library of Congress until its procedures changed in 1978. Although these present a maze of contradictions—for many years, for example, the catalogs didn't bother to index contributions by lyricists—these books, now available online, contain many answers. There follows a list of published books I consulted, which, mind you, make interesting reading for those so interested.

Abbott, George. *Mister Abbott*. New York: Random House, 1963.

Asch, Amy. *The Complete Lyrics of Oscar Hammerstein II*. New York: Knopf, 2008.

Bergreen, Laurence. *As Thousands Cheer: The Life of Irving Berlin*. New York: Viking, 1990.

Bloom, Ken. *American Song: The Complete Musical Theatre Companion, Second Edition, 1877–1995*. New York: Schirmer, 1996.

Bordman, Gerald. *Days to Be Happy, Years to Be Sad: The Life and Music of Vincent Youmans*. New York and Oxford: Oxford University Press, 1982.

———. *Jerome Kern: His Life and Music*. New York and Oxford: Oxford University Press, 1980.

Dietz, Howard. *Dancing in the Dark: An Autobiography*. New York: Quadrangle Books, 1974.

Duke, Vernon. *Passport to Paris: An Autobiography*. Boston and Toronto: Little, Brown, 1955.

Feinstein, Michael. *Nice Work If You Can Get It: My Life in Rhythm and Rhyme*. New York: Hyperion, 1995.

Fordin, Hugh. *Getting to Know Him: A Biography of Oscar Hammerstein II.* New York: Random House, 1977.

Friedwald, Will. *Stardust Melodies: A Biography of Twelve of America's Most Popular Songs.* New York: Pantheon, 2002.

Furia, Philip. *Skylark: The Life and Times of Johnny Mercer.* New York: St. Martin's, 2003.

Gershwin, Ira. *Lyrics on Several Occasions.* New York: Knopf, 1959.

Green, Stanley. *Encyclopaedia of the Musical Theatre.* New York: Dodd, Mead, 1976.

———. *Ring Bells! Sing Songs! Broadway Musicals of the 1930s.* New Rochelle, NY: Arlington House, 1971.

Hammerstein, Oscar, II. *Lyrics by Oscar Hammerstein II.* New York: Simon & Schuster, 1949.

Hart, Dorothy, and Robert Kimball. *The Complete Lyrics of Lorenz Hart.* New York: Knopf, 1986.

Jablonski, Edward. *Gershwin: A Biography.* New York: Doubleday, 1988.

———. *Harold Arlen: Rhythm, Rainbows & Blues.* Boston: Northeastern University Press, 1996.

Kimball, Robert. *The Complete Lyrics of Cole Porter.* New York: Knopf, 1983.

———. *The Complete Lyrics of Ira Gershwin.* New York: Knopf, 1993.

Kimball, Robert, Barry Day, Miles Kreuger, and Eric Davis. *The Complete Lyrics of Johnny Mercer.* New York: Knopf, 2001.

Kimball, Robert, and Linda Emmet. *The Complete Lyrics of Irving Berlin.* New York: Knopf, 2010.

Kimball, Robert, and Steve Nelson. *The Complete Lyrics of Frank Loesser.* New York: Knopf, 2003.

Loesser, Susan. *A Most Remarkable Fella: Frank Loesser and the Guys and Dolls in His Life.* New York: Donald I. Fine, 1993.

Meyerson, Harold, and Ernie Harburg. *Who Put the Rainbow in the Wizard of Oz?: Yip Harburg, Lyricist.* Ann Arbor: University of Michigan Press, 1993.

Nolan, Frederick. *Lorenz Hart: A Poet on Broadway.* New York and Oxford: Oxford University Press, 1994.

Pollack, Howard. *The Ballad of John Latouche: An American Lyricist's Life and Work.* New York: Oxford University Press, 2017.

———. *Marc Blitzstein: His Life, His Work, His World.* New York and Oxford: Oxford University Press, 2012.

Rimler, Walter. *The Man That Got Away: The Life and Songs of Harold Arlen.* Urbana, Chicago, and Springfield: University of Illinois Press, 2015.

Rodgers, Richard. *Musical Stages: An Autobiography*. New York: Random House, 1975.

Sanders, Ronald. *The Days Grow Short: The Life and Music of Kurt Weill*. New York: Holt, Rinehart and Winston, 1980.

Schwartz, Charles. *Cole Porter: A Biography*. New York: Dial, 1977.

Sheed, Wilfrid. *The House That George Built: With a Little Help from Irving, Cole, and a Crew of Fifty*. New York: Random House, 2007.

Shipton, Alyn. *I Feel a Song Coming On: The Life of Jimmy McHugh*. Urbana and Chicago: University of Illinois Press, 2009.

Stubblebine, Donald J. *Broadway Sheet Music*. Jefferson, NC: McFarland, 1996.

Sudhalter, Richard M. *Stardust Melody: The Life and Music of Hoagy Carmichael*. Oxford and New York: Oxford University Press, 2002.

Taylor, Theodore. *Jule: The Story of Composer Jule Styne*. New York: Random House, 1979.

Wilder, Alec. *American Popular Song: The Great Innovators 1900–1950*. New York: Oxford University Press, 1972.

Wilk, Max. *They're Playing Our Song: From Jerome Kern to Stephen Sondheim—The Stories Behind the Words and Music of Two Generations*. New York: Atheneum, 1973.

INDEX

Songs with separate entries in this book; the discussions of those songs; and songwriter listings are denoted in **boldface**.

Aarons, Alex A., 30

Abbott, George, 39, 92, 170

Abrahams, Maurice, 4

"Ac-cent-tchua-ate the Positive," **1-2**, 80

Adams, Lee, 107, 140, **215**

Adamson, Harold, 38, 91, 134, 143–44, 182, 202, **215**

"After You've Gone," **2-3**

Ager, Milton, 47, **215**

"Ain't Misbehavin'," **3-4**, 54

"Ain't She Sweet," 48

"Ain't We Got Fun?," 89

"Alexander's Ragtime Band," 71, 141

"All of Me," **4**

"All the Things You Are," xv, xix, **5-6**, 86, 149

"Alone Together," **7**, 75

Alter, Louis, 134, **215**

"Always," 141

American in Paris, An, 61

Americana, 20, 81

"And This Is My Beloved," 179

Anderson, Maxwell, 144–45, **215**

Annie, 107

"Another Autumn," **8**

Anything Goes, 15, 54, 64

"April in Paris," **9**, 11, 92

"April Showers," 77

Arden, Eve, 59

Are You with It?, 178–79

Arlen, Anya, 29, 69

Arlen, Harold, xv, xxii, 1–2, 10, 11, 16–17, 19, 28–29, 32, 44, 45, 59, 69, 74, 76, 78, 79, 81, 86, 92–93, 95–96, 118–19, 132, 133–34, 146, 147–48, 163–64, 172, 173–73, 179–80, 188, 190, **205-06**

Arlen, Jerry, 16, 32

Armstrong, Louis, 33, 96

Arodin, Sidney, 100–01, **216**

"Arthur Murray Taught Me Dancing in a Hurry," 74

"As Long as I Live," **10**

Astaire, Adele, 58, 117, 182

Astaire, Fred, 26, 29–30, 37, 38, 42, 58, 86, 101, 104, 117, 127–28, 139, 154–55, 182, 183, 202

Atkinson, Brooks, 21, 92, 203
Austin, Gene, 124
"Autumn in New York," 11, 203

Babes in Arms, 55, 125, 191
Babes on Broadway, 55
Bacall, Lauren, 120
Baker, Belle, 4
Balanchine, George, 170
"Ballad of the Sad Young Men, The,"
   12, 159
Ballard, Kaye, 41
Ballets Russes, 9
"Baltimore Oriole," 120
Band Wagon, The, 7, 31, 45
"Barney Google," 29
Barrie, J. M., 127
Bayes, Nora, 134
Beggar's Holiday, 94
Bells Are Ringing, 97, 135
Bennett, Robert Russell, 80, 130
Berigan, Bunny, 59
Berlin, Irving, 4, 26, 29, 37, 39, 46, 47,
   70, 71, 77, 78, 101, 104, 111, 112,
   137, 141–42, 166, 180, 187, 194,
   205
Bernie, Ben, 166–67, **216**
Best Foot Forward, 39, 198
"Best Is Yet to Come, The," 13
"Best Things in Life Are Free, The," 14,
   186
Between the Devil, 75
Big Broadcast of 1938, The, 172
Big Country, The, 93
"Bill," 193
Billy Rose's Crazy Quilt (1931), 63, 92
"Birth of the Blues, The," 14, 25, 77,
   102, 186
Bizet, Georges, 94
"Black Bottom," 25, 186
Blackbirds of 1928, 34, 60
Blackbirds of 1936, 34

Blackbirds of 1939, 34
Blake, Eubie, 25
Blane, Ralph, 19, 39, 50, 198, **216**
Blitzstein, Marc, 112–13, **216**
Bloom, Rube, 34, **216**
"Blow, Gabriel, Blow!," 1
"Blue Day," 15
Blue Skies," 4
Blues: An Anthology, 16
Blues in the Night, 16, 118, 179
"Blues in the Night (My Mama Done
   Tol' Me)," xviii, xix, 1, **16-17**, 86,
   118, 132, 146, 150, 173, 179, 190
Bock, Jerry, 189, **216**
"Body and Soul," **17-18**, 61, 77, 107,
   154, 194, 235
Bogart, Humphrey, 120
"Born Too Late," 18
Bowman, Brooks, 37–38, **217**
"Boy Next Door, The," **19**, 39, 198
Boyd, Elisse, 46, **217**
Boys from Syracuse, The, 200
Brecht, Bert, 112–13, **217**
Brice, Fannie, 63, 92, 134, 203
Brigadoon, 51, 52, 174–75, 183
Brooks, Harry, 3, **217**
Brooks, Melvin J., 46
"Brother, Can You Spare a Dime?,"
   20-21, 81, 92
Brown, Les, 143, **217**
Brown, Lew, 14, 77, 102, 141, 186, **217**
Brown, Nacio Herb, 77
"Buckle Down, Winsocki," 39
Bullock, Walter, 15, **217**
Burke, Billie, 188
Burke, Johnny, 33, 53–54, 76, 121–22,
   137, 138, 168, **206**
Burke, Sonny, 202
Burns, Ralph, 36, **218**
"Button Up Your Overcoat," 14
Bye Bye Birdie, 107, 140
"Bye Bye Blackbird," 63

Cabin in the Sky, 18, 39, 94, 108, 170
Caesar, Irving, 30–31, 165–66, 171, **218**
Cahn, Sammy, 121, 122, 168
"California, Here I Come!," 77
"Can This Be Love?," 21
"Can't Help Lovin' Dat Man," 22, 193
"Can't We Be Friends?," 20, **23**
Cantor, Eddie, 102, 116, 202
Capitol Revue, 165–66
Capote, Truman, 147–48, **218**
Capra, Frank, 74
Cardinal, The, 93
Carmelina, 183
Carmen Jones, 94
Carmichael, Hoagy, xv, 43, 65, 7, 91, 100–01, 120, 126, 146–47, 157, 162–63, **206**
Carnival in Flanders, 54–54, 121
"Carolina in the Morning," 24, 89, 116, 124
Caron, Leslie, 154
Carousel, xxii, 42, 109
Carter, Desmond, 153
Casey, Kenneth, 166–67, **218**
Casino Royale, 120
Cat and the Fiddle, The, 149
Channing, Carol, 95
Chaplin, Charles, 97
Chaplin, Sydney, 97
Charlap, Moose, 136, 195, **218**
"Charleston," 25, 166, 186
Chasing Rainbows, 48
"Cheek to Cheek," 26, 37, 112
"Chicago (That Toddling Town)," 27
Clare, Sidney, 98, **218**
Clippety Clop and Clementine, 69
"Cocktails for Two," 137
Cohan, George M., 110
Coleman, Cy, 13, 195, **218**
Comden, Betty, 9, 115, 126–27, 135, 151–52, **207**

"Come Rain or Come Shine," 15, **28–29**, 69
Concerto in F, 98, 164
Connecticut Yankee, A, 23, 180–81
Conquering Hero, The, 135
Conrad, Con, 29–30, **219**
"Continental, The," 29–30
Cook, Barbara, 32
Cook, Joe, 21, 80
Cooper, Marilyn, 4
Copland, Aaron, 93
Corned Beef and Roses, 134
"Cotton Blossom," 129–30
Cotton Club, 10, 32, 95, 163, 190
Cotton Club Parade (21st edition), 95
Cotton Club Parade (22nd edition), 163–64
Cotton Club Parade (24th edition), 10, 81
"Cracker Barrel County," 62
"Crazy Rhythm," 30–31
Creamer and Layton, 2
Creamer, Henry, 2, **219**
Crosby, Bing, 33, 83, 12, 138, 168

Dames, 73
"Dancing in the Dark," 7, **31–32**, 4, 75, 114
Dancing Lady, 38
"Dardanella," 27
Darling of the Day, 110
"Darn That Dream," 32–33
Date with Judy, A, 91
"Daughter of Sweet Georgia Brown, The," 167
Davis, Sammy, 107
"Day In—Day Out," 34
De Lange, Eddie, 32–33, 122, 219
Death of a Salesman, 46
Deathtrap, 105
"Deep Purple," 157
Delilah, 95
Desert Song, The, 149

DeSylva, B. G., 14, 77, 102, 141, 166, 186, **219**

Diaghilev, Serge, 9

"Diamonds Are a Girl's Best Friend," 172

"Did You Ever See a Dream Walking?," 178

Die Driegroschenoper, 112

Dietz, Howard, 7, 18, 23, 31–32, 68, 75, 114, 153–54, **207**

Disney, Walt, 33, 191, 194

Dixon, Mort, 63, 92, **219**

Do I Hear a Waltz!, xxiii

Do Re Mi, 115

"Don't Get Around Much Anymore," 35

Donaldson, Walter, 24, 107–08, 116, 124, **219**

Donnybrook!, 122

Dorsey, Jimmy, 32

Drat! The Cat!, 105

Dream Boy, 68

DuBarry Was a Lady, 77

Dubin, Al, 73, 96, 111, 137, **220**

Duke, Vernon, 9, 11, 18, 39, 59, 94, 108–09, 114, 153, 170–71, 188, 203, **207**

Durante, Jimmy, 102, 106

"Eadie Was a Lady," 77

Earl Carroll's Vanities (10th edition), 67

"Early Autumn," 36

Early to Bed, 94

"East of the Sun (and West of the Moon)," 37–38

Easter Parade, 61

"Easy Come, Easy Go," 61

Edens, Roger, 82

Eliscu, Edward, 123, 197, **220**

Ellington, Duke, 35, 84, 94, 142–43, 157, **207**

Ellstein, Abraham, 15, **220**

Etting, Ruth, 44

Every Night at Eight, 85

"Everything I Have Is Yours," 38

"Ev'ry Time," 39

"Everything's Coming Up Roses," xxiii

Eyton, Frank, 17–18, **220**

"Falling in Love with Love," 200

Falsettoland, 21

Fantasticks, The, 156, 185

Farmer Takes a Wife, The, 97

"Fascinating Rhythm," 26, 30, 40, 153

Ferber, Edna, 129

Fetter, Ted, 170–71, **220**

Feuer, Cy, 62

Fiddler on the Roof, xxii

Fields, Dorothy, 34, 60, 85–86, 114, 139, 187, **208**

Fifth Season, The, 15

Fine and Dandy, 21

Finian's Rainbow, 56–57, 131, 183

Finn, William, 21

Fiorello!, 189

Firebrand of Florence, The, 46, 52

Firefly, The, 149

Fisher, Fred, 27, **220**

Fitzgerald, Barry, 168

Fitzgerald, Ella, 159

Fleet's In, The, 74, 128

Fleming, Ian, 120

"Fly Me to the Moon," 37, 41

Flying Colors, 7

"Folks Who Live on the Hill, The," 42

Follow the Fleet, 101, 104

Fonda, Henry, 97, 199

"Fools Rush In (Where Angels Fear to Tread)," 34

42nd Street, 63, 73

Fosse, Bob, 136

Fowler, Gene, 92

Freed, Arthur, 55, 133

Freed, Ralph, 55, **220**

Freedley, Vinton, 15, 30
Friml, Rudolf, 44, 110, 149
Funny Face, 58, 169, 182
Funny Thing Happened on the Way to the Forum, A, 6

Garland, Judy, 50, 55, 69, 118, 198
Garner, Errol, 121, **221**
Gaxton, William, 53
Gay Divorce, The, 29, 64, 127
Gay Divorcee, The, 29, 74
Gay Life, The, 114
Gay Purr-ee, 69
Gelbart, Larry, 136
Gentlemen Prefer Blondes, 98
George, Don, 84, 221
George White's Scandals (8th edition), 14, 186
George White's Scandals (1st edition), 25
"Georgia on My Mind," 43, 100, 120
Gershwin, Frances, 21
Gershwin, George, xx, xxii, 1, 5, 9, 15, 18, 19, 21, 23, 24, 26, 29, 30, 38, 40, 44, 45, 47, 55, 58, 59, 66, 77, 87, 89, 98, 103, 104, 108, 111, 117–18, 123, 131, 141, 144, 149, 152, 153, 159, 164–66, 169, 176, 177–78, 180, 182, 187, 188, 194, **208**
Gershwin, Ira, 1, 10, 15, 30, 40, 45, 52, 55, 58, 59, 66, 87, 89, 96, 108, 114, 117, 118, 134, 144, 152–53, 159, 164–65, 169, 175, 176, 182, 187, 188, **208**
"Get Happy," 10, 44, 69, 95
Getz, Stan, 36
Gigi, 114, 175
Gilbert, W. S., 58
Gimbel, Norman, 136, **221**
Girl Crazy, 66
Girl from Utah, The, 177
"Give a Little Whistle," 191
"Glad to Be Unhappy," 39

Godowsky, Frances, 21
Going Places, 96
Golddiggers of 1935, 111
Golden Apple, The, 41, 93–94, 100
Golden Boy, 107
Good Morning, Dearie, 27
"Good-bye to All That," 45–46, 175–76
Goodman, Benny, 33, 76
Gordon, Mack, 178, 182, **221**
Gordon, Waxey, 102
Gorney, Jay, 20–21, **221**
Gorrell, Stuart, 43, **221**
Graham, Robert, 199, **221**
Grand, Murray, 46, **221**
Gray, Dolores, 53–54
Great Day!, 44, 123, 197
Great Magoo, The, 92
Great to Be Alive!, 15
Green, Adolph, 9, 115, 126–27, 135, 151, **209**
Green, Bud, 143, **222**
Green, Johnny, 17–18, 61, 154, 194, **222**
"Greensleeves," xvii
Grey, Clifford, 98
"Guess Who I Saw Today," 46, 199
Guys and Dolls, xxii, 78, 182
Gypsy, xxii, 115

Hall, Adelaide, 10
"Hallelujah!," 1, 98
Hamilton, Nancy, 57, **222**
Hammerstein, Oscar, 2nd, xv, x, xxii, 5, 22, 42, 47, 53, 82, 110, 114, 129–30, 148–49, 150, 155, 163, 187, 193, 195, **209**
Hampton, Lionel, 202
"Hand in Hand," 47
Handy, W. C., 16, 150, 161, 166, **222**
"Hang on to Your Lids, Kids," 142
Hanley, James F., 203, **222**
"Happy Days Are Here Again," 48–49

Harbach, Otto, 148–49, **222**

Harburg, E. Y., 9, 10, 11, 16, 20–21, 56–57, 59, 69, 81, 92–93, 96, 110, 131, 133–34, 183, 187, 188, 190, 202, **209**

Harburg, Edelaine, 20–21

Hard to Get, 96

"Harlem Hospitality," 32

Harline, Leigh, 190–91, **222**

Harlow, Jean, 82

Harnick, Sheldon, 46, 189, **222**

Hart, Lorenz, xv, xix, 23, 27, 39, 49, 68, 88, 90, 91, 103, 106, 109–10, 125, 145–46, 154, 159, 160–61, 180–81, 191, 196, 200, 201, **209**

Hart, Moss, 119, 160

Hastings, Hal, 53

"Have You Met Miss Jones?," 49

"Have Yourself a Merry Little Christmas," 39, 50

Heads Up!, 145–46

"Heather on the Hill, The," 51

Hecht, Ben, 92

Helen Goes to Troy, 94

Henderson, Ray, 14, 77, 102, 141, 186, **223**

Herbert, Victor, 44, 110

Here Come the Waves, 1

"Here I'll Stay," 52

Here's Howe!, 30

"Here's That Rainy Day," 53–54, 121, 192

Herman, Woody, 36, **223**

Heyman, Edward, 17–18, 61, **223**

Heywood, DuBose, 164, **223**

"Hi-Diddle-Dee-Dee," 191

High Button Shoes, 127

"High Hopes," 169

High, Wide and Handsome, 42

Higher and Higher, 90

"Hindustan," 165

Hit the Deck, 98, 172

Hodges, Johnny, 84, 223

Hold Your Horses, 80–81

Hole in the Head, A, 169

Holliday, Judy, 97, 135

"Holmes and Watson," 1–5

Homer, Ben, 143, **223**

"Honeysuckle Rose," 3, 54

Hooray for What!, 133

Hoover, Herbert, 48

Hope, Bob, 59, 138, 172

Horne, Lena, 10, 95

Horwitt, Arnold B., 178–79, **223**

Hot Chocolates, 3

House of Flowers, 147–48

"How About You?," 55

"How Are Things in Glocca Morra?," 56–57

"How High the Moon," 37, 57

"How Little We Know?," 120

"How Long Has This Been Going On?," 58, 144

"How Ya Gonna Keep 'em Down on the Farm," 24

Howard, Bart, 38, 41, **224**

Hudson, Will, 122, **224**

Humpty-Dumpty, 77

"I Believe," 199

"I Can't Believe My Eyes," 118

"I Can't Get Started," 59, 188

"I Can't Give You Anything But Love," 34, 60, 85

I Cover the Waterfront, 61

"I Cover the Waterfront," 61

"I Don't Want to Walk Without You," 62

"I Feel at Home with You," 154

"I Found a Million Dollar Baby (in a Five and Ten Cent Store)," 63, 92

"I Get a Kick Out of You," 64–65

"I Get Along Without You Very Well (Except Sometimes)," 65

"I Got Rhythm," 1, 66

"I Gotta Crow," 127

"I Gotta Right to Sing the Blues," 67, 95, 190

"I Guess I'll Have to Change My Plan," 68, 153

"I Had a Love Once," 69

"I Have No Words (to Say How Much I Love You)," 153

"I Left My Heart at the Stage Door Canteen," 70

"I Love a Piano," 71

"I Love to Lie Awake in Bed," 68

I Married an Angel, 160

"I May Be Wrong But, I Think You're Wonderful," 72

"I Only Have Eyes for You," 73

"I Remember You," 74, 128

"I See Your Face Before Me," 7, 45, **75**, 114

"I Thought about You," 76

"I Want to Be a Minstrel Man," 202

"I Want to Be Happy," 172

"I Want to Be with You," 77, 93

"I Wish I Didn't Love You So," 78–79

"I Wish I Was in Love Again," 191

"I Wonder What Became of Me," 79–80

"I Won't Grow Up," 127

I'd Rather Be Right, 49

"If I Love Again," 80–81

"If You Believe in Me," 92

"I'll Build a Stairway to Paradise," 40

"I'll Say She Does," 166

"I'll See You in My Dreams," 89

"Ill Wind (You're Blowin' Me No Good)," 10, 32, **81–82**, 190

"I'm All Smiles," 82

"I'm an Old Cowhand," 83

"I'm Beginning to See the Light," 84

"I'm in the Mood for Love," 16, **85–86**

"I'm Looking Over a Four Leaf Clover," 63

"I'm Old Fashioned," 86–87

"I'm Yours," 61

"In the Cool, Cool, Cool of the Evening," 120, 146

"In the Shade of the New Apple Tree," 133

"Isn't It a Pity?," 87–88

"Isn't It Romantic?," 88

"Isn't This a Lovely Day to be Caught in the Rain," 26

"It Ain't Necessarily So," 2, 164–65

"It Don't Mean a Thing (If It Ain't Got That Swing)," 122

"It Had to Be You," 89, 116

It Happened One Night, **74**

"It Never Entered My Mind," 90

"It's a Most Unusual Day," 91

"It's Only a Paper Moon," 92–93

"It's the Going Home Together," 93–94

"I've Always Loved You," 94–95

"I've Got No Strings," 191

"I've Got the World on a String," 95–96

"I've Told Ev'ry Little Star," 47

Jablonski, Ed, 69

Jamaica, 10, 69

James, Harry, 84, 224

James, Paul, 21, 23

"Jeepers Creepers," 17, **96–97**

"Jogo Blues, The," 161

Johnny Angel, 120

"Johnny One Note," 191

Johnson, Jimmy, 25, 166, 186

Johnson, Van, 199

Johnston, Arthur, 137

Jones, Isham, 89

Jones, Tom, 156, 185, **224**

Jumbo, 106

"Just in Time," 97

Kahn, Gus, 24, 89, 107–08, 116, **210**
Kahn, Madeline, 199
Kahn, Otto, 30
Kahn, Roger Wolfe, 30–31
"Ka-Lu-A," 27
Kaufman, George S., 45, 119, 175
"Keepin' Myself for You," 98–99
Kent, Charlotte, 134
Kern, Jerome, xv, xx, xxii, 5–6, 9, 18, 22, 27, 29, 42, 47, 77, 82, 85–86, 98, 104, 111, 112, 123, 129–30, 139, 141, 148–49, 150–51, 155, 172, 177–78, 180, 182, 187, 193, 197, **210**
Kid Millions, 202
King of Jazz, 166
Kismet, 179
Kiss Me, Kate, 64, 149
Kiss of Death, 144
Kitt, Eartha, 199
Knickerbocker Holiday, 144
Koehler, Ted, 10, 44, 67, 8l, 95–96, 163, 190, **211**

Lady, Be Good!, 40, 117, 152, 182
Lady in the Dark, 39, 52
"Lady Is a Tramp, The," 191
Lamour, Dorothy, 138
Landesman, Fran, 12, 159, **225**
Lane, Burton, 21, 38, 45, 55, 56, 78, 91, 131, 183, 202, **211**
Latouche, John, 93, 94, 100, 108, 170–71, **211**
Laura, 99
"Laura," 99
Lawrence, Gertrude, 17
Layton, J. Turner, 2, **225**
"Lazy Afternoon," 41, 93, **100**
"Lazy River," 100–01, 120
"Lazybones," 146
Leigh, Carolyn, 13, 126, 195, **225**
Leonard, Michael, 82, 192, **225**

Lerner, Alan Jay, 8, 51, 52, 114, 174–75, 183, 195, 202, **211**
Leslie, Lew, 34, 60
"Let Yourself Go," 101
"Let's Call It a Day," 102
"Let's Do It," 103
"Let's Face the Music and Dance," 101, **104**
"Let's Go," 105
"Let's See What Happens," 110
Levin, Ira, 105, **225**
Lewis, Morgan, 38, 57, **226**
Lipton, James, 118, **226**
"Little Girl Blue," 39, **106**
Little Me, 13
Little Tommy Tucker, 153
Littlest Revue, The, 18
Liza, 167
"Liza," 89
Load of Coal, 3, 54
Loesser, Frank, 62, 78–79, 114, 195, **226**
Loewe, Frederick, 8, 51, 52, 114, 174–75, 183, 195, **226**
Lombardo, Guy, 68
"Look for the Silver Lining," 77
"Lorna's Here," 107
"Losing My Mind," xxiii
Louisiana Purchase, 77
"Love Is a Many-Splendored Thing," 120
Love Life, 52
"Love Me or Leave Me," 44, 89, **107–08**
Love Me Tonight, 88, 109
"Love Turned the Light Out," 108–09
"Lovely to Look At," 86, 112
"Lover," 91, **109–10**
"Lover, Come Back to Me!," 110–11
"Lullaby of Broadway," 111–12
Lyles, Aubrey, 25

"Ma, She's Making Eyes at Me!," 98

Mack, Cecil, 25, 166, 186, **226**

"Mack the Knife," 81, **112-13**

"Magic Moment," 114

Magidson, Herb, 29, **226**

"Make Someone Happy," 115

"Makin' Whoopee!," 89, **116**, 124

Mamoulian, Rouben, 42, 109

"Man I Love, The," xxii, **117-18**

"Man That Got Away, The," 45, **118-19**

Man Who Came to Dinner, The, 119

"Manhattan," 27, 88, 180

Marks, Gerald, 4, **226**

Martin, Herbert, 82, 192, **225**

Martin, Hugh, 19, 39, 50, 198, **210**

Martin, Mary, 126-27

"Maybe It's Time for Me," 119

McHugh, Jimmy, xvi, 34, 60, 85-86, 91, **227**

Me for You, 145-46

Meet Me in St. Louis, 19, 39, 50, 198

"Memphis Blues," 161

"Memphis in June," 120

"Memphis Itch," 161

Mercer, Johnny, xv, xvi, 1-2, 10, 16-17, 28-29, 33, 34, 36, 69, 74, 76, 77, 78, 79-80, 81, 83, 86, 94, 96-97, 99, 114, 118-19, 120, 128, 132, 142, 146, 154, 173-74, 179-80, 184, 190, 202, **212**

Merman, Ethel, 66, 77, 102

Meyer, Joseph, 30-31, **227**

"Midnight Sun," 202

Miller, Flournoy, 25

Miller, Marilyn, 182

Mills, Irving, 122, 157, 227

Minnelli, Liza, 198

"Minnie the Moocher," 113, 163

"Misty," 121-22

"Mood Indigo," 122

"Moonglow," 122

"Moonlight Becomes You," 168

"Moonlight Serenade," 157

"More Than You Know," 44, 98, **123**, 171, 197

Morgan, Helen, 193

"Moritat," 112-13

Moross, Jerome, 93-94, 100, **227**

Most Happy Fella, The, xxii, 78

"Mountain Greenery," 180

Murray, J. P., 80, **227**

Murray Anderson's Almanac, 72

Music in the Air, 47, 155

"My Blue Heaven," 16, **124**

My Darlin' Aida, 94

My Fair Lady, xxii, 51, 175

"My Funny Valentine," xv, **125**, 191

"My Mammy," 24

"My Shining Hour," 133

Nash, Ogden, 18, 115, **228**

"Nearness of You, The," **126**, 191

Nervous Set, The, 11, 159

"Never Never Land," 126-27

"Never No Lament," 35

New Faces of 1936, 198

New Faces of 1952, 46

New Moon, The, 110

Newman, Alfred, 143-44, **228**

Nicholas, Harold, 202

"Night and Day," 29-30, 64, **127-28**

No, No, Nanette, 49, 171-72

North Star, The, 93

"Not Mine," 128

Oakland, Ben, 80, **228**

Odets, Clifford, 107

Of Thee I Sing, 45, 53, 87

Offenbach, Jacques, 94

"Oh, How I Hate to Get Up in the Morning," 70

"Oh, My Goodness," 178

Oklahoma!, 42, 57, 99, 109, 149

"Ol' Man River," xxii, 22, **129-30**, 197

"Old Devil Moon," **131**
"Old Folks at Home," 165
"Old Soft Shoe, The," 57
"Ole Buttermilk Sky," 120
Oliver!, 61
On a Clear Day You Can See Forever, 183
"On the Good Ship Lollipop," 98
"On the Sunny Side of the Street," 85
On the Town, 151–52
"One for My Baby (And One More for the Road)," 12, **132**, 173, 179
One for the Money, 57
One Night of Love, 74
One Touch of Venus, 18, 52, 158
Our Town, 93
"Out of This World," 133
"Outside of That I Love You," 46
"Over the Rainbow," 18, 118, **133–34**, 190
"Overnight," 134

Paint Your Wagon, 8, 183
Pardon My English, 87–88
Paris, 103
Parish, Mitchell, 157, 162, **228**
Park Avenue, 45–46, 75
"Party's Over, The," 135
Passing Show of 1922, The, 24
"Past the Age of Innocence," 136
Peck, Gregory, 82
"Peg o' My Heart," 27
Pennies from Heaven, 137
"Pennies from Heaven," 121, **137**, 168
"People," 135
Perils of Pauline, The, 78
"Personality," 138
Peter Pan, 126–27, 195
"Pick Yourself Up," 139
Pinkard, Maceo, 166–67, **228**
Pinocchio, 126, 190–91
Plain and Fancy, 179

Pomahac, Bruce, 20, 110, 233
Porgy and Bess, 59, 87, 109, 164–65
Porter, Cole, xv, 1, 9, 15, 2, 29, 37, 39, 47, 64–65, 77, 78, 103, 104, 108, 127–28, 149–50, 170, 180, 187, 195, 199, **212**
"Pottawatomie," 39
Pousse-Café, 94
Powell, Dick, 96
Powell, Jane, 91
"Praise the Lord and Pass the Ammunition," 78
Preminger, Otto, 99
Present Arms!, 201
"Pretty Baby," 89
Proud Rebel, The, 93
"Put on a Happy Face," 140
Puttin' on the Ritz, 141
"Puttin' on the Ritz," 141–42

"Ragtime Cowboy Joe," 4
Rainger, Ralph, 172, **228**
Raksin, David, 99, **228**
Rawlings, Marjorie Kinnan, 82
Razaf, Andy, 3–4, 54, **229**
Ready, Willing and Able, 184
"Reckless," 82
Regan, Sylvia,15
Reichner, Bickley, 199, **229**
Revel, Harry, 178–79, **229**
Reynolds, Herbert, 17, **229**
"Rhapsody in Blue," xx, 40, 98, 117, 152, 164, 166
Rhythm Inn, 136
Rhythm on the Range, 83
Rice, Elmer, 143
Richards, Johnny, 195
Road to Utopia, 138
Robbins, Jack, 37, 170
Robbins, Jerome, 126–27, 151
Roberta, 85, 148
Robin, Leo, 98, 172, **229**

"Rockin' Chair," 120

Rodgers, Richard, xv, xxii, xxiii, 5, 9, 18, 23, 27, 39, 49, 53, 78, 88, 90, 91, 99, 103, 106, 108, 109–10, 111, 125, 144, 145–46, 154, 159, 160–61, 169, 177, 180–81, 191–92, 195, 196, 200, 201, **213**

Rogers, Ginger, 26, 101, 103, 139

Romberg, Sigmund, 110–11, 149

Ronell, Ann, 194, **229**

Room Service, 80

Rooney, Mickey, 55

Roosevelt, Franklin D., 23, 48, 144

Rosalie, 58, 118, 194

Rose, Billy, 63, 92–93, 123, 134, 197, **213**

"Rose of Washington Square," 203

Rose-Marie, 149

Rosemary's Baby, 105

Rosenthal, Laurence, 119, **229**

Rourke, M. E., 17, **229**

Royal Wedding, 183, 202

Runnin' Wild, 25

Ruskin, Harry, 72, **229**

Russell, Bob, 35, **230**

Ruth Selwyn's 9:15 Revue, 44

Saint-Saëns, Camille, 94

Samson and Lila Dee, 94

Samson et Dalila, 94

Saratoga, 69

"Satan's Li'l Lamb," 16

"Satin Doll," 142–43

"Savannah," 108

Sawens, Bill, 136

"Say It with Music," 141

Schafer, Milton, 105, **230**

Schertzinger, Victor, 74, 128, **230**

Schmidt, Harvey, 156, 185, **230**

Schwartz, Arthur, 7, 23, 31–32, 45, 68, 75, 78, 114, 153–54, 172, 175–76, 177, **213**

"Second Hand Rose," 203

Sennwald, André, 29

"Sentimental Journey," 143

"Sentimental Rhapsody," 143–44

"September Song," 113, **144–45**, 199

"Shadow of Your Smile, The," 120

Shall We Dance, 176

She Loves Me, xxii

"She Touched Me," 105

Sherry!, 119

"Ship Without a Sail, A," xix, 88, 107, 144, 145–46

"Shortest Day of the Year, The," 200

Show Boat, xx, 22, 110, 123, 129–30, 149, 150, 187, 193

Shuffle Along, 25

Sillman, Leonard, 46, 199

Simons, Seymour, 4, **230**

Sinatra, Frank, xx, 41, 121, 169, 195

"Sing for Your Supper," 200

"Singin' in the Rain," 55

Sirmay, Albert, 6

Sis Hopkins, 62

Sissle, Noble, 25

Sky's the Limit, The, 132

"Skylark," 146–47

"Sleepin' Bee, A," 69, 133, 147–48

"Sleigh Ride," 157

Smarty, 58

Smiles, 182

Smith, Maggie, 199

"Smoke Gets in Your Eyes," 148–49

"So in Love," 149–50

"Solitude," 122

"Some Girl Is on His Mind," 150–51

"Some Other Time," 151–52

"Somebody Loves Me," 40, 77

"Someone to Watch over Me," 152–53

"Something to Remember You By," 153–54

Something's Gotta Give, 154

"Something's Gotta Give," 154–55

"Sometimes I'm Happy," 98, 172
Sondheim, Stephen, xxii–xxiii, 6, 83, 140, 176, 177
"Song Is You, The," 155
"Soon It's Gonna Rain," 156
"Sophisticated Lady," 122, 157
Sour, Robert, 17–18, **230**
South Pacific, xxii
"Speak Low," 18, 52, 113, 158
"Spring Can Really Hang You Up the Most," 159
Spring Is Here, 160, 196
"Spring Is Here," 159, 160–61
"St. Louis Blues," 161, 166
St. Louis Woman, 28, 69, 79
Stags at Bay, 37
"Star Dust," xv, 43, 146, 157, 162–63
Star Spangled Rhythm, 173
"Stars Fell on Alabama," 157
"Steam Is on the Beam, The," 61
Stop! Look! Listen!, 71
"Stormy Weather," xxii, 10, 17, 32, 67, 92, 147, 163–64
Strayhorn, Billy, 142–43, 230
Street Scene, 143–44
Streisand, Barbra, 48, 82, 97, 192
Strike Me Pink, 102
Strike Up the Band, 55, 118
Strouse, Charles, 106, 140, **231**
Sturges, Preston, 53
Styne, Jule, 15, 62, 78, 97, 110, 115, 126–27, 135, 172, 178, 195, **214**
Sugar Babies, 91
Sullivan, Arthur, 58
Sullivan, Henry, 72, **231**
Sullivan, Maxine, 33
"Summer Sequence," 36
"Summertime," 164–65
Sunny, 149, 182
"Swanee," 24, 31, 40, 165–66
Sweater Girl, 62
Sweeney Todd, xxii

Sweet Adeline, 150–51, 193
"Sweet Adeline," 150
Sweet and Low, 134
"Sweet Georgia Brown," 166–67
"Sweet Nevada," 175
Swift, Kay, 21, 23, 44, **231**
Swing Time, 42, 139, 187
Swingin' the Dream, 32–33
"Swinging on a Star," 121, 168–69
"'S Wonderful," 169

Take a Chance, 77, 93
"Taking a Chance on Love," 108, 170–71
"Tangerine," 74
"Tea for Two," 123, 171–72
Tempest, The, 6
Temple, Shirley, 77, 178
"Thanks for the Memory," 98, 172–73
"That Ain't Hay," 62
"That Old Black Magic," 173–74
"There But for You Go I," 51, 174–75
"There's a Boat Dat's Leavin' Soon for New York," 165
"There's a House for Sale in Harlem," 32
"There's No Holding Me," 175–76
"They Can't Take That Away from Me," 176–77
"They Didn't Believe Me," 177–78
"This Can't Be Love," 200
"This Is My Beloved," 178–79
This Is the Army, 70
"This Time the Dream's on Me," 118, 179–80
Thompson, Jane Brown, 65
"Thou Swell," 180–81, 201
Three Little Pigs, 194
Three Sisters, 47
Three to Make Ready, 57
Three's a Crowd, 17–18, 153–54
Threepenny Opera, The, 81, 112–13

Thumbs Up!, 11, 203
"Time on My Hands (You in My Arms)," 91, **182**
To Have and Have Not, 120
"Tonight," xxiii
"Too Late Now," 183
Too Many Girls, 39
"Too Marvelous for Words," 17, **184**
Top Hat, 26
"Top Hat, White Tie and Tails," 26
"Trav'lin Light," 94
Triangle Club, 37
"Trolley Song, The," 39
"Try to Remember," 185
Twain, Mark, 181
Two for the Show, 57

Vallee, Rudy, 68
Vamp, The, 94–95
Van Heusen, James, 32–33, 54–54, 78, 121, 137, 138, 168–69, **214**
"Varsity Drag, The," 14, 102, **186**
Verdi, Guiseppe, 94
Very Warm for May, 5

Walk a Little Faster, 9
Walk with Music, 146
Wallace, Oliver G., 165
Waller, Thomas "Fats," 3, 54, 60, 94, **231**
Warburg, James Paul, 23
Warren, Harry, xv, 44, 45, 63, 73, 92, 96–97, 111–12, 137, **214**
"Washboard Blues," 162
Washington, Ned, 126, 190, **231**
Waters, Ethel, 108, 163, 170
"Way You Look Tonight, The," 139, **187**
Webb, Clifton, 68
Weber, Rex, 81
"Weekend in the Country, A," xxiii
Weeks, Harold, 165

Weill, Kurt, 18, 46, 52, 112–13, 144–45, 153, 158, 183, 199, **214**
West Side Story, xxii
"What Is There to Say?," 188
"What'll I Do," 141
"When Did I Fall in Love?," 189
"When Did You Leave Heaven," 15
"When I'm with You," 178
"When the Sun Comes Out," 190
"When You Wish Upon a Star," 126, **190–91**
Where Do We Go from Here?, 52
"Where or When," 191–92
"White Christmas," xviii
White, George, 14, 25, 186
Whiteman, Paul, 16, 68, 83, 166
Whiting, George, 124, **231**
Whiting, Richard A., 15, 77, 96, 124, 184, **231**
"Who Paid the Rent for Mrs. Rip Van Winkle (When Rip Van Winkle Went Away)?," 27
"Who's Afraid of the Big Bad Wolf," 194
Whoopee!, 44, 107, 116
"Why Did I Choose You?," 192
"Why Was I Born?," 107, 149, **193**
Wildcat, 13
Wildflower, 171
Wilk, Max, 56, 118, 237–38
"Willow Weep for Me," 194
"Witchcraft," 13, **195**
"With a Song in My Heart," 160, **196**
"Without a Song," 197
Wizard of Oz, The, 133, 190
Wolf, Tommy, 12, 159, **225**

"Yankee Doodle," xx, 83
Yearling, The, 82, 192
Yellen, Jack, 48, **231**
"You Are for Loving," 39, **198**
"You Better Go Now," 199

"You Have Cast Your Shadow on the
   Sea," 200
"You Took Advantage of Me," 201
You Were Never Lovelier, 86
"You're All the World to Me," 202
"You've Gotta Eat Your Spinach, Baby,"
   178
Young, Trummy, 94
"Young at Heart," 195

Ziegfeld Follies of 1917, 2
Ziegfeld Follies of 1934, 188
Ziegfeld Follies of 1936, 59
Ziegfeld, Florenz, Jr., 25, 182, 188
"Zing! Went the Strings of My Heart,"
   203